MYSTICAL THEOLOGY

The Integrity of Spirituality and Theology

Mark A. McIntosh

Blackwell
Publishing

350 Main Street, Malden, MA 02148-5018, USA
108 Cowley Road, Oxford OX4 1JF, UK
550 Swanston Street, Carlton South, Melbourne, Victoria 3053, Australia
Kurfürstendamm 57, 10707 Berlin, Germany

First published 1998 by Blackwell Publishing Ltd
Reprinted 1999, 2000, 2003

Library of Congress Cataloging-in-Publication Data

McIntosh, Mark Allen, 1960–
    Mystical theology : the integrity of spirituality and theology /
Mark A. McIntosh.
        p. cm. — (Challenges in contemporary theology)
    Includes bibliographical references and index.
    ISBN 1–55786–906–5 (hardcover : alk. paper). — ISBN 1–55786–907–3
(pbk. : alk. paper)
    1. Mysticism.   2. Theology—Methodology.   3. Spirituality.
    I. Title.   II. Series.
BV5083.M37   1998
248.2'2—dc21   97-44977
                                                                        CIP

A catalogue record for this title is available from the British Library.

Set in 10½ on 12½ pt Bembo
by Ace Filmsetting Ltd, Frome

For further information on
Blackwell Publishing, visit our website:
http://www.blackwellpublishing.com

For Elizabeth Katherine and Nathan Anthony

CONTENTS

PREFACE

Most of the undergraduates whom I have the pleasure of teaching are quick to make a distinction in describing their interests to me. It is a distinction that poses a contemporary challenge to theology – but perhaps it does so by opening a new possibility. 'I'm really not religious, at least not in any institutional sense,' students often say to me. Then they add, with varying degrees of urgency, 'But I have a strong commitment to spirituality.' And they are not alone. The vast proliferation of books, groups, courses and many (disconcertingly lucrative) schemes – all proposing to lead seekers on a new spiritual journey – testifies to the contemporary hunger for some kind of contact with mystery and deeper meaning. A common denominator of many such quests is their more or less pronounced allergy to established patterns of theological reflection, whether in church or academic form.

While the churches may very reasonably be scrambling to offer such seekers new access to their own rich spiritual traditions, academic theology seems dangerously liable to settle into one or the other of two reactions to the challenge posed by contemporary interest in 'spirituality'. One response is simply to co-opt this new interest, not so much as a conversation partner, but as a new specimen for scholarly analysis, dissection and categorization. Needless to say, there is much useful knowledge gained by scrutinizing the psychological states present in various forms of meditation or the social and literary embeddedness of popular spiritual practices. The problem is that such an approach, in isolation, allows academia to avoid the actual and sometimes painfully concrete word that spiritual practitioners are trying to speak – a word that academia in particular may need to hear.

The other kind of academic response to contemporary spiritual hunger takes the form of an uneasy shoulder-shrugging; there is an often unarticulated agreement that the texts and practices of spirituality are simply not suitable for involvement in the academically respectable tasks of religious studies or theology, they represent a different kind of discourse with a different kind of public and can have no real place in the scholarly genres of logical argument. Once again, the challenge posed by spirituality to theology is evaded here, and not without reason, for it is a dangerous challenge: a challenge that questions the standard modern accounts of what should be accepted as legitimate religious reflection.

This book attempts to see the various challenges that spirituality poses to theology as new possibilities. It begins from the assumption that spirituality and theology are far more closely related than we sometimes think, and it goes on to see how a new dialogue between spirituality and theology might lead not only to a new way of thinking about their mutual relationship, but also to fruitful paths of theological analysis and reflection. Suppose, for example, that all the artists of the world suddenly went colour-blind. Their works would continue to be marvels of structure and movement, but the rest of us 'amateurs' would constantly feel that the artists had lost touch with something vital, that some mysterious language for expressing the vitality of the real had been forgotten. We might try to describe to the artists our own encounters with colour and its evocative power, but they would tend to dismiss us as hopelessly undeveloped in our tastes or as willfully avoiding the higher claims of true art. My suggestion in writing this book is that something analogous to the artists' colour-blindness has happened to theology. And when theology loses its sensitivity to the 'colours' of spiritual practice and mystical speech, when it tends to overlook them as mere religious kitsch, it is gradually losing touch with that mysterious language by which humanity and the ultimately meaningful have access to each other and are able to enter into dialogue.

In order to make sense of this suggestion of mine, I have devoted the first part of the book to questions of history and method. This means trying to understand something of what 'spirituality' in fact is, at least in the Christian case, and what is at stake in its relationship with theology. It also means considering some of the historical models that highlight the integrity of spirituality and theology as that integrity is grounded in their relationship with each other – as well as habits of mind in which that integrity tends to get dissolved. Finally it means considering how one might go about the (herme-neutical) process of theologically interpreting, assessing and appropriating spirituality in the work of contemporary constructive theology. In the second part of the book I offer some examples of how this renewed dialogue of spirituality and theology might work in practice. There are many ways indeed by which such constructive work might be done, and I have merely suggested, in three different kinds of problematics, what the fruit might be of re-contextualizing theological issues in an appropriate spiritual matrix.

I hope that readers primarily interested in spirituality will be led to ask themselves about what kind of theological settings give rise to what kind of spiritualities and what the theological implications of those spiritualities might be. For not to consider the theological significance of the spiritual journey is to short-circuit its most authentic goal, which is not to arrive simply at inner peace or some mode of coping with the status quo, but to seek the entire living truth – and, by sharing in the life of truth, to understand something of its meaning (and surely to do this is to engage in theology in its profoundest sense?). And I hope that theologians who may have considered spirituality primarily as a source for anthropological studies, or who may have simply felt unsure of spirituality's theological significance, may be enticed into a real dialogue with mystical thought. For the aim of Christian spiritual teachers has never been to point to their own states of consciousness but to the self-disclosive God who arouses their testimony.

I am deeply grateful to the many who have helped me to think about these things. I extend my thanks to Loyola University of Chicago for granting me a research leave of absence during which most of the final draft was written, to my colleagues there in the Theology Department, to my many students, and especially to my graduate research assistants for all their hard work. Above all I thank my wife, Anne, who always teaches me much about the love that holds all things together, and our dear children, Liza and Nathan, to whom this book is dedicated.

Part I

ISSUES OF HISTORY
AND METHOD

Chapter 1

SPIRITUALITY AND THEOLOGY: THE QUESTIONS AT ISSUE

Two SS officers arrived at the door of a Carmelite convent in Holland. It was five in the afternoon on 2 August 1942. They had come to transport two of the sisters on a fateful journey; within a week the two had both perished at Auschwitz. Both nuns were Jews. One had been a leading intellectual in pre-war Germany, a graduate assistant to the highly influential phenomenologist Edmund Husserl, with a growing scholarly reputation of her own. Her name was Edith Stein (1891–1942). The other nun was her sister by birth, Rosa. At the moment of arrest, Rosa apparently began to grow deeply distressed. To comfort her sister, and perhaps the rest of her convent, Stein is reported to have taken her sister by the hand and said, 'Come, Rosa. We're going for our people.'[1]

The afternoon of the arrest, Edith Stein was working on her study of a major mystical writer, John of the Cross (1542–91).[2] In fact she was at the point of discussing John's death when she was called away to her own. John had developed a highly nuanced understanding of the soul's abandonment into the darkness of an unknown and imperceptible divine presence. Stein's analysis of this spiritual trajectory had now reached the point of intersection with her own spiritual journey, and it is most appropriately at this crossing that this book begins – at the point where the integrity of spirituality and theology is made manifest.

Was Edith Stein a spiritual writer or a theologian? The explicit dichotomy of this question is undone by the unflinching integrity with which Stein held these two elements of her vocation together. Her work as an interpreter of major theologians such as Pseudo-Dionysius the Areopagite (c.500), Thomas Aquinas (c.1225–74), and John of the Cross was all of a piece with her spirituality. The mysterious beckoning of divine love in Stein's life led her out

of herself towards the other, both the divine other and the human other, and
especially the divine by way of responsibility for the human other: 'Come,
Rosa. We're going for our people.' Her *theological* understanding of what she
saw as the self-sacrificing pattern of divine life grew increasingly more
incarnate in her own *spiritual* stance. She repeatedly articulated her belief that
a spirituality of compassion and responsibility for others enabled one to
contribute in some limited personal way to the unlimited self-giving that she
understood to be constitutive of God's existence – a self-giving embodied for
her in the history of Jesus. On at least three occasions she made official requests
to her superiors to offer herself 'as a sacrifice of atonement' for peace and for
the deliverance of her fellow Jews.[3] Her theological perceptions and her
spirituality of self-giving love represented the theoretical and the practical
forms respectively of one unified journey of encounter with God.

The themes manifest in Stein's life are issues at the heart of this book. How
can one best understand the relationship of theology and spirituality? How
have they grown so far from one another? What would their integration mean
for contemporary theology? In the time of Edith Stein and perhaps since that
time the usual definitions of spirituality and theology as separated disciplines
seem less persuasive. This may be, therefore, an appropriate moment for
questioning the status quo of their divorce. It has been suggested that the name
we often give to this era – postmodernity – was born in Auschwitz, out of the
death of the old certainties about reason as purely discursive rationality, about
history as progressing according to some clear and coherent narrative, about
truth as the supposed adequacy of propositions to purely objective entities.[4]
All these old verities of modernity demanded for their pure observance a harsh
and pristine separation of thought from feeling, form from content, and most
devastatingly, theory from practice. In the maelstrom of the twentieth century
such clinical divisions of existence have come to seem dangerously naive,
repressive of wholeness, and hopelessly flatfooted in negotiating both the
traumas and the possibilities of real life. Perhaps today the grounds upon which
spirituality and theology were clinically isolated from each other no longer
exist. It was doubtful whether we could ever afford to maintain such a division
in any case. The question now is whether we may find, in such examples as
Edith Stein, the pattern for the re-weaving of spirituality and theology.

It may seem, however, that another kind of division is being tacitly
endorsed here. Precisely because I am concerned in this book with the
integrity of spirituality and theology within Christianity, I will not be able
(even were I appropriately equipped) to pay attention to the spiritualities of
other religious traditions nor even to argue from analogies between the
spirituality/theology relationship in those traditions and the Christian case.

Far from thinking that Christian theology can operate very adequately without reference to its global context, I am inclined to believe that other religious traditions, as contrasted with Western secular ideologies, are likely to become some of the most significant dialogue partners in Christianity's future. So I am hopeful that analogies between the spiritual practices and conceptual patterns of Christianity and those of other religions will emerge in continuing dialogue. I am unconvinced, however, that all actual religions are limited cultural articulations of a supposedly deeper, universal common core of truth – which some scholars seem able to liberate from its allegedly constraining formulations in particular religions. The agenda of such scholarship seems little different from the missionary aims of previous centuries, namely the conversion of the benighted to a higher understanding; in this case, the 'higher religion' is usually one associated with post-Enlightenment Western academia. Generally speaking, I am concerned here to articulate the concrete particularities of Christian spirituality and theology as a basis for rediscovering their integrity, precisely because I doubt very much whether there *is* any such thing as spirituality or theology apart from their concrete historical life.

Some Definitions

Now there are certain perils in proposing postmodernity as a frame for the discussion of spirituality and theology today. The postmodern is sometimes also conceived as the lazy pluralism of late capitalism, flying off into privatized 'lifestyles' lacking any common ground for the hard work of talking and working together. Certainly much that passes today for 'spirituality' smells suspiciously of just such a tendency. A quick tour of the local bookshop will likely display all these proclivities for individualistic quests for something 'inner' – inner self, inner child, even (in one case I noted recently) the inner wolf. In the consumerist consciousness of much of the northern hemisphere, such shopping for a private inner world seems to correspond all too well with the enormous growth of private security firms!

If spirituality were defined adequately in such terms, it would be hard to imagine how it might relate to theology, except as an object of rigorous analysis and critique. Perhaps it is a hallmark of pseudo-spirituality that it deals in escape, in avoidance of the reality of the other. This book will develop an understanding of spirituality as a discovery of the true 'self' precisely in *encountering* the divine and human other – who allow one neither to rest in a reassuring self-image nor to languish in the prison of a false social construction of oneself. The truly life-bestowing other who beckons one into heightened wakefulness can also liberate one from the bitterly oppressive constructions of oneself enforced by dysfunctional families and broken societies. Understood in this sense, spirituality as the transformation and discovery of the self always happens in encounter, it is an activity constantly stirred up and sustained by the other who calls one out of one's 'self' and into the truth of one's mission in life, out of provisionality and into the adventure of incarnation.

I want to suggest, then, that spirituality so conceived is inherently oriented towards discovery, towards new perceptions and new understandings of reality, and hence is intimately related to theology. Perhaps one might think initially in terms of encounter with God as the common ground of spirituality and theology: spirituality being the impression that this encounter makes in the transforming life of people, and theology being the expression that this encounter calls forth as people attempt to understand and speak of the encounter.

Now how does this working definition of spirituality comport with the historical range of meanings that the term has acquired? Both Bernard McGinn and Philip Sheldrake have already provided lucid surveys of the historical permutations of 'spirituality' as a term.[5] The qualifier *pneumatikos* (spiritual) in the New Testament is obviously connected to the *pneuma* who is understood to be in Jesus and to be the gift of the risen Lord to the community. 'The "spiritual" is what is under the influence of, or is a manifestation of, the Spirit of God.'[6] It is important that in both the Pauline and later Christian writings 'the "spiritual person" (e.g., 1 Cor 2. 14–15) is *not* someone who turns away from material reality but rather someone in whom the Spirit of God dwells.'[7] It is worth noting two very significant points about the early Christian use of the term.

First, the spiritual is that dimension of life which is engendered and empowered by God; God is the primary agent who animates and releases new life and understanding in the believer. Spirituality, in other words, is not something the believer *has* but is a new pattern of personal growth taking place in the community of those who have been sought out, converted and cherished by the risen Christ. 'In this is love, not that we loved God but that God loved us . . . . We love because God first loved us' (1 John 4. 10, 19). Second, the spiritual is connected with the active presence of God and not primarily with extraordinary inner experiences, though God's presence may certainly arouse such feelings. Spirituality in this early sense, therefore, is not connected with the cultivation of particular interior experiences but with the new network of communal relationship and perception that the presence of

God makes possible for each spiritual person. John Zizioulas comments on this ecclesial matrix of spiritual life:

> The idea of new birth or birth in the Spirit was associated in the early church with baptism. The deeper meaning of baptism for Christian existence involved on the one hand a death of the 'old person,' that is, of the way in which personal identity was acquired through biological birth; on the other hand it involved a birth, that is, *the emergence of an identity through a new set of relationships, those provided by the church as the communion of the Spirit.*[8]

None of this means that the experience of an individual person was unimportant in this early conception of spirituality. What it means rather is that personal experience is not in itself the goal of spirituality. Individuals are not so much seeking to discover their own feelings as to live into the knowledge and love of God through the hard work of being members one with another of the Body of Christ. Spirituality in this early Christian sense is inherently mutual, communal, practical and oriented towards the God who makes self known precisely in this new pattern of life called church.

In the twelfth century the term *spiritualitas* (which translated the Greek *pneumatikos* and is the Latin precursor of our 'spirituality') came to be used not only in its early sense, as the power of God animating Christian life, but as whatever 'pertains to the soul as contrasted with the body'; and this new connotation lies behind 'those conceptions of spirituality which willy-nilly used it as the reason for giving the physical world and especially the human body a largely negative role in what they conceived of as authentic Christian life.'[9] This initiated a privatizing tendency in the history of Christianity. Spirituality came to refer to a highly refined state of the soul, with the focus on how one achieves such states of inner purity and exaltation. 'During the course of the sixteenth and seventeenth centuries there seems to have been a gradual shift of "spirituality", both in Latin and in the vernaculars, toward signifying only the inner dispositions, the interior states of the soul.'[10] A moment of crisis occurred in 1695 with the condemnation of the allegedly Quietist teachings of the French spiritual writer, Madame Guyon (1648–1717). Her thought undoubtedly highlighted the drift towards spirituality seen in terms of interior states of being. Guyon's writings, with their recommendation of extreme resignation and disconnection from the external world, provoked a suspicion of spirituality as 'too refined, rarified and separated from ordinary Christian life'.[11]

Partly in reaction to the era of Madame Guyon, a new focus developed on the ordered theorization of the individual's struggle for perfection. And in keeping with this neo-scholastic pursuit of order and classification there was a new terminological profusion. The term 'mystical theology' was appropriated from Pseudo-Dionysius the Areopagite. Whereas for him the term referred to the 'knowledge' disclosed to Christians as they themselves are known and transformed by the unknowable God, now it comes to be used as a technical term for theoretical teaching about the soul's process of sanctification. Here was a double irony, for just as Madame Guyon's language about the utter *resignation* of the self was in fact an elaborate *rhetoric* of the self, so what might have seemed a turn away from this perspective (to the supposedly more scientific 'mystical theology') turns out to be a new and ever more baroque *technology of the self*.

Conceived in such a manner, spirituality could be safely categorized as a sub-specialization of moral theology, which, while important for the growth of the individual soul, could hardly be imagined to be a source of theological insight or discovery. The mystical dimension of the spiritual life remained even more isolated from theology: instead of being considered as the depth dimension of all spirituality, the *mystical* (as now distinct from the ascetical) came to be seen either as the revered and chilly reward of grace after untold ascetical struggle or else as a suspect panoply of paranormal experiences and quirky behaviours. Indeed, the Dutch Carmelite Kees Waaijman remarks of modernity's attitude towards the mystical:

> It had to eliminate mysticism – precisely to the degree that mysticism lays bare man's inner powerlessness – as an unproductive element, often falsely labeled as quietistic, irrational, and occult. In reaction, mysticism – a living indictment against every form of self-interest, self-will, and technicalism – developed a language and a logic of its own which in turn rendered it unintelligible to cultural rationality.[12]

So the mystical dimension of Christian spirituality, that transforming knowledge of God which early Christian writers often saw as the very foundation of theology, grew ever more estranged from theology.

In this century the term 'spiritual theology' was often used interchangeably with ascetical/mystical theology, though it continued largely to describe the mechanics of the spiritual quest. By the middle of the century the term 'spirituality' was itself brought back into scholarly and, increasingly, popular usage. This development coincided with a much broader existential approach to spirituality, concerned to articulate believers' experiences of transcendence across all aspects of life and across ecumenical and religious boundaries. This contemporary notion of spirituality 'does not so much concern itself with defining perfection as with surveying the complex mystery of human growth in the context of a living relationship with the Absolute.'[13] While this more recent understanding of spirituality is much more flexible and open to many approaches of study – psychological, phenomenological, sociological and so on – its connection with theology remains problematic. Definitions of spirituality framed in such general terms as the human search for transcendence, fulfilment, and authenticity make it hard to distinguish spirituality from religion generally, or ethical life. As McGinn comments wryly: 'if spirituality is everything that is good and positive about what is human, then all it needs is a round of applause rather than cultivation and study.'[14]

While no one would want to discount the significance of experiential phenomena in the spiritual life, if these are seen as the defining features then spirituality seems to lose its theological voice. It becomes seen as a particularly powerful expression of human subjectivity. The analysis of spirituality in terms of that subjectivity washes out the theological implications of the subject's transformation – the trace of the divine other vanishes behind one or another aspect of human self-consciousness. So for example, Meister Eckhart's (c.1270–1327) teaching about the soul's 'breakthrough' into the divine ground would not be interpreted in terms of what this implies theologically about the remarkable relationship of human existence to infinite divine existence, but chiefly in terms of an ascent of the mind to a form of pure consciousness common to many religious traditions.

This approach is immensely (perhaps seductively) attractive, first because it permits the study of spirituality purely in terms of the human sciences, and hence seems to legitimize spirituality in the politics of academia. Furthermore its openness to an implicit commonality among religions is beguilingly ecumenical and modern. Indeed, it would be fair to say that this represents a growing consensus regarding the nature and proper study of spirituality. Whether such an approach is as inclusive as at first appears, or whether it tends to foreclose prematurely the possibility of spirituality's contribution to theological reflection, we must carefully consider.

The Issues at Stake

In the last section I proposed thinking of spirituality as the new and transformative pattern of life and thought engendered in people by their encounter with God. In early Christianity we saw the communal matrix for this transforming process: spirituality as growth into a new network of relationships wherein the struggle to love the human other in all his or her angularity and difference from oneself becomes the process by which one is drawn into the knowledge and love of God. The focus of later eras on the inner experiences aroused in this process of encounter gave rise to an ever more elaborate 'science' of the soul. This was conducted via neo-scholastic categories through the early part of the twentieth century and via more psychological and generally anthropological modes in the more recent period. This has led in varying degrees to an understanding of spirituality that is less transparent to the other who engenders the transformational process and hence less expressive as a source of theology. So before we consider the problems and the possibilities of the present state of the question, it will be useful to recall what exactly is at stake. Why is a divorce between spirituality and theology of concern anyway?

Put as bluntly as possible, theology without spirituality becomes ever more methodologically refined but unable to know or speak of the very mysteries at the heart of Christianity, and spirituality without theology becomes rootless, easily hijacked by individualistic consumerism.[15] Part of the difficulty is that the ramifications of such a divorce are obscure until one sees the proper integrity of contemplative encounter and dogmatic theology; for apart from their mutual interaction the true functioning of each becomes easily miscon- ceived. In other words, when a culture has grown used to the divorce between theology and spirituality, between doctrine and prayer, then the mutually critical function of the two breaks down. Neither is in sufficient dialogue with the other to keep it honest. And after a long period of such separation it becomes increasingly difficult to see what is missing in so much of the pale pretenders that pass fairly often for theology and spirituality today. But if one can catch sight of their natural interrelationship, then the problems inherent in their divorce become painfully apparent.

In his highly illuminating short paper on 'Theology and Spirituality', Andrew Louth quotes a telling passage from Thomas Merton:

> Contemplation, far from being opposed to theology, is in fact the normal perfection of theology. We must not separate intellectual study of divinely revealed truth and contemplative experience of that truth as if they could never have anything to do with one another. On the contrary, they are simply two aspects of the same thing. Dogmatic and mystical theology, or theology and 'spirituality', are not to be set apart in mutually exclusive categories, as if mysticism were for saintly women and theological study were for practical but, alas, unsaintly men. This fallacious division perhaps explains much that is actually lacking both in theology and spirituality. But the two belong together. Unless they are united there is no fervour, no life and no spiritual value in theology, no substance, no meaning and no sure orientation in the contemplative life.[16]

So what is the natural relationship of spirituality and theology? Earlier I suggested that the two have their common ground in the believing community's encounter with God. Spirituality is the *impression* that encounter has in the continual transformation of the members of the church; theology is the *expression* of that encounter in the attempt to understand and tell something true of the mystery whom the believing community encounters.

Louth specifies this model further by reference to the activity of contemplation. Today we often use the term 'mysticism' though this is really something of an academic invention; earlier eras referred to the most intimate and transforming encounter with God as 'contemplation'. It is a term that holds together two elements we often see contrasted as though they were mutually exclusive, namely the affective or loving impulse and the intellectual or knowing impulse. Louth quotes the medieval mystical theologian Richard of St Victor (d. 1173): 'Contemplation is a free and clear vision of the mind fixed upon the manifestation of wisdom in suspended wonder.'[17] There are at least three vital points to note about this definition.

First, contemplation is not like normal thinking only muddled and tentative, on the contrary it is seen as an activity in which the mind is liberated to perceive clearly, freed from the usual constraints of distraction, self-preoccupation or prejudice. If what is perceived in the mind's clear vision is dark and mysterious this is not because pious emotions have muddled things to a murk, but because of the shocking intensity of the vision of reality that has broken through.

Second, the use of the term 'mind' here ought not to suggest that which is exclusively discursive, a manipulative rationalism that subjects whatever it encounters to its own control. The more classical notion of mind refers to the desire of our whole being for deep understanding and relationship with all that is intelligible. In this definition of contemplation, the mind's vision is said to take place in 'suspended wonder'. Now if, as I have just suggested, the activity of mind does not mean a rationalist manipulation of concepts, then for the mind to act in 'suspended wonder' does not entail some kind of abrogation of the mind or the Enlightenment's dreaded *sacrificium intellectus*, but rather the mind's profound engagement. If, for example, you are enraptured by the marvel of musical structure in Bach's *Two and Three Part Inventions* this does mean, it is true, that your mind is strongly inclined towards knowing these compositions, but it does *not* mean that your mind has ceased to reflect critically in the process; on the contrary the activity of the mind in 'suspended wonder' may be all the more intense, engaged and resourceful in analytical perceptivity.

Third, this understanding of contemplation says that *what* the mind is fixed upon in clear vision by an act of suspended wonder is 'the manifestation of wisdom'. In other words, the contemplative act is not in the first instance a moment of especially excited feelings, though these may be involved; it is rather an event of being grasped by the self-disclosure of wisdom. Contemplation is not particularly concerned with the inner states of the contemplative (however interesting, unusual and worthy of study they may be in their own right), but with the breaking through of wisdom into the contemplative's consciousness. This is one of those subtle differences that matters enormously. First because it makes clear that the whole event of contemplation is not primarily something that one does but that one is invited into. Second, to speak of contemplation as the breaking through of wisdom makes clear that the event of contemplation issues in new *understanding*, a new encounter with wisdom. It is inherently theological.

The point of all this elucidation is to give us a common frame of reference for asking the question: What is at stake in the divorce of spirituality and theology? For, if we return to Louth with this notion of contemplation in mind, we begin to see the natural relationship of spirituality and theology and the implications of their separation. 'It is in *contemplation* that theology and spirituality meet. Theology is one of the fruits of contemplation, the attempt to express and articulate what is perceived in this "free and clear vision"; spirituality is the preparing of the soul for contemplation. And contemplation, in this sense, is not something we can attain.'[18] Louth would not, I think, mean to imply that spirituality is something we simply decide to have a go at but rather that it is itself (from the very first stirring of desire to pray) engendered within us by the beckoning of God's address to humanity. In such a view, spirituality is intrinsically oriented towards theology and theology is organically emergent from spirituality. They are related to each other as the preparation for and articulation of the event of contemplation, the most intimate encounter with God.

This being so, their separation from one another is mutually debilitating. At first glance it might seem that spirituality is not necessarily affected; after all, it is theology that depends on spirituality as its source. Yet in real life we have no 'freeze frame' picture to deal with, but a living community of prayer and reflection. If the contemplative's encounters are dismissed as so much 'devotion' which can have no place in academic theology, then a significant public forum for mystical insight is closed. The call to unfold the communal, theological import of the contemplative event is no longer heard by the mystic. In such a case, it would hardly be surprising if 'the mystic's world became increasingly private, subjective, psychological, and ascetic'.[19]

Christians such as Gregory of Nyssa (*c*.330–*c*.395) or Augustine (354–430) were able, prior to this tendency to separate spirituality and theology, to find 'the appropriate dogmatic clothing for their very personal experience; everything became objective, and all the subjective conditions, experiences, fears, strivings, the "shock" in a word, were made to serve a fuller understanding of the content of revelation'.[20] We might almost say that the ability to discern and formulate the meaning of mystical encounter is something that must be acquired, like a skill, and that without a culture in which such a skill is forged and fostered it may be lost. Take, for example, the case of the great mystical theologian Julian of Norwich (c.1342 – after 1416). According to her own report, on the night of 13 May 1373, in her thirtieth year, she was very near the point of death when she received fifteen 'showings' from God. But her now famous book, the *Revelations of Divine Love*, with all its fertile theological analyses of human existence, the meaning of Christ, and the doctrine of the Trinity, was the product of a long, hard, struggle of elucidation. This theological fruitfulness was the result of twenty years rumination on what might have remained purely private spiritual experiences. Throughout her work, Julian is aware that her effort of theological articulation may receive a frosty reception. The ecclesiastical and academic culture of her era was already less than open to the insights of someone situated far from the impressively authoritative halls of the university – and a woman at that.

Hans Urs von Balthasar has suggested that mystical thinkers in later eras became so conditioned by this isolation of academic goals from contemplative life that they no longer thought of making the effort that Julian did, nor would they perhaps have had the skill to achieve what she accomplished.

> The saints, intimidated by the conceptual entanglements drawn round the gospel truth, no longer dare to collaborate in the necessary work of exposition of doctrine, or think themselves qualified to do so. They leave dogma to the prosaic work of the School, and become – lyrical poets. But just as poetry has developed from an objective art interpreting reality, the conception of the Greeks and Romans, to a subjective art describing inner states, the expressionistic and impressionistic art of modern times, so also have the saints come to speak a religious language which is not dogmatic. Or else they obey instructions and respond to demands made on them, which are more and more of a subjective and psychological nature. The saints in modern times are required to describe the way in which they experienced God, and the accent is always on experience rather than on God.[21]

It is not, in other words, simply the fault of the contemplative that spirituality loses its theological voice; this is a part of larger cultural shifts (particularly in the academic version of theology) that redirect persons of prayer away from the public reception of their insights.

The problem with this separation from theology is that it tends to disorientate spirituality, to deprive it of some stable communal goal and reference, and hence render it susceptible to the idols, compulsions, or fears of the individual. There is another danger as well: the intensity of mystical experience can easily lead to a kind of absolutism that oppresses the lives of mystics themselves or of cultures receptive to them. Theology reminds spirituality that 'interpretation is intrinsic to experience'.[22] And therefore every spiritual consciousness must be contextualized and appraised in terms of its context; claims to a putatively absolute experience, free from the interpretive matrix of one's cultural location are always problematic.

Yet my primary concern in this book is the challenge that spirituality issues to theology for, apart from its spiritual source, theology tends to enervation and desiccation. In his presidential address to fellow theologians of the Catholic Theological Society of America, Michael Buckley asked very pointedly,

> is it not extraordinary that so much Catholic formal theology for centuries, its divorce between spirituality and fundamental and dogmatic theology, has bracketed this actual witness [the spiritual experiences of holy lives] as of no cogency. . .? Is it not a lacuna in the standard theology, even of our day, that theology neither has nor has striven to forge the intellectual devices to probe in these concrete experiences the warrant they present for the reality of God and make them available for so universal a discipline?[23]

Buckley and others have submitted that the divorce between spirituality and theology at the very least involves a serious 'lacuna', and this in two respects. First there is simply the problem of a gap in theology's sources. As spirituality and theology have each grown more focused on particular dimensions of their respective spheres (inner experience on one hand and the criteria of 'scientific' scholarship on the other), theology has correspondingly felt less sure of what exactly to do with either the spiritual life of theologians themselves or with the lives and texts of spiritual writers. 'The questions that Christianity's mystics raise for theology visibly embarrass too many academic theologians.'[24] From the concrete patterns of a saintly life to the particular imagery of a mystical text, the vast range of spiritual sources available to theology can hardly be ignored if theology is to do its job of articulating a critical understanding of the faith community's beliefs. So for example, it would seem peculiar to analyse the meaning of Jesus Christ without reference to that unfolding realization of his significance embodied in the life of a martyr or the consciousness of a mystic – especially if they have each intentionally defined their mission in terms of participation in Christ.[25]

The other aspect of this lacuna is that, as von Balthasar suggested, theologians cut off from spirituality may not only lose contact with important sources of religious reflection but may also lose the proper skills for speaking of the doctrines of Christianity – doctrines conceived not simply as propositions for analysis but as living mysteries to be encountered. This is not a call for theology to cloak its bafflements with an unctuous tone of voice or, as Paul Tillich once warned against, 'to fill in logical gaps with devotional material'.[26] Quite the opposite, spirituality calls theology to an honesty about the difficulty of understanding what is unfathomable (that 'suspended wonder' spoken of by Richard of St Victor), an openness to what is never a puzzle to be solved but always a mystery to be lived. The question is whether, apart from spirituality, theology remembers very well how to do this, to discern the nature of the mystery – and to leave others not simply in reliance on the theologian's words but to lead them well enough in the right direction that believers may truly enter into transforming understanding themselves.

This brings us to what is perhaps the deepest concern, namely that when theology is divorced from spirituality it is likely to begin talking about a different god, a deity who depends on theological performance for vitality and verisimilitude. If I spend any length of time describing someone I've met to a friend, pretty soon my description begins to be the defining framework within which both I and my friend will consider this other person. Yet the description is not the reality and it tends easily to usurp the place of the concrete human being on whom it depends. Apart from continuing reflection on the transforming encounter with God, it is easy enough for me as a theologian to forget that the divine 'object' of my study is never simply that but always the living self-disclosing ground of my own understanding. God is always the source of all other agency. Yet my theological exposition of God may have all the liveliness of a laboratory specimen – and then I may begin thinking about God in those terms even without realizing it. The God I want to talk about imperceptibly becomes an object susceptible to the intricate theories I propound. Surely it is right for theology to offer as clear and critical an exposition of God's reality as possible. The perilous possibility is that theology, apart from spirituality, may be fooled by its very success as a human discourse into talking about a reality who is no longer the acting subject of self-disclosure. What kind of god does theology divorced from spirituality end up describing?

By way of an example of the problem, one might recall the laborious patience with which Cleanthes in David Hume's *Dialogues Concerning Natural Religion* struggles to construct an enlightened understanding of God. Just as we can note the construction of an elegantly designed building, observes Cleanthes, and infer from that something of the existence and nature of the architect, so close examination of the miraculous harmony of the universe points us quite reasonably to the beneficent divinity who is its 'architect'. From this theological perspective, any advertence to the community's spiritual encounter with the living presence of God is a distraction (possibly a dangerous one since not every right-thinking person can be assumed to have had the same spiritual experiences). Michael Buckley traces the intricate patterns of just such arguments wherein the community's spiritual encounter with the living Christ is banned from the discussion as an improperly sectarian and devotional line of thought. Speaking of the development of modern theology into the eighteenth century, Buckley writes: 'In the absence of a rich and comprehensive Christology and a Pneumatology of religious experience Christianity entered into the defense of the existence of the Christian god without appeal to anything Christian.'[27] And indeed, in Hume's little theological tragi-comedy, Cleanthes's effort is pulled to pieces by the sceptical Philo. The deity your theological reasonings have arrived at, says Philo to Cleanthes, might very well turn out to be a strange god, rather different indeed from the Christian assumptions which you have left so politely unspoken. Separated from the interpretive framework of the spiritual encounter with God, the world is hard to judge. Perhaps the universe, says Philo, 'was only the first rude essay of some infant deity who afterwards abandoned it', or perhaps it is 'the production of old age and dotage in some superannuated deity; and ever since his death has run on at adventures'.[28]

Cleanthes's theological edifice, with all its doors firmly shut against the community's experience of God's mystery in Christ, has become a trap – within which no encounter with the living reality of God is possible. Herbert McCabe puts it with his customary acuity:

> If we are to enter into the mystery of God it is not information that we need, and in principle we could not have information – our language and concepts break down in the presence of God. What we need is to be taken up by God himself, to share in his knowledge of himself, a sharing that to *us* must just look like darkness. So that our faith seems not like an increase of knowledge but, if anything, an increase in ignorance. We become more acutely aware of our inadequacy before the mystery as we are brought closer to it. So it is God's initiative that is needed. Not that we should speak more about him, but that *he* should speak to us.[29]

This is the perspective of theology rooted in spirituality, of theology growing organically out of God's own knowing and speaking of Godself.

So while it is very true that theology provides an indispensable critical function for spirituality, it is no less true that spirituality affords a radically critical perspective equally necessary for the health of theology. How easy it is for theologians to evade the hard question, 'Who is God?'. Who is this God who makes self known in the intimate helplessness of an infant born all untimely to poor people and the forsakenness of one being executed as an enemy of the state? Where does theology venture in its task of searching for critical understanding of this God? Will it risk exposure with the faithful women at the foot of the Cross, or does it seek more secure and acceptable (more academically respectable?) company? Spirituality grounds theology ever anew in this place of human waiting and speechlessness at the foot of the inestimable speaking of God. It is true that what takes place there defies human understanding and would hence seem to defeat the purpose of theology; yet the hope with which spirituality imbues theology enables it to persevere there, to wait not for a clever resolution of its own, but for the 'theology' that God articulates in the resurrection of Jesus of Nazareth from the dead: 'So spirituality − prayer − is, I suggest, that which keeps theology to its proper vocation, that which prevents theology from evading its own real object. Spirituality does not exactly answer the question, Who is God? but it preserves the orientation, the perspective, within which this question remains a question that is being asked rather than a question that is being evaded or elided.'[30] Perhaps we might say simply that spirituality contextualizes theology in the mystery of Jesus' dying and rising which is God's self-disclosure and therefore the matrix of honest theological reflection.

The critical function which spirituality serves for theology is not a matter simply of adding one more source for theology to consider; it is not a matter of judiciously taking people's *experiences* seriously along with supposedly more 'rational' thought, but a matter of exposing theology to the profound questioning that animates the very heart of the community's struggle to be faithful. In the words of Rowan Williams:

> The questioning involved here is not our interrogation of the data, but its interrogation of us. It is the intractable *strangeness* of the ground of belief that must constantly be allowed to challenge the fixed assumptions of religiosity. . . . And the greatness of the great Christian saints lies in their readiness to be questioned, judged, stripped naked and left speechless by that which lies at the centre of their faith.[31]

It is spirituality's vocation, in countless struggles and whole lives, in acts of compassion and contemplation, in mystical texts of every kind, to be drawn out of provisionality into real life precisely by this divine questioning at its centre. It is this questioning that spirituality carries within itself ('always carrying in the body the death of Jesus' [2 Cor 4.10]) as its animating source. Apart from constant exposure to that questioning, theology risks losing touch with the very God who has given it life. 'One will not long believe in a personal God with whom there is no communication, no interaction.'[32]

Problems and Possibilities Today

The current state of the relationship of spirituality and theology depends of course on a long history of interaction, but there are also contemporary factors that shift the terms of the discussion. Many of these relate to massive cultural shifts, the study of which is quite beyond the scope of this book. There is for example the apparently growing disparity of resources between regions of the world; the desperately poor have a spirituality of their own, of survival in the face of brutal daily violence and appalling need.[33] As these forms of spirituality become known in their practices and texts, how will theologians react? In other parts of the world, an abundance of material resources and the banalization of life have led to a new quest for popular spirituality that is highly consumerist and individualist in orientation. Best selling books on angels, 'near-death' experience and a ritual use of 'crystals' are merely the more glamorous items in a search for sacred personal totems. Is this popular mentality a new form of spirituality that will endure across and beyond all boundaries of institutional religions (as the 'New Age' movement), or is it more like a faddish expression of cultural boredom? Whatever the answer, it would be hard to avoid the conclusion that institutional religions have often failed to invite people into the depths of their own spiritual traditions as sources for inner growth and self-transcendence. How exactly do these and similarly wide-ranging cultural crises or shifts (e.g., the growth of fundamentalisms) shape the context in which spirituality and theology interact today? At the very least we could say that theologians will not want to work in ignorance of such features of the cultural landscape. The question is how to sift and appraise in constructive acts of theology such disparate and massive spiritual trends. There are, however, two other factors more easily construed within the scope of this book which are already shaping the relationship between spirituality and theology.

Spirituality as an academic discipline

Until now I have talked of spirituality primarily in terms of the lived encounter with God. Yet one of the most salient features of the contemporary discussion is not only steadily rising *popular* interest in spirituality, but the emergence of a revised *academic* discipline that studies spirituality. How is this related to spirituality as living encounter and what are its implications for the integrity of spirituality and theology? In three important articles Sandra Schneiders, a founder and director of one of America's leading graduate academic programs in the study of spirituality, has proffered her views on spirituality as an academic discipline and its relationship to theology.[34] Because of the influential perspectives enunciated by Schneiders it will be worthwhile considering her views carefully.

Schneiders usually offers two, sometimes three, dimensions to her use of the term 'spirituality'. First, just as one says that a person has a certain 'psychology', a shape or pattern to their psychic life, so one could well say that every human being has a spirituality, that is, a 'fundamental dimension of the human being'.[35] Hence, in her view, 'the primary application of the term spirituality is to that dimension of the human subject in virtue of which the person is capable of self-transcending integration in relation to the Ultimate, whatever the Ultimate is for the person in question.'[36] Note the polarity evoked in this description: spirituality in itself is an aspect of the human subject, yet it is precisely that dimension of the human which is oriented towards self-*transcendence*; or again, the integration of the human subject is the telos of spirituality, yet that integration is achieved not solipsistically but 'in relation to the Ultimate'. The second form of usage Schneiders highlights is 'the lived experience which actualizes' one's spirituality.[37] So Schneiders would have us distinguish at least theoretically between spirituality as an inherent feature of human existence and the particular processes by which this possibility moves towards fulfilment. The third way in which she sees the term used is in reference to 'the experimental and theoretical study of human efforts at self-transcending integration and to the pastoral practices aimed at fostering the spirituality of individuals and groups'.[38]

The inescapable trajectory of these terminological clarifications is towards a notion of spirituality as *innate human aspiration towards ultimacy*. 'In short, spirituality refers to the experience of consciously striving to integrate one's life in terms not of isolation or self-absorption but of self-transcendence towards the ultimate value one perceives.'[39] There is a very good reason, in Schneider's view, for highlighting the innately human status of spirituality.

As we saw above in considering the history of the term, spirituality was treated (from the beginning of the modern era) as a sub-discipline of dogmatic or moral theology; in that conception, spirituality derives its principles directly from revelation and follows these as norms in working towards Christian perfection beyond the level of the basic morality required of all. Schneiders rightly views this earlier conceptuality as out of touch with a more existential outlook in theology, and as quite removed from 'most of what ordinary people are talking about' when they use the word.[40]

This explains her preference for what she forthrightly calls an 'anthropological' approach in which 'the structure and dynamics of the human person as such are the locus of the emergence of the spiritual life.'[41] Besides opening the door for a wide interdisciplinary range of scholarship to participate in the study of spirituality (hence integrating it more widely in the university setting), this anthropological approach has the advantage of leaving the ultimate value towards which the subject is striving as an open space which can be filled in quite differently depending on one's religious preference or non-religious perspective. I agree that these are advantages in fostering the study of spirituality in a contemporary academic setting. My question at this point is whether the theological effect of this approach is quite so unproblematic as may appear.

Schneiders herself rightly warns against an obvious false step; namely the assumption that one could ever have an academically convenient 'spirituality in general' available for study and theorization, such that the particularities of a given religious (or secular) form of spirituality might be allowed to fade in favour of what are, allegedly, the deeper values or patterns hidden at the heart of all spiritualities.

> There is no such thing as 'generic spirituality.' Spirituality as lived experience is, by definition, determined by the particular ultimate value within the horizon of which the life project is pursued. Consequently, it involves intrinsically some relatively coherent and articulate understanding of both the human being and the horizon of ultimate value (i.e., in Christian terms, theology), some historical tradition, some symbol system, and so on.[42]

Even after she offers this admonition, however, Schneiders points out that 'by focusing on the common experience of *integrating self-transcendence within the horizon of ultimacy* one keeps open the possibility of dialogue among people of very different world views'.[43] Again, it seems to me perfectly useful to highlight patterns in spirituality that find analogies across religious or secular traditions, but this approach has deeper ramifications.

Schneiders accepts the role of theology (along with other disciplines such as history, hermeneutical theory, psychology, etc.) in helping to construe spiritual texts or practices. She is also supportive of the intent to draw on spirituality as a theological source. But the anthropological approach outlined in her articles, with the most well-meaning intentions, seems likely to perpetuate the divorce between spirituality and theology. In identifying the human search for wholeness as the true subject matter of spirituality (as academic discipline), the anthropological approach would seem to render God peripheral. Whatever ultimate value orients any given spiritual life would be very useful to know about, rather as it is useful to know about a spiritual seeker's historical setting – interesting points, no doubt, but once clarified, issues not really at the heart of the matter. Clearly this is going to make it hard to highlight the theological implications of spirituality, since all the details of the spiritual journey are going to be read as data of human experience, while their polyvalence as signs of the divine in the transformation of human life might easily be left unexplored.

Furthermore, who is this wonderfully transcending self who happens to have an Ultimate Value of some kind as the reference for the self's higher integration? The existence of such a self seems at least as much in doubt today as the existence of its mirror image: the autonomous, self-referential god of eighteenth-century deism. The notion that 'I' would even be able to understand myself as an I, apart from interaction with others, seems to be an outlook from which the mask is slipping to betray the questionable longings of the Enlightenment for a stable, order-imposing self. In other words, the whole project of an anthropological approach to spirituality seems to rest on a dubious metaphysical entity called the transcending self; indeed it is, ironically, every bit as dependent on this self as the older dogmatic approach to spirituality that it wishes to escape – the latter bustled this self off on a neo-scholastic progression to perfection, whereas the anthropological approach depends on an existentialist self which aspires towards wholeness. The very existence of such a self is, for postmodernity, very much in question. The anthropological approach to spirituality would seem to be a continuation of the post-Cartesian preoccupation with the individual subject, complete with its private mental states and experiences, so that it is exactly these fascinating experiences that become identified as one's 'spirituality' and are counted therefore as the subject matter for the academic discipline that studies spirituality. As Fergus Kerr remarks, however, participation in the real world constantly reminds us 'that we are agents in practical intercourse with one another – not solitary observers gazing upwards at the celestial realm of eternal forms, or inwards at the show in the mental theatre. *What constitutes us as human beings is the regular and patterned reactions that we have to one another. It is in our* dealings with each other – in how we *act* – that human life is founded.'[44] It is for this reason that I proposed thinking of spirituality specifically in terms of encounter, spirituality as a form of life engendered and initiated by the other – the human other of the neighbour and the divine other whom I meet through my love for the neighbour. It is this beckoning of the other (and the response this beckoning elicits in us) that draws us from provisional existence into real life, into the unfolding of true personhood, and so ultimately into the most real form of life there is, namely the interpersonal trinitarian life of God.

The focal point in *this* view of spirituality as an academic discipline would not be the states of inner transcendence experienced by the self, but rather the patterns, structures and images that embody the beckoning of the other and the response this invitation evokes. We would ask what these features suggest about the one who initiates and sustains this process and about the one who comes to be as a result of the process. In fact, as our reading of mystical texts proceeds throughout this book, we will see that the whole scheme of inner subjectivity by which modernity has tended to interpret spirituality may need to be relinquished in favour of a more embodied and contextual model. We will consider mystical writers, for example, who evoke a play of mutuality in which the one who initiates (God) and the one who comes to be (human being) are drawn into a union that, paradoxically, does not deprive them of voice or face but constitutes them or identifies them ever more fully as persons.

Besides being less provincially bound by post-Cartesian mythologies of the self, this approach seems more congruent with the concerns of many of the spiritual and mystical writers themselves. As the historian of late medieval mysticism Paul Mommaers comments:

> The mystics themselves appear to be fascinated not by their own feelings but by *something* felt, by *someone* from without becoming present within. As a perceptual phenomenon, the mystical state no doubt testifies to a magnificent capacity of human consciousness. But this matters less to the mystic than who or what appears on the perceptual field. Consciousness is valuable not because of what it is but because of the other that it can experience as not identical with itself or at its disposal.[45]

Mommaers gives an example of the kind of subtlety with which this consciousness of the other is signalled within the human perceptual field, but not identical with that consciousness. Commenting on the remarkable use of the figure of love (*Minne*) in the writings of the Flemish poet and visionary Hadewijch (mid 1200s), Mommaers notes that while her experience of *Minne* is very personal, it is not simply an expression of inner feelings. *Minne* 'is not subjective in the sense of valuing and enjoying the emotion of love as such. For Hadewijch, *Minne* as a movement of the soul is never detached from *Minne* as the Other who causes it. To feel love is to meet the Beloved.'[46] Hadewijch is intensely aware of her transforming encounters, but it is not the feelings aroused in these encounters that interest her so much as the indication they give of the one who arouses them. The spiritual experience – in our usual sense of some sensation of inner feelings – is for her only a by-product of her participation in God, a manifestation in terms of her humanity of God's secret presence and activity.

Why is it that language about God or the cosmos so often comes to be interpreted as language about the self and its 'experiences'? In a profoundly insightful monograph, Denys Turner has pointed to some of the impulses at work in our constant tendency to treat the language of spirituality in a positivistic manner. Mystical writers again and again warn against paying much attention to religious feelings or preoccupation with various experiential states. Such writers do this by using imagery of withdrawal, darkness, inner abandonment and so on. But their interpreters very often mistake this imagery for a kind of literal report of, or prescription for, actual religious experience. The language of negativity in spiritual texts, intended as a critique of all religious experience, is read as encouragement to pursue the achievement of negative *experiences*. If a mystic said for example that, 'Darkness is the only way to God', the experientialist interpreter takes this to mean that one must seek some inner state of 'darkness', rather than hearing it as a warning against reliance on particular beliefs, aspirations, feelings, or idols of any kind whatsoever in the encounter with the living God.

> Experientialism is, in short, the 'positivism' of Christian spirituality. It abhors the experiential vacuum of the apophatic [the way of negation], rushing in to fill it with the plenum of the psychologistic. It resists the deconstructions of the negative way, holding fast to supposititious experiences *of* the negative. It is happy with commendations of the 'interior' so long as it can cash them out in the currency of experienced inwardness and of the practices of prayer which will achieve it.[47]

The anthropological approach to spirituality as described in Schneiders's articles seems unintentionally open to this manner of distortion – not just in regard to this or that mystical text, but to the phenomena of spirituality as a whole. What an irony it would be if the academicians finally allowed the return of spirituality as a conversation partner in the university, only to consign it – as did many late medieval ecclesiastical and university authorities – to a non-theological realm labelled, appropriately, 'private devotion'.

Feminist and liberation perspectives

Another major development that shapes how we consider these issues today is much broader than the disciplinary question we have been looking at. It is the new perspective brought to theological studies by developments in liberation and feminist thought. A number of important insights have been crystallized in these areas of theology. Perhaps most broadly construed, the central vision has to do with the overcoming of modernity's impulse to isolate theory from practice, and to regard the former as theologically preeminent. Feminist and liberationist religious perspectives have recovered a fundamental assumption of earlier eras; namely, that living, practical involvement in reality is not a recipe for subjective beclouding of our understanding but is rather the prerequisite for true insight in conceptualization.

As the remarkable work of Pierre Hadot has shown, this was the assumed perspective of the ancient world. Wisdom itself was understood to be embodied in a certain manner of living according to particular practices and exercises. Ancient philosophical teachings, as we now think of them – highly theoretical doctrines about reality – were, in fact, second-order derivations. The great philosophers and their schools developed very concrete patterns of life. These practical exercises or forms of being in the world were what characterized the philosophical schools most definitively. What we think of as their 'philosophy' was the attempt of disciples to give an account in theory of the forms of life being practised by lovers of wisdom. These doctrinal and theoretical works were essentially teaching tools, designed to give the philosophical schools' students something with which to habituate their minds to the patterns of living that a given school enacted. Hadot summarizes:

> Theory is never considered an end in itself; it is clearly and decidedly put in the service of practice. Epicurus is explicit on this point: the goal of the science of nature is to obtain the soul's serenity. Or else, as among the Aristotelians, one is more attached to theoretical activity considered as a way of life that brings an almost divine pleasure and happiness than to the theories themselves. . . . Or, as among the Platonists, abstract theory is not considered to be true knowledge: as Porphyry says, 'Beatific contemplation does not consist of the accumulation of arguments or a storehouse of learned knowledge, but in us theory must become nature and life itself.'[48]

In this scheme of things, transforming practices of life give rise to a theoretical account of reality as it is understood by those practitioners. This account, in turn, is intended not as a higher ascent towards reality by means of theorization, but as a preliminary guide for those seeking to follow the transforming way of life themselves.

Granted that the transforming practices of life envisaged by feminist and liberation theology are rather different from those enjoined by the ancient philosophical schools, there is nonetheless in our contemporary movements a rediscovery of this balance of theory and practice. Feminist thinkers have for a long time now been unmasking the very idea of a purely objective consciousness or the supposed preeminence of pure theory over the 'merely' categorical. Both these modern shibboleths are seen to emerge from very concrete contexts of male-dominated approaches to reason, contexts whose practical shaping of thought – feminists point out – cannot honestly remain unacknowledged. So, for example, feminist scholars have argued that the academic study of spirituality requires a holistic and participative approach that involves the student and scholar in some personal existential contextualization of the material. In response, some members of the academy have raised serious questions about this proposal, hinting that there is a hidden religious agenda involved. Feminist scholars have in response pointed out that the real issue is the lingering myth of an objective consciousness, which actually hinders both practical and theoretical understanding.[49] Feminist theology has provided a new context for theological reflection in which the community's lived experience is granted a voice. These deeply contextualized construals of reality are helping to shape theology as a more supple and inclusive discipline, able to hear the multiple spiritualities of people not as raw data to be abstracted from, but as having theological substance and import in themselves.

Political and liberation theologies have emphasized the need for theology not simply to reflect doctrinally *upon* the situation of the poor in the light of revelation, but to understand revelation as an interpretive framework, a call to obedience and solidarity in which God's voice can be heard in the lives of the poor themselves. It is, in other words, a question of allowing the 'dangerous memory' of the exodus of slaves from their masters, and the radical interruptive suffering of Jesus among the poor and condemned, and the liberative empowerment of the small persecuted community of disciples, all to operate as lenses that can disclose the continuation of God's liberating work among the poor today. This means that, in the perspective of liberation theology, it is normal and even necessary for theology to emerge directly as a public reflection on, and sharing of, the people's spirituality. Gustavo Gutiérrez writes:

> Spiritual experience is the terrain in which theological reflection strikes root.
> . . . The solidity and energy of theological thought depend precisely on the

spiritual experience that supports it. This experience takes the form, first and foremost, of a profound encounter with God and God's will. Any discourse of faith starts from, and takes its bearings from, the Christian life of the community. Any reflection that does not help in living according to the Spirit is not a Christian theology. . . . This fact does not weaken the rigorously scientific character of theology; it does, however, properly situate it.[50]

It is worth noting here a feature prominent also in Hadot's description of ancient philosophy; namely that the goal of the theoretical reflection must be not only to articulate people's encounter with reality but also to assist people in 'living according' to that reality.

It has sometimes been the case that academic theology, as we have seen, is suspicious of spirituality as far too subjective, as purely a kind of poetic language of devotion that, were it to have any utility for theology, would require translation first into more abstract language. This assumption is prominently featured in the work of Friedrich Schleiermacher (1768–1834), often thought of as the founder of modern theology. Indeed, Schleiermacher counts it as a the very goal of scientific theology 'that the figurative expression be either exchanged for a literal one or transformed into such by being explained, and that definite limits be imposed on the corresponding element in the rhetorical expressions'.[51] This assumes that the religious symbols and imagery of spiritual texts are important but 'early' stages in the expression of religious experience and that academic theology needs to free the essential meaning of these expressions from their primitive representations.

What liberation theology suggests in reply is that the spiritual practices, imagery and patterns of thought emerging in the lives of the poor cannot so easily be dispensed with if theology is going to remain an accurate construal of God's revelation in real history. The symbols and imagery of a people's spirituality are not moving but hopelessly unscientific descriptions of religious reality; they are the interpretive framework that allows the religious reality to be experienced and recognized as such. A story, for example, bears a gift of meaning that draws the listener into a new vision of things which could never be conveyed or achieved by purely discursive or propositional expositions of the story's 'meaning'. From this perspective, doctrines are not the scientifically manipulable 'meanings' of person's lives, rather the lives and spirituality of people are the meaning of doctrine. Jon Sobrino notes: 'The basic change in a theology that had been purely doctrinal came from the realization that the whole warp and woof of the theological task must be shot through with hope, and thus with a call for Christian practice.'[52] Already we can see here a very strong call for the reintegration of spirituality and theology. They are seen as distinct expressions of one and the same encounter with God, each having particular tasks to perform but always informing each other and leading back to each other.

The ancient technical term for teaching that does not merely speak *about* the divine mystery but helps to lead others to a participatory understanding of it themselves is 'mystagogy'. And it seems fairly clear by now that this is in fact what many liberation theologians are advocating. It is a stance that doubtless raises questions for academic theology today: what would be the truth status of theological discourse if it were oriented in such a fashion towards praxis? What would be the impact on theology's standing in the university? It seems to me that these questions already belong to another era. Many theorists, even the kind one finds in universities, would reckon perfectly intelligible a *participatory* model of truth rather than a purely propositional *adequacy* model. Is my discourse only true, in other words, if I can somehow offer propositions that adequately correspond to a given 'object' out there? But what if the reality I desire to speak of is no 'object', indeed does not exist as one of the items of the universe, but is rather the answer to the question why there is a universe at all rather than nothing? Then it would be the case that the most adequate truth-telling would attempt to guide one into participative encounter with that reality, not to offer an impossible series of descriptive propositions about it.

Truthful discourse about God would thus seem to require a particular way of knowing and stating things, namely a knowing that does not point at something (for there is literally no-thing at which to point) but participates in the mystery of the reality it desires to know. For example, I cannot really know a friend by demanding a listing of particular pieces of information about her, but must in some way come to participate by her invitation in her life. So too with the ever deeper divine mystery at the heart of human personal mystery – understanding requires involvement, practice, participation. In a typically clarifying passage, Sobrino observes:

> It is not enough merely to speak of God. Theology must allow God to speak. Theology must move the human being to speak with God. . . . In order to do this, theology must see to it that its doctrine on God, and its doctrine on whatsoever theological content, genuinely facilitate the experience of God. A theologal theology [i.e., speech *of* God not just *about* God] must be a mystagogy – an introduction into the reality of God as God is: transcendent mystery, utterly resistant to manipulation, and yet our Father, near at hand, good, and saving. The doctrine of God must be such that it both respects God's mystery, and introduces its addressee into that mystery. Theology must know how to speak of God while letting God be God. Theology must integrate into a knowledge

of God the ignorance corresponding to that knowledge. Otherwise it will not be genuine knowledge of God.[53]

Sobrino's insights are well worth pondering. If theology is to do its job, he argues, it must preserve a kind of transparency to the encounter with God in which it is rooted. This is not simply a question of using pious language, as if a devotionally-tinged prose were somehow specially good theology. That is not the idea at all. Because theology is intended to be truthful talk of *God*, it must take account of the peculiar requirements of knowing and speaking of God. As I suggested above, this particularly includes the awareness that God is not an object which we could simply describe in the usual ways; as if God were like all the other items in the universe only bigger and invisible. Rather, to know and speak truly of God requires being drawn to share in God's own self-knowledge (what that might mean we shall consider in the rest of this book). And so theology, if it is to be of much use as theology, needs to maintain an openness to the spirituality whence it springs, and to orient people towards that encounter themselves.[54] In short, it needs to recover its integrity with spirituality.

Another contribution of liberation and feminist theology to our discussion needs to be highlighted. For besides the focus in these forms of theology on the wholeness and contextuality of all theology, and on the integral link theology has with the spirituality of the people, we are also reminded of the importance of relationality. By this I mean not simply that people and ideas and history are all bound up together in real life, but that we exist *at all* and we know *at all* precisely because we are not 'individuals' in some privatized, autonomous sense but because we live by encounter, by relationship.[55] Feminist thinkers have pointed out the perils of suggesting that we are *only* by virtue of our relationships, for many women have been trapped by this very construction of their own beings as dependent on some (male) other. The idea is rather that, in the first place, what makes us really human is that we have this capacity for relationship (to a more complex and volitional degree than the genetic hard-wiring of the herd or pack found in other parts of the animal kingdom); and, in the second place, that we can choose to exercise our relationality in ways that bestow life upon ourselves and others.[56] Relationality does not mean fusion with the other but rather mutuality. This capacity to be one-with-another-in-love-and-freedom is what characterizes us most definitively as humans; it is embedded, therefore, in the very structures by which we exist and by which we know.[57]

Sobrino, for example, speaks of spirituality as a fundamental willingness to face what is *real*, rather than the projected fears or wishes of the ego. The real is never an abstraction, but living truth that calls for response. To avoid this call, to prefer the security of a putatively self-constructed world, is a kind of dishonesty. 'This dishonesty is not simply a noetic error with regard to the truth of things. Rather it consists in doing things an injustice – violating them in their very being, refusing to be honest with them, refusing to deal with them honorably.'[58] From this perspective, spirituality is embedded in the very structure of reality, because everything that exists calls and beckons towards honest relationship; I exist humanly in my truthful encounters with the real. And at the heart of these encounters always lies encounter with the One who is the continual source of reality – both what I think of as my *own* reality and what I am drawn *out of myself* to encounter honestly as the reality of the other.

So we could say that 'I' come to exist and to know by relating to reality in ways that do not attempt to control reality for my own devices. This is an 'act of correct, converted intelligence, intelligence that identifies as its primary interest the objective service of reality, not the service of the thinking subject'.[59] But, as Sobrino puts it, since so much of what is real today 'lies prostrate in the death of subjection', an honest relationship to this call of reality demands not just observation but a bestowal of life, a practice of love towards the reality of the other. In a sense, reality calls this loving response forth from us; or we could say that the reality of the other calls us out from one moment of selfhood into a new form of life. This is what Sobrino calls the 'more' of reality, the momentum of new possibility and of hope 'with which reality trembles'. To face reality honestly is to allow oneself to be drawn into this momentum that carries us into new activity. 'Thus the subject is not only challenged by that reality, but borne along by it as well, and this sweep, this pull, is a gift from reality, a mediation of gratuity.'[60]

Interestingly, this approach to epistemology bears some resemblance to theories of knowing in Christian mystical traditions. Here knowing and loving are often held together, so that the ultimate form of 'knowledge' is not an event in which certain information is imparted to the mind but rather the mind is drawn to a new level of perception by being transformed in love. For these mystical traditions, knowledge or wisdom is never a merely noetic factor but involves a new way of living, a practical or (to use the old term) 'habitual' kind of knowledge that is acquired through one's manner of life and sensed perhaps more intuitively than propositionally.[61]

What is the significance of all this for theology? If knowing reality is an act of this 'converted intelligence' which does not seek to defend itself against reality but allows itself to be drawn out in love and justice towards the other, then theology as a form of knowing and speaking of God must in some manner follow this path itself. Such an analysis would seem, at least, to disclose

something of *theology's inner character as itself a form of spirituality*, and as aptly
fitted therefore to articulate the perceptions of spiritual and mystical journeys.

We have considered how the debate over spirituality as an academic
discipline highlights some crucial issues in the relationship of spirituality and
theology. Especially significant is the possibility that a scholarly focus on the
self's own states might elide the theological import of spirituality, ironically
preserving the divorce between the two disciplines just when they might be
rediscovering a common mission. The perspectives of liberation and feminist
theology have pointed towards a more contextual and relational understanding of both spirituality and theology, suggesting a close correlation between
their mutual endeavours to know and speak of God. But all this has been
begging a rather large question, namely, what in fact I am talking about
whenever I refer to this 'encounter' with God. How might we conceive this
divine–human interaction so as to make sense not only of spirituality itself, but
of the particular relationship of theology and spirituality? Having sorted
through a good number of the points at issue in this relationship, it is now time
to take a preliminary gaze into the heart of the matter.

The Divine–Human Encounter: Some Heuristic Thoughts

What I want to propose now is a tentative approach to the question, 'How
does the encounter with God, in its most intimate and intense form, actually
take place – and what does our conceptual picture of that encounter suggest
about the integrity of spirituality and theology?'

As a kind of itinerary for this section, consider the preliminary heuristic
definition of mysticism suggested by Bernard McGinn in his magisterial
history of Western Christian mysticism, *The Presence of God*: 'the mystical
element in Christianity is that part of its belief and practices that concerns the
preparation for, the consciousness of, and the reaction to what can be
described as the immediate or direct presence of God.'[62] In some recent public
lectures, McGinn has continued to refine and revise this statement, moving
towards a more actualist language of *divine grounding of consciousness*. The issues
here involve a concern that 'presence' language may connote a kind of static
divine essence that does not comport well with the mystical awareness of
God's freedom and non-objectifiable reality. Divine 'grounding' language, by
contrast, would suggest a more transcendental idea, a sense of God being
newly appreciated by the mystic as the continual source or ground of all life.
As McGinn says, these are questions that can only be refined by continued

historical study. His point at this stage is to invite us away from fixation with various interpretations of 'union' language; the mystics do refer to their intimacy with God using a range of union images, but this is by no means the only framework in which they discuss a far more dynamic and complex phenomenon than the image of 'union' might by itself suggest.

By his heuristic sketch, McGinn wishes to emphasize a number of critical points. First, the mystical is not a peculiar moment that exists in a cultural vacuum; it is rather always an *element* in a given religious tradition. Christian mystics have always seen themselves as practitioners of Christianity, shaped in all their experiences, perceptions and insights by Christian scripture, worship and teaching. This helps to avoid from the start any idea that the mystics somehow exist in a realm quite beyond Christian theology.

Second, this mystical element of Christianity should 'be seen primarily as a *process* or way of life rather than being defined solely in terms of some experience of union with God'.[63] In other words, while it is true that there comes to be a most intense moment of encounter with God, which we might be tempted to think of (not quite correctly) as mysticism proper, this moment is really part of a life-long spiritual journey – all the preparations for, and reflections upon which, comprise mysticism in its fullest sense. It is specially important for our purposes to see that, in McGinn's view, the mystical is not completed in a given moment of intense experience. All the reflection and transformation that such a moment engenders 'for the life of the individual in the belief community is also mystical, even if in a secondary sense'.[64] So the texts of mystical writers are themselves features of the mystical, and their theological insights are direct expressions of the mystical.

McGinn suggests we speak of mystical *consciousness* rather than mystical experience. This raises a helpful point. It would be undesirable, and impossible, to rule out experience as a category. But the term 'mystical experience' unfortunately has tended 'to place emphasis on special altered states – visions, locutions, raptures, and the like – which admittedly have played a large part in mysticism, but which many mystics have insisted do not constitute the essence of the encounter with God.'[65] The problem has been that, as a generic concept, experience tends to place the focus on these extraordinary inner conditions; furthermore the emphasis seems to verge on the purely affective, as though the noetic content inherent in the mystical encounter were entirely a matter of some later thematization. By contrast, consciousness (here McGinn points to the thought of Bernard Lonergan) is a more capacious term suggesting the full process of cognition: experience (or the 'raw data'), questioning, understanding, judgement. Studies of mystical writers have shown that what is often referred to as 'experience' in their texts includes all four of these stages of cognition that together constitute consciousness.[66]

So to refer to mystical *consciousness* is a way of taking seriously the language and texts of the mystical writers themselves. They are, in other words, giving voice not to a contentless sensation of the inner self but to a transforming perceptivity — a perceptivity that is being drawn into a mind-*fullness* which exceeds what we usually refer to as 'thought'. To think of mystical consciousness as supra-conceptual does not, obviously, imply a *less* than conceptual form of knowing but something that is in itself even greater in clarity, expressivity, truthfulness and coherence than what we normally understand by the term 'concept'. Of course to say that mystical consciousness participates in greater clarity and expressivity than our usual forms of understanding does suggest the possibility that we may *experience* this supra-conceptual knowing as unknowing and darkness. To revert to a favourite mystical analogy, when we suddenly gaze at the sun after being in a dark room our vision is dazzled — not because sunlight is intrinsically dark, but because our eyes are not adjusted to such light. Analogously, then, to note that mystical consciousness is sometimes *experienced* in terms of darkness and unknowing, does not mean that there is an intrinsic incoherence or void of meaning in the One being encountered.

Yet many scholars have suggested that at the highest levels of mystical encounter, the mystic is drawn into a realm that, *in itself*, is pure noetic silence, absent of all 'word' and devoid of all expressivity.[67] But this would seem exactly to confuse the *experience* of mystical consciousness with the nature of the reality encountered. Surely for the Christian mystic, while God may be experienced in absolute silence (a total absence of form or imagery), God's existence in itself is inherently self-expressive. The speaking of the divine Word is eternal and is never silence in itself but the gloriously infinite effulgence of meaning — a divine meaning-*fullness* that shatters the deathly silence of nothingness in creation and the silence of death itself in the resurrection of Jesus of Nazareth from the dead. This means that mystical consciousness is the impression in human existence of infinite coherence, expressivity and meaning, namely the trinitarian life of God. Mysticism bears this speech of God, God-talk, theo-logy, within it and is therefore inherently theologically fruitful.

The task of the theologian must not be to turn away from the painful and ecstatic silences or the unlooked-for words of mystical speech, or to confuse them with the very being of God. Instead the theologian can draw correlations and show analogies between the impression made by the infinite trinitarian expressivity in the consciousness of the mystic and the impression that the same expressive activity of speaking and loving, Word and Spirit, has made in the wider history of revelation as witnessed in the Scriptures. These analogies might, in turn, become the basis for new and deeper perceptions of Christian faith.

But how can this actually happen? How does a theologian come to sense such analogies between mystical consciousness and the biblical and doctrinal traditions of Christianity? The foundational theological insights of the patristic era seem very often to have been the fruit of teachers who combined theological acuity and mystical perceptivity in their own persons. They knew how to draw such mystical-doctrinal analogies because they lived them themselves. Whether the cultural location of theologians today is very conducive to this kind of mystical-doctrinal personal integrity is debatable.[68] Perhaps the rarity of this kind of personal integration is a sad commentary on the exigencies of those divisions of scholarly labour that so characterize the contemporary academic world.

And yet growing interest in the contextualization of thought and increasingly positive views of interdisciplinary study are both hopeful signs; perhaps they may lead to a new awareness of the fundamental complementarity of mystical thought and theological endeavour. Andrew Louth quotes a highly pertinent text on this point from Diadochus of Photike (mid 400s):

> The theologian whose soul is penetrated and enkindled by the very words of God advances, in time, into the regions of serenity (*apatheia*). . . . The contemplative (*gnostikos*), strengthened by powerful experience, is raised above the passions. But the theologian tastes something of the experience of the contemplative, provided he is humble; and the contemplative will little by little know something of the power of speculation, if he keeps the discerning part of the soul free from error. But the two gifts are rarely found to the same degree in the same person, so that each may wonder at the other's abundance, and thus humility may increase in each, together with zeal for righteousness.[69]

In this view, the mystic and the theologian are always being led to a perception of the same mysteries, only from different perspectives. More than this, the very patterns of their respective vocations lead them towards convergence if never quite identity. And how refreshing to think that in recognizing their different callings, the contemplative and the theologian would not only tolerate one another but regard with wonder and humbling admiration something of each other's gifts.

The point of all this is to suggest that the inherent momentum of theology is towards contemplation, and that this is no abdication of academic rigour or the critical function; the most rigorous and critical turn theology takes may flow from the passionate desire to know the living truth. Christians believe that the ultimate truth of reality is God's triunity, the infinite personal activities of God's knowing and loving who constitute God as Trinity. Therefore, Christianity holds, at the heart of reality lives an eternal bestowal, expressivity and embrace. Christians perceive this trinitarian life as beyond their understanding yet infinitely full of meaning. The impression made in the consciousness of the mystic by that infinite triune generation of meaning cannot, if it is at all truthful to its source, remain silent or contentless but needs to find the words in which the Word can dwell. So too the expression that theologians seek to give to God's own expressivity should encourage them to renew their formulations and revise their understandings in close conference with mystical thought, which springs with theology from the same source. Theologians are not called to render God's Word yet more 'wordy' — surely the goal of theology is not a sententious banalization of mystery; rather theology fulfils its task by explicating not just the words of Scripture and tradition, but ultimately that living *encounter* with the Word in which the Spirit fills the community with the mind of Christ.

Notes

1 The account is given in Waltraud Herbstrith, OCD, *Edith Stein: A Biography*, trans. Bernard Bonowitz, OCSO 2nd edn (San Francisco: Ignatius Press, 1992), 180.

2 *Kreuzeswissenschaft*. Translated by Hilda Graef as *The Science of the Cross* (Chicago: Regnery, 1960).

3 Herbstrith, 168–9.

4 See, e.g., Ann W. Astell, 'If modernity ended in Auschwitz, and if postmodernity was born there, then the place to look for the defining traits of a truly postmodern Christian spirituality is also there, in the concentration camps, prisons and battlefields of the second World War and, more precisely, in the lives of the saints who were formed there.' ('Postmodern Christian Spirituality: A *Coincidentia Oppositorum?' Christian Spirituality Bulletin* vol. 4, no.1 [Summer 1996]: 3).

5 See especially Bernard McGinn, 'The Letter and the Spirit: Spirituality as an Academic Discipline,' *Christian Spirituality Bulletin* vol. 1, no. 2 (Fall 1993):1–10; and Philip Sheldrake, *Spirituality and History: Questions of Interpretation and Method* (New York: Crossroad, 1992), particularly chapter 2, 'What is Spirituality?', 32–56, and for further discussions of definitions see the citations Sheldrake gives in n. 3, p. 53.

6 Sheldrake, *Spirituality and History*, 34.

7 Ibid., 35.

8 John D. Zizioulas, 'The Early Christian Community', in *Christian Spirituality: Origins to the Twelfth Century*, ed. Bernard McGinn, John Meyendorff and Jean Leclercq. *World Spirituality: An Encyclopedic History of the Religious Quest*, vol. 16

(New York: Crossroad, 1987), 23–43, here p. 28. My italics.

9   McGinn, 'The Letter and the Spirit', 3.

10   Ibid.

11   Sheldrake, *Spirituality and History*, 35.

12   Kees Waaijman, 'Towards a Phenomenological Definition of Spirituality', *Studies in Spirituality* 3/1993: 5–57, here 35.

13   Sheldrake, *Spirituality and History*, 50.

14   McGinn, 'The Letter and the Spirit', 6.

15   Cf. Hans Urs von Balthasar, 'Theology and Sanctity', chapter in *Explorations in Theology*, vol. 1: *The Word Made Flesh* (San Francisco: Ignatius Press, 1989), 208: '"Scientific" theology became more and more divorced from prayer, and so lost the accent and tone with which one should speak of what is holy, while "affective" theology, as it became increasingly empty, often degenerated into unctuous, platitudinous piety.'

16   Thomas Merton, *Seeds of Contemplation*, Anthony Clarke Books, 1972, 197–8. Quoted in Andrew Louth, 'Theology and Spirituality', revised edn (Fairacres, Oxford: SLG Press, 1978), 4

17   In Louth, 'Theology and Spirituality', 7.

18   Ibid.

19   Harvey D. Egan, SJ, *Christian Mysticism: The Future of a Tradition* (New York: Pueblo Publishing Company, 1984), 375.

20   Hans Urs von Balthasar, 'Theology and Sanctity', 190.

21   Ibid., 192.

22   Egan, *Christian Mysticism*, 376.

23   Michael J. Buckley, SJ, Presidential Address: 'The Rise of Atheism and the Religious *Epochē* in *The Catholic Theological Society of America* [vol. 47]: *Proceedings of the Forty-Seventh Annual Convention, Pittsburgh, June 11–14, 1992*, ed. Paul Crowley, 1992, 77.

24   Egan, *Christian Mysticism*, 376.

25   William M. Thompson, among others, has noted signs of a new openness to spirituality as a theological source and has attempted some efforts in demonstration of the possibilities inherent therein. See his works, *Fire and Light: The Saints and Theology. On Consulting the Saints, Mystics, and Martyrs in Theology* (New York: Paulist Press, 1987) and *Christology and Spirituality* (New York: Crossroad, 1991).

26   Paul Tillich, *Systematic Theology* I (Chicago: University of Chicago Press, 1951), 118. Quoted in John Macquarrie, *Paths in Spirituality* (London: SCM Press, 1972), 63.

27   Michael J. Buckley, SJ, *At the Origins of Modern Atheism* (New Haven: Yale University Press, 1987), 67. See also William Placher commenting on the theology of the period as exemplified in the preaching of John Tillotson (1630–94): 'Thanks to Christianity, we can reason our way to God more easily [than by natural theology alone], and our moral struggles too will be less difficult, but the God Tillotson urges Christians to worship was not in any central sense either the

God self-revealed in Christ or the source of a grace so amazing as to astonish every human ethical understanding, but essentially reason's God, the orderer of things both physical and moral.' (*The Domestication of Transcendence: How Modern Thinking about God Went Wrong* [Louisville, Kentucky: Westminster John Knox Press, 1996], 173.)

28   David Hume, *Dialogues Concerning Natural Religion and the Posthumous Essays*, ed. Richard H. Popkin (Indianapolis: Hackett Publishing Company, 1980), 37. It is deliciously ironic, of course, that Hume has Philo enlist as his unwitting ally in the campaign against the 'enlightened' Cleanthes none other than the rather dimwitted Demea, whose views Philo refers to with (mock?) admiration as rather *mystical*.

29   Herbert McCabe, OP, *God Matters* (London: Geoffrey Chapman, 1987), 20.

30   Louth, 'Theology and Spirituality', 4.

31   Rowan Williams, *The Wound of Knowledge: Christian Spirituality from the New Testament to St. John of the Cross*, 2nd edn (Cambridge, Massachusetts: Cowley Publications, 1991), 1.

32   Buckley, 'The Rise of Atheism', 83.

33   Cf. K. C. Abraham and Bernadette Mbuy-Beya, eds, *Spirituality of the Third World: A Cry for Life* (Maryknoll, New York: Orbis Books, 1995) for some essays suggesting the shape of this emerging spirituality.

34   In order of publication, the articles by Sandra M. Schneiders, IHM, are: 'Theology and Spirituality: Strangers, Rivals, or Partners?', *Horizons* 13/2 (1986): 253–74; 'Spirituality in the Academy, *Theological Studies* 50 (1989): 676–97; 'Spirituality as an Academic Discipline: Reflections from Experience', *Christian Spirituality Bulletin*, vol. 1, no. 2 (Fall 1993): 10–15. (Because of the similarity of these articles' titles, I shall refer to them below by the author's surname and year of publication.) Another important collection of essays by a range of scholars on the general issues of spirituality as an academic discipline was edited by Bradley C. Hanson, *Modern Christian Spirituality: Methodological and Historical Essays*. American Academy of Religion *Studies in Religion* 62 (Atlanta: Scholars Press, 1990).

35   Schneiders 1989, 678.

36   Schneiders, 1993, 11.

37   Schneiders, 1989, 678.

38   Schneiders, 1993, 11.

39   Schneiders, 1986, 266.

40   Schneiders, 1989, 683.

41   Ibid., 682.

42   Ibid., 684.

43   Schneiders, 1986, 267. The italics are Schneiders's own.

44   Fergus Kerr, *Theology after Wittgenstein* (Oxford: Blackwell, 1986), 65 (first emphasis mine). See also p. 69: 'I discover myself, not in some pre-linguistic inner space of self-presence, but in the network of multifarious social and historical relationships in which I am willy-nilly involved.'

45 Paul Mommaers and Jan Van Bragt, *Mysticism Buddhist and Christian: Encounters with Jan van Ruusbroec*. Nanzen Studies in Religion and Culture (New York: Crossroad, 1995), 18–19.

46 Ibid., 19.

47 Denys Turner, *The Darkness of God: Negativity in Christian Mysticism* (Cambridge: Cambridge University Press, 1995), 259.

48 Pierre Hadot, *Philosophy as a Way of Life: Spiritual Exercises from Socrates to Foucault*, ed. Arnold I. Davidson, trans. Michael Chase (Oxford: Blackwell, 1995), 60.

49 Cf. Joann Wolski Conn: 'I suggest that the real issue behind these questions may not be religious commitment versus objectivity, but the myth of objectivity. The goal of fairness or objectivity in academic disciplines used to be measured by the researcher's distance from the subject matter. I suggest that only when a researcher is critically aware of her or his actual commitments and assumptions, and acts to make them assist rather than prevent insight, can the researcher be objective.' ('Towards Spiritual Maturity', chapter in *Freeing Theology: The Essentials of Theology in Feminist Perspective*, ed. Catherine Mowry LaCugna [San Francisco: Harper Collins, 1993], 239.)

50 Gustavo Gutiérrez, *We Drink from Our Own Wells: The Spiritual Journey of a People*, trans. Matthew J. O'Connell (Maryknoll, New York: Orbis Books, 1984), 35–7.

51 Friedrich Schleiermacher, *The Christian Faith*, ed. H. R. Mackintosh and J. S. Stewart (Edinburgh: T. & T. Clark, 1986), 81.

52 Jon Sobrino, *Spirituality of Liberation: Towards Political Holiness*, trans. Robert R. Barr (Maryknoll, New York: Orbis Books, 1988), 48.

53 Ibid., 71–2.

54 Ibid., 75–6: 'If theology does not . . . have recourse to the locus of the realization of the faith of a poor people, it will be a truncated theology. Ever and again it will become abstractivist and elitist, thus depriving itself of an irreplaceable font of theological cognition. . . . A theology isolated from the people of God – or even worse, at odds with that people – and feeding only on its own resources, will betray its irreality, however true its propositions.'

55 Ibid., 13: 'spirituality is not something absolutely autonomous on the part of the subject; it stands in relationship with reality. . . . I think it important to underscore the "relational" character of spirit vis-à-vis the sum total of reality.'

56 Conn, 'Towards Spiritual Maturity', 254–5, points out that women's need for autonomy is not in service to a post-Cartesian model of the self-referential subject but in order to achieve the detachment requisite for free and faithful relationality and mutuality.

57 So suggests Denise Lardner Carmody, 'Feminist Spirituality as Self-Transcendence', chapter in *Rising from History: U.S. Catholic Theology Looks to the Future,* ed. Robert J. Daly. Annual Publication of the College Theology Society 1984, vol. 30. (Lanham, Maryland: University Press of America, 1987), 139–55.

58 Sobrino, *Spirituality of Liberation*, 14.

59 Ibid., 15.

60   Ibid., 20.

61   For a helpful survey of the attitudes towards knowledge in the Western mystical traditions see Bernard McGinn, 'Love, Knowledge, and *Unio Mystica* in the Western Christian Tradition', chapter in *Mystical Union and Monotheistic Faith: An Ecumenical Dialogue* (New York: Macmillan, 1989), 59–86.

62   Bernard McGinn, *The Foundations of Mysticism*, vol. 1 of *The Presence of God: A History of Western Christian Mysticism* (New York: Crossroad, 1991), xvii.

63   Idem., *The Growth of Mysticism*, vol. 2 of *The Presence of God* (New York: Crossroad, 1994), x–xi.

64   Idem, *Foundations*, xvi.

65   Ibid., xvii–xviii.

66   I am happily indebted to Edward Howells for clarifying this matter for me; see his forthcoming dissertation at the University of Chicago under the direction of Bernard McGinn, 'Mystical Consciousness and the "Mystical Self" in Teresa of Avila and John of the Cross'.

67   See, e.g., the collection of essays, *The Problem of Pure Consciousness: Mysticism and Philosophy*, ed. Robert K. C. Forman (New York: Oxford Univeristy Press, 1990).

68   William Johnston comments fairly bleakly: 'One might draw the conclusion that the primary need is for Christian theologians who are also mystics. . . . Yet I will refrain from drawing any conclusions of this nature. The reason is that from the time of Thomas à Kempis better men than I have been attempting to convert the theologians – and they have been conspicuously unsuccessful. The theologians remain unregenerate.' (*The Inner Eye of Love*, [London: HarperCollins, 1990], 195–6).

69   Diadochus of Photike, chapter 72 of the *Century of Gnostic Chapters*. Quoted in Louth, 'Theology and Spirituality', 14.

Chapter 2

MYSTERY AND DOCTRINE: THE HISTORICAL INTEGRITY OF SPIRITUALITY AND THEOLOGY

If, as I suggested in the last chapter, the integrity of spirituality and theology has a naturalness and coherence to it, then we might expect to find some illuminating examples in the history of Christian thought. And that is the task of the present chapter. I am not proposing to offer a summary history of the Christian mystical tradition, but to study some examples showing what this integrity of spirituality and theology looks like in practice, how (in the West at least) it came to be dissolved, and finally what approach might lead to a healing of the breach.

What exactly are we looking for? Perhaps I might call it a characteristic theological stance: a way of grounding all the doctrines of Christianity in God's plan to draw the whole world to Godself in Christ. It is a way of writing about the depth of revelation that equips the believing community to live into the mystery. The Orthodox theologian Vladimir Lossky proposed the following as an ideal: 'We must live the dogma expressing a revealed truth, which appears to us as an unfathomable mystery, in such a fashion that instead of assimilating the mystery to our mode of understanding, we should, on the contrary, look for a profound change, an inner transformation of spirit, enabling us to experience it mystically.'[1]

As Lossky goes on to point out, this is not a theology whose only criterion is the evocation of piety. On the contrary, mystical theology is characterized by the very definite plumbline it uses to measure all theological discourse: namely, how well does it safeguard the possibility for all Christians of becoming 'partakers of the divine nature' (2 Peter 1.4). The concern of mystical theology 'is always the possibility, the manner, or the means of our union with God'.[2] That does not mean that mystical theology is only interested in, say, theories of prayer; indeed it is likely to regard these as for the most part quite secondary. What is paramount are the central doctrinal truths of Christianity: that there has been a true incarnation in true humanity of the true God, and that the church can only live as the true body of this incarnate Word by living ever more truthfully into Christ's dying and rising – thus to participate in that self-giving love which is truly the life of the triune God. 'All the history of Christian dogma unfolds itself about this mystical centre,' and it is this approach to theology that, following Lossky, I would term mystical theology – doctrinal reflection that is constantly alive to its spiritual sources and goals.[3]

If theology is able to do this, to show the spiritual seeker that the very heart of the Sought is precisely the source and goal of Christian theology, then it might suddenly find a great many people being interested, both in church and academy, in Christian theology. If, as William Temple put it, faith or spirituality is 'personal fellowship with the living God,' then 'correct doctrine will both express this, assist it and issue from it; incorrect doctrine will misrepresent this and hinder or prevent it'.[4] What theology has to say about the divine should be an enormous help in relating oneself to the divine. Mystical theology in this sense is theology that lets its own speech be questioned and even stripped away by the mystery of God – who can never really become the scientific 'object of study' for theology, but always remains the acting Subject.

This kind of theology would not feel embarrassed about being theological, for it is addressing the very realities people find at the centre of their own lives. It means thinking of doctrines not so much as symbols for something deep and universal in every human person; for in such a case the doctrines and narratives could quickly be dispensed with. Rather, doctrines would be seen, in Rowan Williams's words, as 'a set of instructions for performance'.[5] The performance in question is not an isolated event but the life-long drama of the journey into union with God. Doctrines are interpreted by mystical theology as a language for describing and participating in this encounter with God, as an itinerary giving an indication of the major landmarks along the journey.

In the case of academic theology, this means not simply listening to classical mystical writers and contemporary spiritual seekers as theological consultants;

it also means that theology attempts to elucidate Christian doctrines by showing how they both orient and are shaped by the Christian experience of God. Reflection on the doctrine of the Trinity or christology, for example, takes place by critical analysis of the ecclesial experience of being drawn into the pattern of Jesus' life and his relationship with the One he called 'Abba'. What does this kind of theology look like in practice, and how did its undoing come about?

The development of mystical strands in early Common Era Judaism and Platonism should remind us that the emergence of mystical elements in Christianity took place in a richly multicultural era – the history of which is well-detailed in other places.[6] Here at least we can note that the visionary impulse in strands of Judaism and the theme of ecstatic *erōs* (yearning) in Neoplatonic sources was not without echo in early Christian texts. Certainly the sense of passionate and ecstatic desire is less obvious in the early Christian scriptural texts. Yet even here the process of knowing God certainly is understood as entailing a loving attachment to Christ. One comes to enter into God's presence precisely by an ecstasy cast in obediential terms, a leaving of self behind in order to follow Christ.

Much more central to this early stage of Christian thought is the figure of the Word (*logos*) in John and the Lord in Paul as the one in whom, for whom, and through whom everything comes to be and journeys to fullness. In one crucial instance this relationship to Christ is transposed from obediential terms to contemplative ones: 'And we, with unveiled faces reflecting like mirrors the brightness of the Lord, all grow brighter as we are turned into that image (*eikon*) that we reflect' (2 Cor 3.18). Bernard McGinn comments on this text: 'The word translated as "reflecting" (*katoptrizomenoi*) was often understood as "gazing" or "contemplating" (*speculantes* is both the Old Latin and the Vulgate translation). Thus, the text could be read to mean that it is by contemplation of the glory of the risen Christ that the image of God in us is being conformed to the Word.'[7]

So in addition to the Johannine trajectory of abiding in the Word, we have the germ here of a new christological focus for contemplation. Ultimate knowledge of God comes about in both cases through a fellowship of both mind and heart with Christ. The contemplative activities of ultimate knowing and loving, in other words, are interpreted by early Christians in terms of sharing in the paschal mystery: 'If we have been united with him in a death like his, we shall certainly be united with him in a resurrection like his' (Romans 6.5). As I will show in later sections of this chapter, this becomes the crucial interpretive framework for many mystical writers – a passing beyond the self by means of sharing in Jesus' crucifixion. This is a dark knowing of God by sharing in the patient and suffering yet desiring love of Jesus for the Father, a knowing which at its climactic moments seems to take the form of forsakenness.

In the welter of influences and trends, some distinctive patterns of Christian usage begin to emerge. Christians sought to explore the hidden depths of meaning in the revelation of God in Christ, and the cultural milieu of the ancient Mediterranean world afforded a range of spiritual paths, genres and conceptual stances. Louis Bouyer's now classic essay 'Mysticism: An Essay on the History of the Word' pinpoints some of the salient features in the developing exploration of these depths of mystery in God's self-disclosure in Jesus.[8] Our word 'mystical' comes from the Greek *mustikos*, a qualifier deriving from the verb *muō* meaning 'to close' (especially the eyes). It refers to that which is secret, hidden. According to Bouyer, the earliest pre-Christian use we find of the term is in connection with the Hellenistic mystery cults; here 'the mystical [things]' (*ta mustika*) are the secret ritual actions of the cults which it was utterly forbidden to reveal to any uninitiated person. The emphasis here seems to be not on any secret knowledge about the ultimate, but simply the secrecy with which the ritual practices were guarded. By the Christian era, the collection of terms related to 'mystical' had come into common parlance, used in a very wide-ranging and often quite generic sense of religious secrets. Still, it is surprising that when Christian authors do adopt the term, their initial use of it has nothing to do with ritual activities, but preeminently with the Bible.

Early Christian writers such as Clement (*c*.150–*c*.215) and Origen (*c*.185–*c*.254) seem, in this regard, to follow their fellow Alexandrian Philo (*c*.20 BCE–*c*.50 CE) in their concern to point to the hidden depth of meaning in the Scriptures. For Philo, the divine Logos is the hermeneutical focus of all scripture, and Clement and Origen, believing Christ to be the incarnation of the Logos, follow the same path. For them, the whole history of God's people and the textual unfolding of that in scripture finds its secret meaning unlocked, revealed and articulated in Christ. To read the Scriptures with this aspiration of allowing Christ to open what has been closed is now referred to precisely as a 'mystical' interpretation. It is worth noting the presuppositions at work here: Christ is the hermeneutical key who opens a vast treasury of meaning, giving access to God's eternal will for creation; the exegetical process of arriving at this new knowledge is referred to as mystical, and the knowledge itself comes also (for Origen) to be designated as such. In effect the exegetical process itself becomes the mystical journey in which communion with the living Christ (encountered through scriptural meditation) leads the Christian towards God.

What is mystical is not the inner experience of the Christian but the hidden meaning and transformative understanding discovered in Christ. As Bouyer summarizes: 'For the Greek Fathers the word "mystical" was used to describe first of all the divine reality which Christ brought to us, which the Gospel has revealed, and which gives its profound and definitive meaning to all the Scriptures. Moreover, mystical is applied to all knowledge of divine things to which we accede through Christ, and then by derivation to those things themselves.'[9] What is interesting, as Bouyer suggests, is the spreading application of the term. The hidden mystery of God's plan to re-unite creation with God's own existence is embodied in Christ, discerned in the Scriptures, and sacramentally enacted in the eucharistic community. 'Mystical', as a term, begins its Christian career by referring simply to the hidden depths of meaning in the Scriptures; it comes to refer to the meditative exegetical practices by which the Christian community encounters the meaning of this hiddenness in Christ, and then extends from the exegetical to the liturgical forms of this encounter. In these contexts the mystical also comes to refer to all teachings or doctrines that touch on the more mysterious, even difficult, points of Christian faith.

A number of salient features should be noted here. First, the underlying basis of all this language seems to be something like St Paul's notion of a *mustērion*, a mystery 'which was kept secret for long ages but is now disclosed' (Romans 16.26), a mystery regarding God's infinite love for the creation: 'For he has made known to us in all wisdom and insight the mystery (*mustērion*) of his will, according to his purpose which he set forth in Christ as a plan for the fullness of time, to unite all things in him, things in heaven and things on earth' (Eph 1.9–10). In other words, 'mystical' refers principally to the hidden and now revealed divine will to re-unite all things in Christ.

The gospel of God's love for humanity is secret, 'mystical', because it is the manifestation of *God's* love and is therefore always full of unfathomable depths and richness of meaning. This is the incomprehensible love that is not *imprisoned* in heavenly mystery, but races to rescue the lost sheep and hurries out to welcome and embrace the lost prodigal child. What renders this divine love '*mustikos*' or hidden, mystical and beyond comprehension, is not merely its infinity but the fact that *this infinity discloses itself in the activity of self-giving love*, in God's decision not to be God apart from the lost creation. As Louth puts it, this infinite outpouring of rescuing love is 'inexhaustible and inaccessible in the very event of its being made known in the life, death and resurrection of Christ.'[10] Indeed, the contrary and arresting sign of the Cross is the fitting revelation of this hiddenness, for it marks the very real, concrete, historical point at which this love passes into a darkness beyond human understanding.

It is worth highlighting this point, for it serves, in my view, to distinguish the Christian mystical thought which has been most deeply immersed in the gospel. In this view, the mystical is not simply the ineffable incomprehensibility of God (no matter whether that incomprehensibility is thought of in ancient Neoplatonic terms or modern post-Kantian ones); rather what is most *mysterious* is not the divine being per se but precisely the infinite self-giving of God which is the fundamental characteristic of the divine Trinity and is enacted in history in the life, death and resurrection of Jesus.

There is a second feature of the early development in Christian mystical thought that Bouyer's study highlights. Christ as the agent of the mystery of divine love seeks out the people of God 'mystically', that is, by means of the unveiling of the gospel in the veiled words of the Scriptures and liturgical rites. And by extension, the activity by which this hidden meaning comes to life in the community is also termed mystical, and this is a communal event rather than, in the first instance, a private experience. It is oriented towards a transformed communal life in response to God's plan of salvation; the inner psychological state of individuals involved is not connected at this point with the term 'mystical'. Ultimately, therefore, 'mystical' in this early usage refers to the decisively transforming practices of the church, by which it comes to be drawn into the dying and rising of Jesus. For the early Christians, the church 'is nothing other than the world in the course of transfiguration' as the mystical presence of Christ effects the re-creation of all the members of his Body.[11] In the following two sections, I would like to ground us in this approach, to develop a real conversance with some classic forms of mystical theology.

The Growth of Mystical Theology: Pseudo-Dionysius the Areopagite

Now the first question to ask is how we got from this early *practice* of mystical theology – so communal, practical and oriented towards the activity of God in the church's midst – to our common modern *conception* of the mystical as having to do with individualistic states of heightened inner experience. The usual answer points an accusing finger at that mysterious body of texts, probably composed in the late fifth or early sixth century, by an unknown writer who identified himself with an Athenian convert of St Paul's, one Dionysius the Areopagite who is mentioned along with a woman convert named Damaris in Acts 17.34. As Jaroslav Pelikan remarks of this figure from the pages of scripture, 'what is surprising . . . is not that some writings were eventually fathered on him, but that it took so long'.[12] Whoever the author of the texts was, he does not manipulate his pseudonymity as some ironic mask, archly posing as something he is not. Rather he disappears (perhaps as an act of monastic humility) behind the apostolic figure of Dionysius. His joy in the radiance of God's glory, his contemplative unfolding of how the church manifests this light, and his profound analysis of how best to speak of this radiance all made him an irresistible figure to generations of theologians. But was his adoption of Neoplatonic thought in the service of Christian theology also the thin end of the wedge that pried Christian spirituality loose from its communal, scriptural moorings?

Take one of the examples that sounds closest to the idea of mysticism as a heightened or visionary state of inner experience. In a description of his beloved teacher, Hierotheus, Dionysius observes that what set his spiritual master apart from other great figures was precisely the profundity of his spiritual experience: 'He surpassed all the divinely rapt hierarchs, all the other sacred initiators. Yes indeed. He was so caught up, so taken out of himself, experiencing communion (*koinōnia*) with the things praised, that everyone who heard him, everyone who saw him, everyone who knew him (or, rather, did not know him) considered him to be inspired, to be speaking with divine praises' (DN 684A, p. 70) This certainly sounds as if the focus of the mystical is coming to rest on a spiritually gifted individual's inner experience. But recent studies by Andrew Louth and Paul Rorem have suggested that this construal is an anachronistic one, a superimposing of our more modern notion of 'mysticism' upon a more ancient practice. That Hierotheus is described here as having an extraordinary experience is unquestioned, but when the language is compared to that used by Dionysius in other contexts it suggests not so much an *interior state of soul* as a *liturgical event*. 'Not only is "communion" an occasional designation of the eucharist, but other passages also specify "the things praised" as the bread and the cup.'[13] So, for example, Dionysius speaks of the chief celebrant proclaiming God's saving acts; then the celebrant 'lifts into view the things praised through the sacredly displayed symbols. Having thus revealed the kindly gifts of the works of God, he himself comes into communion (*koinōnia*) with them and exhorts others to follow him. After receiving and then distributing the divine communion (*koinōnia*) he concludes with the sacred thanksgiving (*eucharistia*)' (EH 428A, p. 211). This passage along with others cited by Rorem suggests that the mystical depth encountered by the spiritual seeker is not found by a purely interior ascent of the soul, but rather that such a Neoplatonic itinerary has been re-contextualized in the sacramental life of the community.

But what about the reference to Hierotheus being 'caught up' and 'taken out of himself'? As we have just seen, this language immediately precedes the reference to 'communion', a communion which turns out to be not less but all the more ecstatic for being eucharistic in context. 'The Areopagite himself simply did not understand the notion of *ekstasis* to mean a private, emotional, and supra-rational experience.'[14] In fact one of his clearest references to this ecstatic state is found in an analysis of the dynamism of scripture. Dionysius explains that he prefers to speak of God using a dialectical language of negation, one notion always being surpassed by another; 'here, of course,' he adds reassuringly, 'I am in agreement with the scripture writers'. Why? Because 'their preference is for the way up through negations, since this stands the soul outside everything which is correlative with its own finite nature' (DN 981B, p. 130). In Dionysius's view, scripture bears within itself a momentum leading its interpretive community through an exegetical transformation that is essentially ecstatic in nature; not ecstatic in a purely psychological sense, but ecstatic in a noetic sense of being led continually beyond the idols of thought most in need of being left behind during the community's exodus into deeper relationship with God.

But to make the most sense out of this liturgical and exegetical context of mysticism, two central features of Dionysius's thought need to be explored. First, we need to consider the cosmos and the ecclesia as the radiance of God's glory. Second, we want to understand theology as the interpretive activity by which the community seeks to enter into the hidden depths of divine glory and thus, carried along by the momentum of that glory, enter into its divine source. This is mystical theology in Dionysius's sense, namely theology that fulfils itself by leading the community into the unfathomable reality of God's love.

The radiance of God's glory

Let me start with the bad news. Without doubt the single aspect of Dionysius's thought that has occasioned most distaste in the modern era is his very own invention, the concept of 'hierarchy'. All our least favourite connotations are suggested: the tendency to identify order, in both cosmos and ecclesia, with the institutionalization of a potentially static and exclusionary male clerical authority structure; the tendency to legitimize oppressive and highly gendered power arrangements as the very reflection of the divine being in time and space.[15] It would be dangerously naive to comment on Dionysius without keeping a wary eye on the unhappy career of his notion of 'hierarchy'. It would also seem unfortunate, however, not to seek out what Dionysius was trying to put his finger on by adopting such a concept.

In his first direct attempt at definition, Dionysius says that hierarchy is a holy ordering of life that intends to seek understanding 'and an activity approximating as closely as possible to the divine' (CH 164D, p. 153). It is meant to enable every creature to be drawn into the 'beauty of God'. This happens as they participate in the divine light by pouring it out to other creatures, so that all come 'to be clear and spotless mirrors reflecting the glow of primordial light and indeed of God himself' (CH 165A–165B, p. 154). Hierarchy, in other words, is an ordered society of transfiguring activity, and Dionysius speaks harshly against any who misuse their particular place in this ordered structure by failing to draw others into the light: 'It would be quite wrong for those granting initiation in the sacred things, as indeed for those sacredly initiated, ever to do anything or even to exist against the sacred orderings of him who is after all the source of all perfection' (ibid.). Highly significant here is the language of initiation; the catechetical process of baptismal initiation into the dying and rising of Jesus is seen as the defining and critical feature by which all hierarchical activity is judged.

It is not hard to recognize the wellspring of this ordering activity in which each pours divine glory upon another: 'The source of this hierarchy is the font of life, the being of goodness, the one cause of everything, namely the Trinity (trias) which in goodness bestows being and well-being on everything' (EH 373D, p. 198). In the era of Origen, trinitarian life as the source and archetype of hierarchy would undeniably connote a strictly descending cascade of being; but after the Arian controversy and the theological efforts of the Cappadocians to ensure the full and co eternal status of all three divine hypostases, the picture is not quite so simple. At the heart of all reality there is now understood to be the life of eternal mutual self-giving. Although the first person of the Trinity is still understood as the source of divine existence, this life is never *not* being poured out to the 'other' in God.

In fact, Dionysius even seems to suggest that the very existence of God is constituted not by a primordial divine 'possession' somehow belonging to the Father (or some logically pre-existent divine ground), but rather by the eternal activity of *mutual self-bestowal of the three Divine Persons*. Far from implying that the three are only a vestigial Neoplatonic triad that emanates from the absolutely prior One, Dionysius describes the triune relationality of God as itself the *source* of the divine unity. He refers to 'the abiding and foundation of the divine persons who are the source of oneness as a unity which is totally undifferentiated and transcendent' (DN 641A–B, p. 61). And he goes on to say: 'Let me resort here to examples from what we perceive and from what is familiar. In a house the light from all the lamps is completely interpenetrating, yet each is clearly distinct. There is distinction in unity and there is unity in distinction. When there are many lamps in a house there is nevertheless a single undifferentiated light and *from all of them comes the one undivided brightness'* (ibid., my emphasis). If we may press the logic of Dionysius's metaphor, then here at least he clearly indicates that the undivided *unity* of God is the eternal 'effect' of this shining-together of the radiant eternal *threefold* event of God's loving. The dialectical quality of Dionysius's thought is unmistakable. The more God is one, the more God is triune (because the unity of God is not an arithmetical oneness but the oneness of complete and absolute mutual love which always gives life to the other); and conversely the more God is triune, the more God is one (because the trinitarian relationality of God is not a conjunction of post-Cartesian autonomous selves but the threefold event of a single love – giving, receiving, returning eternally).

For Dionysius this trinitarian fecundity, in its eternal joy in giving away to what is other, is the sole explanation for why there is a universe at all rather than nothing. The divine Three 'united even within this divine differentiation are the acts by which it irrepressibly imparts being, life, wisdom and the other gifts of its all-creative goodness' (DN 644A, p. 62). I stress the language of 'acts' because it helps to remind us that for Dionysius, God is never a *static* One. God may be, as Dionysius never tires of saying, beyond being, but that is because in Dionysius's view there is a reality even prior to existence. Love is the reason for existence. The divine yearning (*erōs*) for the other is what causes there *to be* an other, both in Godself and beyond. Despite all his connections with Neoplatonic thought, these views very definitely distinguish Dionysius's notions from more general Hellenistic ideas and mark the Christian cast of the Areopagite's thought.

For by the time of Plotinus (*c*.205–270 CE), the Neoplatonic One may have come to be thought of as 'erotic'; and, as the final cause which attracts the erotically striving cosmos back to Itself, the One is the Source of all. But for Plotinus the One is utterly unconcerned with what is below it and is in no way drawn towards what is below. 'Plotinus explicitly denies that God loves the world' (e.g., *Ennead* 5.5.12).[16] This can be contrasted with Dionysius's view that God's yearning desire for the other is the very source of creation, indeed draws God 'out of' Godself in ecstatic love towards the beloved other – both the other *in* God and the other *than* God. In what has justly become one of the Areopagite's most famous passages, he writes:

> The divine longing (*theios erōs*) is Good seeking good for the sake of the Good.
> That yearning (*erōs*) which creates all the goodness of the world preexisted

superabundantly within the Good and did not allow it to remain without issue. It stirred him to use the abundance of his powers in the production of the world [DN 708B-C, pp. 79–80]. . . . This divine yearning (*theios erōs*) brings ecstasy so that the lover belongs not to self but to the beloved. . . . And, in truth, it must be said too that the very cause of the universe in the beautiful, good superabundance of his benign yearning (*erōs*) for all is also carried outside of himself in the loving care he has for everything. He is, as it were, beguiled by goodness, by love (*agapē*), and by yearning (*erōs*) and is enticed away from his transcendent dwelling place and comes to abide within all things, and he does so by virtue of his supernatural and ecstatic (*ekstatikē*) capacity to remain, nevertheless, within himself [DN 712A–B, p. 82].

This crucial text is worth some pondering. Given the trinitarian perspective we have seen above, this text suggests that the triune relationality may be conceived of as productive *erōs*. This desire for the other, for there *to be* other to love 'stirs' God to extend existence to otherness, including the other which is the cosmos. But that is not all. For this *erōs* does not leave the giver of love/existence aloof from the beloved recipient. Rather it includes an *ekstasis*, a standing outside oneself to be all the more available to the beloved. And this, says Dionysius, with a feeling for the shock of what he utters ('in truth, it must be said'), is how the self-bestowing desire which is God's triunity leads God into the very heart of every creature. How is it that God also remains within the divine being in the very act of this ecstasy? Again, the key is the fact that trinitarian *erōs* is constitutive of God's existence; in other words, if God 'comes to abide within all things' this is no change or abandonment of God's deity, for to give away life and dwell in the other is the very definition of the Trinity. God is eternally existing ecstatically in other, and to do so in the finite play of creation is a small thing compared to the infinite communion of the divine hypostases.

At this point a rather crucial distinction is worth making. Throughout his works, Dionysius refers to the descending radiance of the divine glory as at its most powerful at the highest levels of intelligible existence and then radiating at ever dimmer levels as it descends to the purely material creation. Indeed it is this ordered 'echoing' of glory that makes the whole cosmos a symphony of praise, since each level of the hierarchy resounds with its own unique voice. But given the intimacy of divine presence suggested in the extended passage above, can it be that *existence* (as for Neoplatonic thought generally) is also an emanation of a descending power — with each creature progressively more distant from its creator and hence dependent on higher levels of being for its existence rather than on divine existence itself? Louth answers this question in the negative; the cosmic hierarchies are the effulgence and emanation of divine glory, but they are not themselves the order of creation – that is a direct and immediate relation between the Creator and each creature. 'Being is derived from God alone,' and so we have Dionysius's 'understanding of emanation simply in terms of illumination and not communication of being.'[17] So rather than referring to the cosmos as an emanation, suggests Louth, we would more accurately describe the relation of the cosmos to God by use of the term 'theophany':

> The world is a theophany, a manifestation of God, in which beings closer to God manifest God to those further away. The world is God's glory made manifest: it exists to display his glory and draw everything into contemplation of his beauty. The doctrine of creation is necessary to such an understanding of the world as theophany: God is immediately present to his whole creation as its creator; created reality is not, as created, an obstacle to his glory, neither because it owes its being to something other than (or even alien to) God, nor because it is an increasingly remote echo of God's original creative urge. But if God is to manifest himself outside himself, that implies multiplicity, which in turn implies difference, which must be either ordered or disordered: and for Denys, only an ordered hierarchical creation could manifest the glory of the One.[18]

It is precisely because the yearning triune love gives existence immediately to each creature that the whole creation is *not* opaque to God but is luminous with divine glory; and it is because this creative love is the effulgence of God's *triune relationality* and order that the cosmos itself has a sacred mutuality and order – it is not, in other words, a monochromatic indistinctness but the reciprocal play of unique creatures that together reflect the infinite play of the divine persons. Undoubtedly the negative historical connotations of hierarchy make it hard for us to imagine a structure of mutuality. Yet the word 'hierarchy' is not derived from terms implying oppressive relations but from two Greek words, *hier* meaning sacred, and *archē* meaning principle of origin or source. Perhaps we could think of the cosmic hierarchy as the sacred triune relationality expressing itself by means of the beautiful patterns of creation of which it is the origin. It is in this sense that the cosmos is a theophany, a manifestation of God – or more precisely, of God as the eternal event of self-giving love.

   With this understanding we can see more clearly what Dionysius is getting at when he writes that God 'has bestowed hierarchy (*hierarchia*) as a gift to ensure the salvation and divinization of every being endowed with reason and intelligence' (EH 376B, p. 198). As the reflection of the triune activity of self-bestowing love, hierarchy is not a static or passive affair. Every creature has received its fill of 'the sacred gift' from God, 'then the divine goodness sent them to lead others to this same gift. Like gods, they had a burning and generous urge to secure uplifting (*anagōgē*) and divinization for their subordinates' (EH 376D, p. 199). Reflecting the triune yearning for the other, each member of the hierarchy fulfils its own gift of life by bestowing light and meaning on another, uplifting the other and assisting in its *ekstasis* towards truth (and in this particular *ekstasis* lies the germ of theology itself as we will see below). Louth comments on the society of mutuality that Dionysius's vision suggests:

> Hierarchy is the outreach of God's love, it is not a ladder we struggle up by our own efforts. . . . To depend on God and his love means to depend on other people. It is the members of the hierarchy who purify, illumine, and perfect, and themselves stand in need of such purification, illumination and perfection. The hierarchy is a community that is being saved and mediates salvation. Denys is often accused of a narrow individualism, because he seems concerned to show how the hierarchical arrangements meet the needs of the individual. But it is not so often noted that the hierarchical arrangements themselves are emphatically not impersonal, but are the arrangements of a community, or group of communities, whose members are seeking to draw near to God and draw others near to God.[19]

What really makes the cosmos a hierarchical theophany is not, in other words, simply its ordered structure in itself, but the fact that the members of the structure are alive with the desire of God for the other, mediating God's desire for the other's ultimate good – and this, in the case of creatures, means salvation.

Now it might seem that in such an aesthetic vision of reality there could be little place for the weak, the unlovely and the lost. It is certainly true that Dionysius does not have much to say concretely about the needs of the poor and oppressed. But there is a hint, at least, that they too are crucial members of the hierarchy. With his usual downward emphasis, one might fear that Dionysius envisions as the primary role for little ones in the church as simply being the objects of the tender ministrations of everyone else. But in passing on the divine light, Dionysius says, each level of the theophany needs to render God's glory more accessible to the level below it. So the immaterial is expressed in material images and forms of life, the purely intelligible is enacted in physical relationships, and so on; because, says Dionysius, we all need 'perceptible things to lift us up into the domain of conceptions' (EH 377A, p. 199).

There is a curious dialectic at work here, for the further revelation passes into the cosmos, the more it will be clothed in words, interpretations and theories. These are all necessary to give expression to the revelation of glory in terms of which our minds are capable, but they inevitably end up dimming and veiling what is infinitely clear and perspicuous in itself. As Karl Barth would insist long after Dionysius, revelation itself is an unveiling of God by means of a veiling (not because of the *creatureliness* of finite being per se, but because of its fallen proclivity to understand everything in separation from the Creator).

Yet there is something inherently revealing about this veiling in and of itself; it is not simply a loss to be bemoaned or avoided. The dimmed and nearly silenced embodiments of God's glory are signs of perhaps the greatest truth of God, namely the ultimate hiddenness and incomprehensibility of divine life.[20] In other words, there is a pivotal point here at which God comes to illumine just as much the weakness, fallibility and misery of the world but now in a form which such a context can bear. And what is revealed there in greatest humility is the greatest majesty, the unfathomable mystery of rescuing love. For, as Dionysius writes:

> The transcendent (*huperousios*) has put aside its own hiddenness and has revealed itself to us by becoming a human being. But he is hidden even after this revelation, or, if I may speak in a more divine fashion, is hidden even amid the revelation. For this mystery (*mustērion*) of Jesus remains hidden and can be drawn out by no word or mind. What is to be said of it remains unsayable; what is to be understood of it remains unknowable (Ep. 3, p. 264).

Christ is the true coming forth of God to humanity, revelation itself. And yet at this point the helpless child of peasant parents, the broken body on the cross, remind us that what Jesus unveils is revealed in painful darkness and unknowing; for what is unveiled is the most veiled, the most secret, the most mysterious – divine love which refuses to be God apart from what is most alienated from God. Jesus is the hidden pivot, the mystical turning point of the whole cosmic hierarchy, because in him is revealed both the going out of God's love and its will to return with the lost in its embrace. In a remarkable passage, Dionysius uncloaks this mystery of God's innermost being as rescuing love by describing its culmination in the utter self-giving of the Cross:

> Is it not characteristic of his unspeakable, incomprehensible goodness that he fashions the existence of things, that he draws everything into being, that he wishes everything to be always akin to him and to have fellowship (*koinōnikos*) with him according to their fitness? Does he not come lovingly (*erōtikōs*) to those who have turned away from him? Does he not contend with them and beg them

not to spurn his love? Does he not support his accusers and plead on their behalf? He even promises to be concerned for them and when they are far away from him they have only to make a backward turn and there he is, hastening to meet them. He receives them with completely open arms and greets them with the kiss of peace (Ep. 8, 1085D–1088A, p. 271).

Note how Dionysius moves from the outflowing goodness of God in creation, to the seeking of those who turn away (in the prophets), to the Lukan themes of Christ's forgiveness of his executioners and the warm embrace of the Lost Prodigal.

So the ordered relations of cosmos and ecclesia are the manifestation of this outgoing love of God, of God's triune self-giving love in motion towards humanity. Implicit in each level of the hierarchy are two entirely correlate motions: on one hand there is the outgoing (ecstasy) of God's love, and on the other hand there is God's intention to embrace and uplift the other into the divine life. The fact that these two motions are really different aspects of *one* divine momentum is disclosed in their complete integration in Jesus. Christ embodies both God's ('descending') love in pursuit of the other who turns away, and also God's ('ascending') love within the other, uplifting and drawing her or him into the embrace of peace. Theology, in Dionysius's view, is the communal activity of recognizing and responding to this hidden or mystical presence of God.

Theology as entering into the mystery

If God is ecstatic in love towards the creature, theology is an expression of the creature's reciprocal ecstasy in *discerning* this love in all its manifestations, and in *returning* to God through interpretations of the theophany of God. For Dionysius, revelation both in the order of the Scriptures and in the order of the liturgy is the manifestation of God's outgoing desire for relationship with the other. The task of theology, then, is to pass by way of these signs into the depth of the Mystery who speaks them. Theology is, in a real sense, the common task of all hierarchy:

> The common goal of every hierarchy consists of the continuous love (*agapē*) of God and of things divine, a love which is sacredly worked out in an inspired and unique way. . . . It consists of a knowledge (*gnōsis*) of beings as they really are. It consists of both the seeing and understanding of sacred truth. It consists of an inspired participation in the one-like perfection and in the one itself, as far as possible. It consists of a feast upon that sacred vision which nourishes the intellect and which divinizes everything rising up to it (EH 376A–B, p. 198).

unic between theology and mystery

The goal of hierarchy is responding to the divine love in the unique manner of each member of the hierarchy. It involves a movement into the depths of reality, a process of understanding the ever-richer meaning of reality (manifested in scripture and liturgy). This is an uplifting process, a unitive process that draws the participants into the unity of the Trinity; it is a kind of feasting that makes the guests come to life. This is mystical theology.

Regarding the logic of the Areopagite's mystical theology, Hans Urs von Balthasar suggests, 'the aesthetic transcendence that we know in this world (from the sensible as manifestation to the spiritual as what is manifest) provides the formal schema for understanding theological or mystical transcendence (from the world to God).'[21] So the aesthetic and hermeneutical process of contemplating the hidden meaning of scripture and liturgy is the framework for the theological journey into the mystery of God. Speaking for example of the angelic hierarchy, Dionysius observes, 'I must behold the sacred forms attributed to it by the scriptures, so that we may be uplifted by way of these mysterious (mustikōs) representations to their divine simplicity' (CH 177C, p. 156). This kind of formulation is found frequently and is the animating drive behind Dionysius's well-known predilection for negative or apophatic theology; the affirmative self-expression of God in the theophany must become the matter for the return to God – each level of representation is 'negated' as one passes through and into the depths that it manifests.

Paul Rorem's detailed study of the role played by biblical and liturgical symbols in Dionysius clarifies this process. The ascending dynamic of mystical theology 'is not away from the images as undesirable but precisely through them as the means to a higher realm'.[22] Reflection on the patterning of the biblical imagery or the sequence of a liturgical rite opens the mind to the uplifting and unitive mystery at work within them.

Perhaps Dionysius's most famous account of this process is that short and compelling work which he actually titled, Mystical Theology. The structure of the work as a whole encapsulates the Areopagite's vision of reality and the theological task. It begins with a prayer to God the Trinity, the outpouring of life who is the source of all creation and the source of all the cosmic signs of truth (especially as manifested in scripture and liturgy). Dionysius beseeches the Trinity specifically to 'lead us up beyond unknowing and light up to the farthest, highest peak of mystic scripture' (MT 997A–B, p. 135). So Dionysius sees God in God's self-differentiation as the source of that uplifting journey through the theophanic symbols. This theological ascent is dependent upon the prior 'descent' of God's self-disclosure as the cause of all things, and theology appropriately begins by tracing this descent from the most transcendent to the most humble.

But next theology must, in a fully existential and practical way, begin to ascend these same levels of divine self-disclosure, being drawn through each into the deeper meaning beyond it, and ultimately beyond the mind's ability to grasp or control the meaning. Moses' ascent into the mystical darkness of unknowing is described as the model of this process. In Rorem's view, Dionysius describes Moses' ascent in terms of the celebrant's entrance into the heart of the liturgical mystery: Moses 'moves beyond the trumpet sounds and the many lights, just as the hierarch knows how to transcend the bare sounds of the scriptures and the material lights of worship', and so on for each element of Dionysius's description.[23] Thus the example of Moses is not a description of an individual's inner experience so much as a model for the ascending consciousness of a liturgical community as it enacts together the eucharistic rite and reflects on its journey of deeper participation in the mystery of Jesus' self-oblation.

After the model of Moses has been opened up as the proper and secure context for the theological process, Dionysius turns to reflect more theoretically on the crucial transition – the shift from the descending (cataphatic) affirmations of God's self-disclosures to the correlative ascending (apophatic) negations. For Dionysius this apophatic journey takes place as the community participates in the hidden meaning of the symbols ever more deeply. This always leads the theological community out of itself, beyond its ability to name and articulate the mystery, precisely because now it is encountering God not as disclosed in the theophany but in the full mystery of that love which expresses itself in all theophany:

> Now as we plunge into that darkness which is beyond intellect, we shall find ourselves not simply running short of words but actually speechless and unknowing. In the earlier books my argument traveled downward from the most exalted to the humblest categories, taking in on this downward path an ever-increasing number of ideas which multiplied with every stage of the descent. But my argument now rises from what is below up to the transcendent, and the more it climbs, the more language falters, and when it has passed up and beyond the ascent, it will turn silent completely, since it will finally be at one with him who is indescribable (MT 1033C, p. 139)

Theology does its job, in Dionysius's view, by leading the community beyond where human words can go. But the crucial point is that the final stage of this journey is not the silence which is utterly null and void of meaning but the silence of embrace, unity with God who unspeakably comes forth from divine life in order to draw what is not divine into divinity.

All this suggests that far from initiating a privatized conception of mysticism as a range of interior states of experience, Dionysius understands the mystical life as essentially a corporate journey into the depths of meaning implicit in all the works of God's outgoing love. Mystical theology is the discernment of this hidden presence and the attempt to enter into an understanding of who God must be if God so truly loves the world as to create it and become present to it in Christ. Such an understanding leads the theological community beyond its concepts and into God's own supra-conceptual form of understanding, namely unitive *relationship with the other.*

Mystical Knowledge and the Role of Christ: Maximus the Confessor

Dionysius provided a visionary and fertile model for faith in search of understanding. In his conception, cosmic and ecclesial outpouring of divine love is not simply a vast backdrop for theology but the inner dynamic of theology itself. Theology does not so much need to develop a 'method' in Dionysius's view as to discover its true identity. For theology is really an aspect of the mystical journey by means of which God is leading creation back into unity with the divine life. Theology is the attempt to notice how this is happening, to articulate the stages of the community's journey, to point ahead to the One who alone could mystically arouse the uplifting ecstasy that always leads beyond.

There are, however, some points that might well be clarified in such a vision of mystical theology. And perhaps chief among them are the nature of 'knowledge' in mystical theology (especially in terms of the soul's ultimate state of union with God) and the role of Christ in the mystical journey. As the writings of Dionysius made their appearance in the early Byzantine world, the question of their construal became a matter of some debate. One of the most profound interpreters of this integrated view of doctrine and prayer was Maximus the Confessor (c.580–662), and it is to his treatment of these particular questions about knowledge and the role of Christ that we now turn.[24]

Mystical knowing

As with Dionysius, there is in Maximus a strong sense that the motive force of mystical knowing is the divine love itself. Just as the *agapē* in which the faithful share is first God's, so also there is a desirous (erotic) aspect of love which is God's too. That is in the end what gives love its ability to enrapture the believer into the divine life. What can raise the mind most of all is this divine *erōs*, which is able through prayer to reach the mind and give it wings to fly towards God.[25] God's *agapē* itself is described as the means by which the *gnōsis* (knowledge) of God is able to ravish (*harpzo*, snatch, seize) the mind.[26]

Significantly, Maximus rarely moves into such talk without weaving it through with the language of knowledge, light and infinity. The topic is irradiated for him by the intensity of God's effect on the soul. He speaks of the contemplative life (*theoretikos*) as occasioned by 'divine *eros* and maximum purification,' in which the mind is 'rapt by the divine and infinite light', conscious 'only of him who through charity (*agapē*) effects such brightness in it. Then being concerned with the properties of God, it receives impressions of him, pure and limpid.'[27] The mind is taken up and flooded with light, and most suggestively, made capable thereby of receiving divine impressions. This is certainly no dissolution of the mind, but rather its utter delight in the divine being, and undoubtedly its astonishment at being made able to enjoy the divine mode of life.

All of which brings us to the question of how, in the coincidence of love and intellect, one comes in some sense to 'know' God. As we have just seen, in the ultimate state of knowing the desirous love of God catches the mind up and draws it ecstatically beyond itself into a new 'kind' of knowing. But what kind of knowing is this? Maximus, following Evagrius (346–99), assumes that these ultimate forms of knowing have been prepared for as the mind has learned to practice more preliminary forms of mystical contemplation. Specifically the mind needs to develop the detachment and freedom to discern the inner principles (*logoi*) of all material things.

This interpretive practice is integral to the Maximian appropriation of Dionysius's scriptural and liturgical interpretation. In all these cases the pattern is of an ascent into truth by means of a descent into the hidden (mystical) meaning of the object. But we have to realize that for Maximus the mystical *logoi* in all created realities are whispers of the Logos, the divine Word who is the speaking source of all creation. And so at the highest levels of desirous love, knowledge comes about because the mind receives an impression of divine life directly from *the* Logos. The problem is whether the mind is free enough (from the intellectual desire to possess everything) that it can pass through the *logoi* of creatures to the mystical presence of the divine Speaking.

Of course, the human faculties are not operating in a vacuum, and just as the divine glory captivates the eye, so the mystical meaning of that glory may be able to beckon the believer onwards. 'Just as the beauty of visible things draws the eyes of sense, so also the knowledge of invisible things draws the pure mind to itself.'[28] In the later *Chapters on Knowledge* Maximus offers another elaboration of this theme: 'Just as straight lines which proceed from the center are seen as entirely undivided in that position, so the one who has been made worthy to be in God will recognize in himself with a certain simple and undivided knowledge all the preexisting principles of things.'[29] In other places Maximus is clearly speaking of a movement from visible objects to contemplative awareness of their *logoi*. Here, however, Maximus has moved to a new level of contemplation in which the *logoi* are not present to the mind because it has first beheld them visually, but rather because now the contemplative comes to be centred in God. From this centre the contemplative can see all things from their inner source, the Logos of them all. This knowledge is the contemplative's own, but because it is a knowledge enjoyed from the divine perspective, as it were, it is a simple and undivided knowing, patterned after God's knowing.

The role of Christ and union with God

The resurrection of Christ is central to the thought of Maximus the Confessor. His teaching on human deification is, throughout, an expression of confidence that the mystery of the Word Incarnate is a living, attractive, inclusive and powerfully transformative reality. It may be profitable to begin by distinguishing, on the one hand, the role of the eternal Word as the bearer of existence and inner rationale for all creation, and, on the other hand, the Word's salvation-historical mode. For Maximus, all that the Word accomplishes hiddenly through the process of creation – and its fulfilment by the grace of deification – is achieved concretely in the Word's salvation history.

This means that each gift of existence and deified existence bears within it the power and character of Christ's paschal mystery. So for example when Maximus talks of the soul passing from death to life in Christ, he is not using the resurrection of Christ as a metaphorical aid in describing deification; rather, he is saying that what deifies the believer is precisely a sharing in Christ's dying and rising. The creative and deifying power of the Father's Word is at work in the believer's life; and this inner work, itself a gift of the Spirit, effects deification. It does so by filling the believer with the salvation-historical mystery of Christ, thereby enabling human nature to live according to the mode of the Son.

Something of this is conveyed in a rather mysterious passage describing the interconnectedness of creation, incarnation and deification: 'The mystery (*mustērion*) of the Incarnation of the Word bears the power of all the hidden meanings and figures of Scripture as well as the knowledge of visible and intelligible creatures. The one who knows the mystery of the cross and the tomb knows the principles of these creatures. And the one who has been initiated into the ineffable power of the Resurrection knows the purpose for which God originally made all things.'[30] As with Dionysius, an important epistemological principle is at work here: the mystery of the Incarnation is the hermeneutical key that discloses the mystical presence of God in the theophany of cosmos and ecclesia. But one can also sense an ontological grounding: the very same divine *ekstasis* at work in creation comes to full concrete expression in the Incarnation, and in the ongoing assumption of creation into the divine life which the Incarnation inaugurated: 'For the Word of God who is God wills always and in all things to work the mystery of his embodiment.'[31]

Maximus sets the achievements of Christ in the framework of the Sixth, Seventh and Eighth Days of creation, making the usual correlations between the 'fulfilment' of Christ's work and the Sixth Day, the Seventh as day of rest (in the tomb), and the Eighth as the new day of resurrection and deification. 'The one who has become worthy of the eighth day is risen from the dead, that is, from what is less than God. sensible and intelligible things, words, and thoughts; and he lives the blessed life of God, who alone is said to be and is in very truth the Life, in such a way that he becomes himself God by deification.'[32] Maximus works out a very detailed correlation between the mystical 'day', the work of Christ, and the stage of spiritual life of the believer, clearly setting the latter in the creation–incarnation context. The passover through creation is accomplished by the Incarnate Lord and this same passover must now be made by the believer. Maximus makes quite clear that the pilgrimage in Christ leads *through* the mystery of the Cross of the Sixth Day, not around it: 'Absolutely no heavenly or earthly power can know these days before experiencing the passion, only the blessed divinity which created them.'[33]

In all, Maximus's emphases in considering the salvation-historical work of Christ are three: the new freedom which Christ's obedience has wrought in human nature, the reunion of creation with itself and with God by incarnation and ascension, and the revelation of these accomplishments and of the Trinity through the accessible historical form of Christ. The whole scheme is seen to hinge on the *transitus* of the paschal mystery, the passover to the Eighth Day.

Maximus envisages the believer being led by Christ into the higher levels of mystical awareness. 'This will enable [the one who prays] to follow the one who has "passed through the heavens, Jesus the Son of God", who is everywhere and who in his incarnation passes through all things on our account. If we follow him, we also pass though all things with him and come beside him if we know him not in the limited condition of his descent in the incarnation but in the majestic splendor of his natural infinitude.'[34] This passage is a good example of the subtlety with which Maximus weaves together Christ's historical and mystical effects upon the believer. Jesus passes through all things, and this opens a way for the believer. But there is also the mystical effect of knowing this Christ as one rises with him, knowing him in the glory of his 'natural infinitude'. This knowledge is transformative and fits the believer to live more and more at the side of Christ.

This mystical presence of Christ in the soul reconstrues Dionysius's notion of God arousing the soul to 'stand outside itself' and so journey into the hidden presence; that is, it sets the uplifting ecstatic movement of theology very definitely in a christological context: it is Christ who awakens the believer and sets in motion the mystical passage into the depths. In the Lord's Prayer commentary Maximus says that Christ 'sets in movement in us an insatiable desire (*orexis*) for himself who is the Bread of Life, wisdom, knowledge, and justice.'[35] Here is one of the clearest witnesses in Maximus to the role of Christ as author of the desirous movement within the believer.

Following the model of the hypostatic union (in the Incarnation), the Confessor sees human fulfilment coming about as human nature is lived out (and reconfigured) according to the divine pattern of the Son's life (i.e., just as Jesus' humanity is 'enacted' according to the pattern of the Son's life and mission, so our humanity is fulfilled as it comes to participate in Christ). This means that the highest stages of mystical life consist in a participation in the triune relationality. The Person of the Word transfigures the soul and raises it up to a new relation with the Father, precisely by drawing the soul ecstatically into the mode or pattern (*tropos*) of filial activity which is what 'defines' the Word as distinct from the other divine hypostases: 'Having God through prayer as its mystical (*mustikos*) and only Father by grace, the soul will center on the oneness of his hidden being . . . [wanting to be only] God's who takes it up becomingly and fittingly as only he can, penetrating it completely without passion (*apathōs*) and deifying all of it and transforming it unchangeably to himself.'[36]

Maximus seems to conceive of deification very much as the soul's ascent, through formation in Christ, to the Father. One can indeed see here an enjoyment of the Father who is the ultimate source of the soul's life, and the one who has adopted the soul in Christ. And because the Father is the source of the other Persons, in 'transforming [the soul] unchangeably to *himself*', the soul is 'formed' now according to the eternal outgoing pattern of trinitarian love. Maximus does not omit, however, to mention that the Father deifies the soul by 'transforming it *unchangeably* to himself'. There is no question for Maximus of a transformation which changes the essential humanity, somehow leaving it behind.

Maximus is pointing us to a new creation of the human act of existence. Through the life of virtue, the activity of love and the ascent of knowledge, the historical and mystical work of Christ has effected a transformation in the human mode of existence, the pattern of activity by which we identify who we are. Human being, precisely *as* human being, is drawn into harmony with the mission of the eternal Son. Mystical theology in this context would seem to involve a momentous transformation in human understanding: maximally it implies perceiving reality from within its eternal trinitarian source; minimally it implies reflecting on reality in its relationship to that eternal event of self-giving love. The key, I believe, to making sense of this idea in our own era is steadfastly to remind ourselves that such a transformation of human perceptivity makes it more fully human, not less.

The achievement of Maximus is to set mystical theology within the framework of incarnational thought, thus suggesting how it could be truly *human knowledge* while being at the same time a sharing in the unfathomable divine pattern of life. The ultimate form of human knowing might seem to eventuate finally in the rapt inexpressibility of the trinitarian embrace. But is that quite how Maximus has taught us to read mystical union? In the passage below, he explains that even after the redeemed soul ceases to need food for growth, it will be fed directly in a mysterious sustenance of its new perfection:

> When it receives through this food eternal blessedness indwelling in it, it becomes God through participation in divine grace by itself ceasing from all activities of mind and sense and with them the natural activities of the body which became Godlike along with it in a participation of deification proper to it. In this state only God shines forth through body and soul when their natural features are transcended in overwhelming glory.[37]

Cessation from natural human activity is only possible because the human nature involved is now capable of being lived out divinely. Because the mystic has been drawn into a deified mode of human nature, God can act and live directly in real human being. Humanity, body and soul, is revealed in all its true perfection. As the perfect humanity of Christ enacted the very identity of the eternal Son, so every deified human being becomes an immediate revelation of God. As Maximus says, 'only God shines forth'. But God shines forth, as in Christ, precisely through the perfections of human existence – and these have ever included the perceptivity of our bodies (note that Maximus does not exclude our material being), the linguisticality of our minds and the sensitivity of our feelings. Mystical theology in this view is not the activity of speechless disembodied automatons but of real human beings who find that their whole humanity 'takes place' more intensely and vitally than ever. In mystical theology, bodily knowing is empowered by the very Word who speaks precisely in excruciatingly bodily form on the cross. So the fully linguistic understanding unlocked in mystical theology flows directly from that eternal trinitarian play of speaking and hearing, knowing and loving, which constitutes the very life of God.

For the early Christians right through Dionysius and Maximus, mystical theology takes place in the setting of the community's participation in Christ. It means the transformation of consciousness through the hard communal praxis of spiritual growth, in mutual openness to the hidden presence of the divine in the ordinary struggles and rituals of ecclesial life. But it does mean a new kind of knowing, an understanding brought to life as believers are drawn ecstatically beyond their usual habits of mind and heart. And this leads to deeper, truer communal life – both in terms of what is taught and how life is lived. The ineffability of life in the Trinity is overflowingly generative of concrete, historical meaning.

Discovery of the Inner Self: The Turn to Experience

So far I have suggested that in its formative period at least, mystical theology was far from a peripheral aspect of ecclesial life; 'it is the fruit of participation in the mystery of Christ, which is inseparable from the mystery of the Church'.[38] It is not coincidental that this period in which the church was drawn more deeply into the mystery of God in Christ was equally the formative period in Christian doctrinal thought. For 'the basic doctrines of the Trinity and Incarnation, worked out in these centuries, are mystical doctrines formulated dogmatically.'[39] It was in the matrix of the community's deepening participation in the paschal mystery that the church began to glimpse more of the meaning of Jesus, and thus to understand something more of the hidden source of all life revealed in the self-giving love of one dying on a cross.

Doctrine, from this perspective, is the transposition into human language of the divine 'language'– namely the eternal giving away of love for the other which constitutes the divine act of existence. Therefore, as personal and intimate as each believer's encounter with that divine reality might be, the meaning of the encounter is communal and cosmic. The questioning and transformation at the heart of the mystical life are personal but, as Rowan Williams has said very well, 'the focus of meaning is not private and particular, but a reality which incorporates and gives an identity and a structure to individual experience, and is never reducible to its limited terms'.[40]

But what happens if the very structures of ecclesial life no longer seem to sustain this integrity of personal encounter and public meaning? Would it become harder for individual experience to be *incorporated*, to find an identity and structure within the *communal* setting? This would not be an implausible reading of the histories of mystical and dogmatic theologies over the course of the Middle Ages. For during this period of the rise of scholastic theology there were also shifting trends in Christian spirituality that made it harder for the two realms of life to communicate, let alone nourish each other. In much later medieval spirituality, the self comes to be construed more and more in terms of its inner life, its experiences and affectivity. Thus, participation in the mystery of God in Christ is likely to seem all the more purely a matter of the 'private and particular'.

Coinciding with the growth of scholasticism, medieval spirituality's intensifying focus on individual experience and affectivity gave rise to a spiralling mutual distrust between spirituality and theology that lingers even today. A large-scale historical analysis of this period of divorce remains to be written. Yet it may be useful to consider briefly two persuasive readings of the issues. From 1948 until nearly the time of his death in 1988, Hans Urs von Balthasar was concerned with the separation, particularly as it takes place in the later Middle Ages.[41] Given his early studies in the history of German literature, it is perhaps not surprising that von Balthasar takes what might well be called a 'tragic' view of the theology–spirituality divorce. The diverging needs of inner-ecclesial formation, on one hand, and apologetic and scientific theology, on the other hand, lead inevitably to the doom of the theology–spirituality matrix. But that is only the external problem, says von Balthasar, it is only the trap in which the real tragedy takes place, namely the growing loss of that fertile receptive ground in which spiritual consciousness could grow into doctrinal truth. The real tragedy, in other words, is that by the later Middle Ages fewer and fewer saints, mystics and theologians still knew how to knit spirituality and theology together in their own life and work. And with that comes the loss of the crucial 'objective spiritual medium' in which the spiritual roots of doctrine can flourish.[42]

But von Balthasar's view needs to be placed in a larger social and political context. In her recent work, *Power, Gender and Christian Mysticism*, Grace Jantzen highlights the disturbing power relations at work in effecting the spirituality–theology divorce.[43] Jantzen has pointed out that when contemplatives were themselves mostly male members of the ecclesiastical power structure, their mystical thought was regarded as central to Christian life (think of Augustine, Pope Gregory the Great, and Bernard of Clairvaux – just to name some authoritative figures). As more women begin to speak as mystical theologians in their own right, is it just coincidental that contemplative life comes to be regarded as primarily a private affair (best kept cloistered and away from the corporate life of the church), as too easily given to 'hysteria' and even madness to merit a role in the theological deliberations of Christendom? So variant forms of popular 'devotion' come to be viewed by eccelsiastical and academic authorities with ambivalence at best, and certainly as far removed from the kind of theologically fertile contemplative teaching of earlier eras.

Commenting on the modern view of 'mysticism' (and its persistent separation of spirituality from public theology), Jantzen writes:

> It was only with the development of the secular state, when religious experience was no longer perceived as a source of knowledge and power, that it became safe to allow women to be mystics. Thus it came about that when mysticism became constructed as private and personal, having nothing to do with politics, it was also possible to see it as compatible with a woman's role. . . . Feminists have every reason, both historical and current, to be suspicious of an understanding of mysticism which allows that women may be mystics, but which makes mysticism a private and ineffable psychological occurrence and which detaches it from the considerations of social justice.[44]

This modern view of 'mysticism' emerges all too easily when spirituality is separated from theology, mystical consciousness from concrete social and intellectual implications. Mystical thought becomes private piety. How did this divorce come about? Or, if one takes Jantzen's darker view, what circumstances made its social construction both possible and plausible? In this section I will consider some of the implications of shifts in the construal of the self, and in the next, shifts in the perceived relationship of love and knowledge – all of which were factors in the divorce.

Certainly part of the answer lies in a strange historical paradox: in the period usually accounted the height of corporate 'Christendom', the corporate metaphors in biblical anthropology seem to have lost their hold in popular imagination – precisely in favour of a concern with individual salvation. In his influential study, *The Discovery of the Individual 1050–1200*, Colin Morris points to a number of cultural trends bearing directly on our question.[45] Eucharistic piety and confessional practices both began to alter by the later eleventh century from a corporate piety towards a more private and personal devotion; especially striking is the mounting penitential concern with inner attitudes and intentions as central to the sacrament.[46] A growing cultural interest in self-knowledge and inner feelings develops into a lively fascination with conflicts in motivation and psychology. An older framework that conceived moral life in terms of a choice between good and evil gives way to a growing awareness of 'the multiplicity of affections and appetites' by which 'the individual's spiritual progress could be more subtly observed'.[47] One notices correlate shifts in theological focus in period treatments of the atonement and eschatology. Earlier formulations of the doctrine of salvation, for example, focused on the cosmic victory of Christ over death and sin; by the high Middle Ages there is intense focus on the painful physical sufferings of Jesus in crucifixion as expiation of the individual sinner's guilt. Similarly, expectations of the end seem to shift from hope in the renewal of all things towards concern for the destiny of the individual.[48]

Chicken and egg games are notoriously vexed in historical questions, but it is at least no accident that parallel developments take place in the understanding of the mystical life during this same period. It is one of history's ironies that Bernard of Clairvaux (1090–1153), a defender of the public and theological role of the mystic if ever there were one, should be connected with the fateful 'turn to experience' in mystical theology – a turn that took mysticism in directions very far, one can surmise, from the mellifluous doctor's intentions. What, for example, did Bernard mean when, in the famous opening of his third sermon on the Song of Songs, he wrote: 'Today the text we are to study is the book of our own experience (*in libro experientiae*). You must therefore turn your attention inwards, each one must take note of his own particular awareness of the things I am about to discuss'?[49] Throughout his writings, Bernard is constant in his 'insistence on the necessity of the personal experience of his listeners as the only way to understand his message'.[50] It would be most unfortunate to misread Bernard in modern post-Cartesian terms, so some clarification regarding what Bernard himself understood by 'experience' is necessary.

As Jean Leclercq has noted, for a monastic figure in Bernard's era 'experience' is essentially a communal reality. It is personal in the sense of a personal appropriation and existential embodiment of the communal faith, but it is environed 'by the conventual experience of a community and it flourishes in the midst of this common fervor'; hence it is fundamentally biblical and liturgical in its sources and 'presupposes nothing more than the pursuit of the spiritual life led in a community whose essential aim is the search for God'.[51] And if the 'bindings' of the 'book of our own experience' are the communal features of monastic life, so too is the content of the experience oriented towards a common public faith. Bernard Bonowitz comments: 'true experience of God is the registration in the human person of a constant divine self-communication; it is the means of educating and converting the heart by mediating to it the knowledge and the love of God; and *it is itself the relationship with God at the time it is occurring,* since what the person meets in his experience is *not his own interiority but the Persons of the Blessed Trinity.*'[52] So, in Bonowitz's reading at least, when Bernard speaks of experience he is not talking about inner states of feeling or a person's 'interiority', but the particular shaping given to someone's life and consciousness by the presence of God. Or, as Bernard himself puts it, the most crucial experience of burning desire for God is a transcription in terms of the self of God's prior desire for the soul, 'it is the result of the soul being already sought and visited' (84, IV.190).[53] The problem is that, given the shifts in cultural consciousness pointed out by Morris, Bernard's inherently communal understanding of experience may indeed have been misconstrued by later eras (not least our own!) – in a privatizing way.

But let us consider some examples that help to give a sense of Bernard's own usage. Explaining for example why the biblical book is not just the Song of Solomon but the Song of *all* songs, the abbot writes: 'only the touch of the Spirit can inspire a song like this, and only personal experience can unfold its meaning. Let those who are versed in the mystery revel in it; let all others burn with desire rather to experience it than merely to learn about it' (1, I.6).[54] Or again, those 'with an urge to frequent prayer will have experience of what I mean' (9, I.58).[55] Or again, 'if you have been attentive I think you will have seen that your inward experience re-echoes what I have outwardly described' (21, II.7).[56] In these examples we can see Bernard clearly trying to stir up his fellow monks to realize within their own lives something of the mysterious relationship of the soul with God. Here the language of experience is designed to remind the reader that the real meaning of the teaching is found in the *living* of the teaching and that only those who have begun to practice this living into the mystery will fully understand. In other words, while all individuals need to have their own experiences of the reality Bernard describes, these experiences do *not* isolate them from each other in private selves but rather draw them together in the common journey into deeper relationship with the one God.

But the language of experience does not stop there in Bernard. Not only does it point towards the intensely personal bordering on the secret and private, Bernard's language also points to experience as a new kind of spiritual tool, a guide by which one begins to chart one's inner spiritual journey. The kind of personal experience lying at the heart of the Song of Songs, says Bernard, is like 'a tune you will not hear in the streets, these notes do not sound where crowds assemble; only the singer hears it and the one to whom he sings – the lover and the beloved' (1, I.7).[57] Note the explicitly 'unpublic' dimension suggested here. Are we moving in imagery at least, if not in intent, from the common public realm of salvation history to the inner private realm of the emotions?

In this atmosphere, the affective dimensions of experience become especially significant, and indeed Bernard proposes them as important pointers in discerning one's spiritual path. So he suggests how certain feelings of enlightenment with regard to scripture should assure the soul 'that the Bridegroom is with me'; and 'if I am filled with a feeling of humility rich with devotion . . . then truly I am aware of fatherly activity and do not doubt the Father's presence' (69, IV.33).[58] Earlier we saw how Bernard refers his readers to their own experience in order to have them discover the depth of meaning in what he was trying to say to them, but here the usage is rather different. Now readers are being urged to assess the emotive structure of their experiences and to draw conclusions thence to their individual relationships with God.

This appeal to affective experience as a principle of discernment is even more marked when Bernard guides his readers through feelings of 'apathy, lukewarmness and fatigue' by exhorting them to reach out to God for support, 'until finally, under the influence of grace, you feel again the vigorous pulse of life' (21, II.7).[59] Bernard is merely directing his readers to an awareness of the divine *source* of their affective experiences, but later spiritual guides will tend almost unavoidably to identify *the experiences themselves* rather than the divine source of the experiences as the principal object of the spiritual life. When we read Bernard with some sense of the history that follows him, it is hard to resist the temptation of later eras to misread him in this way; for even though he admonishes his readers to *avoid* becoming possessive about their spiritual experiences, the more he does so the more the experiences themselves become the preoccupying issue: 'While this state of happiness remains, you must not use it as if you possessed God's gift by right of inheritance, secure in the conviction that you could never lose it; for if he should suddenly withdraw his hand and withhold his gift, you would be plunged into dejection and excessive unhappiness' (21, II.7).[60] In such highly charged language, Bernard's warning against over-attachment to one's inner experience becomes, as it were, the unbidden harbinger of that utterly mesmerizing world, the inner self – whose spiritual dramas would, in the generations following Bernard, become the new locus of meaning in mystical theology.

In his highly suggestive monograph, *The Darkness of God: Negativity in Christian Mysticism*, Denys Turner has shown how this developing experientialist focus gave rise to our modern conception of 'mysticism' and came to supplant mystical theology. The second-order metaphysical dialectic by which authors such as Dionysius describe the *negation of experience* on the journey into God is gradually transformed into a first-order language about *having negative experiences*.[61] What had been a complex and polyvalent language – used both to describe the phases of the spiritual journey and to transcend those experiences – comes to be taken as a language of experience *tout court*. In other words, language for talking about the indescribable wonder of God (who cannot *be* experienced *in se*) becomes the language of having a wonderfully indescribable experience of God. This tendency was recognized by medieval writers themselves. So for example both Eckhart (*c*.1260–1327) and the author of the *Cloud of Unknowing* (later 1300s) attempt to counter this experientialism, which they see as a distorting account of the 'way' to God 'which one-sidedly translates the discourse of "interiority" into essentially psychological categories; that is to say into *experiences of inwardness*'.[62]

The more complex the psychological analysis of this experience becomes, the less transparent to the divine source it grows. By the sixteenth century this process has become so developed that mystical writers no longer authorize their statements by appeal to scriptural or traditional authorities, but by appeal, in Michel de Certeau's words, to the 'I', the particular experience of the speaker. Mystical discourse is understood to emerge from the secret place of the inner self, and so is 'authorized solely by being the locus of that "inspired" speech act, also designated by the term "experience". It claims to produce a present act of saying. In the text, the "I" increasingly becomes the index, at the same time as the instrument, of the question – an initial question – that the mystic discourse must take up: who speaks, and whence?'[63]

In this way mystical theology comes to be all about the life story of a new religious type, the 'mystic', whose own personality and spiritual 'genius' are increasingly seen as the key to understanding mystical texts: 'there is a narrativizing of the speaker, an endless circulation around that productive agency, that infinite and uninsured locus, the "I".'[64] By the time we come to one of the twentieth century's pioneers in the study of mysticism, Evelyn Underhill, this perspective has reached full bloom:

> We do not call every one who has these partial and artistic intuitions of reality a mystic, any more than we call every one a musician who has learnt to play the piano. The true mystic is the person in whom such powers transcend the merely artistic and visionary stage, and are exalted to the point of genius. . . . As artists stand in a peculiar relation to the phenomenal world, receiving rhythms and discovering truths and beauties which are hidden from other men, so this true mystic stands in a peculiar relation to the transcendental world; there experiencing actual, but to us unimaginable tension and delight. His consciousness is transfigured in a particular way, he lives at different levels of experience from other people.[65]

Underhill is articulating the impression of several centuries in her description of 'the mystic' as the experiential artist who lives at a different level from us ordinary people. 'Mysticism' is now understood as an inner drama enacted by the mystic's exquisitely refined feelings on the stage of the interior self.

De Certeau suggests that already by the time of Teresa of Avila (1515–82) this drama of the inner world had become a necessary substitute for a cosmos that, in de Certeau's memorable phrase, 'is no longer perceived as *spoken* by God, that . . . has become opacified, objectified, and detached from its supposed speaker'.[66] The inner self becomes the temporary substitute for the more public 'speech' of God: 'This *I* who speaks in the place of (and instead of) the Other also requires a *space* of expression corresponding to what the world was in relation to the speech of God.'[67] For Teresa, this 'interior mansion' becomes the imaginal realm in which the divine speech can still be heard, but now the language of that speech is constituted by the inner movements of the soul. The soul itself is 'but the inarticulable echo of an unknown Subject', thus it needs a dramatic imaginary inner stage upon which to act out and narrate the mysterious and inexpressible touch of 'Unknownness'.[68]

And so, coincident with the apparent divine withdrawal from the cosmos, mysticism in modernity also withdraws into this inner castle, the world of the inner self—a world whose claims to wisdom, authority and truth could easily be marginalized by religious and academic authorities, even as they have been subborned and co-opted by modern individualistic consumerism. At this point 'the mystic' has, in Western culture more generally, become something of a marginal eccentric at best, whose peculiar inner experience (to use Underhill's words) of 'unimaginable tension and delight' has come to seem a thing of pious curiosity perhaps, but clearly of little relevance for the serious task of academic theology. One has only to think of the unbridgeable gulf separating such fellow Christians and contemporaries as Thérèse of Lisieux (1873–97) and Adolf Harnack (1851–1930). The 'story of a soul' and the history of dogma seemed to have become not simply culturally isolated from one another, but fundamentally and mutually exclusive projects.

Affectivity and the Degrees of Knowledge

Another way of reading this story is in terms of the growing medieval sense of divorce between love and knowledge. It may be hard for us today even to make sense of such a phrase as 'intellectual mysticism'; we have been so conditioned to think of the mystical as the play of a person's inner feelings that the role of the intellect seems obscure. But of course in the ancient world from which the Christian mystical tradition grew, the mind was not primarily a self-referential ratiocination machine. 'We say, "I think, therefore I am", that is, thinking is an *activity* I engage in and there must therefore be an "I" to engage in it; the Greeks would say, "I think, therefore there is that which I think – *to noeta*". What I think is something going on in my head; what the Greek thinks, *to noeta*, are the objects of thought that (for example, for Plato) exist in a higher, more real world.'[69] That is to say, our words 'mind' or 'intellect' suggest a process that is, first, uniquely *our own* (*I* am doing this thinking), and second, fairly mundane and analytical. But for the ancient world the process of *noesis* or (to use our thinner word) 'knowing' is far more intuitive, and less 'private' in that it is not so much 'I' who am knowing but that 'the known' has drawn me into an encounter with itself. In the formative environment of Christian mysticism, knowing reality is associated more with the intimacy, even the desire, that runs between knower and known (as we saw with Maximus), and less with our modern conception of a scientific analysis of manipulable objects by the knower. Indeed for St Paul it is clear that the most complete form of knowledge would not finally be our own act at all, but an event in which I yield myself to God. And God, in this view, turns out to be not the known object but the ultimate Knower in the whole process: 'Now I know in part, then I shall know fully even as I have been fully known' (1 Cor 13.12).

Given this background, it is not surprising that in the tradition passing through Augustine (354–430) and Gregory the Great (*c.*540–604), love and knowledge are at the highest levels utterly coinherent: 'The soul wants to know God more and more because it loves him, and loves him because it knows that he is supreme Truth and Beauty. Love and knowledge of God are united in the kind of knowledge we have of God, namely wisdom, *sapientia.*'[70] And this relationship came to be formulated in the tag from Gregory that 'love itself is a form of knowing' (*amor ipse notitia est*).[71] Thomas Aquinas seems to have accepted this view as the correct one. For the angelic doctor *intellectus* does not, of course, equate to our usual modern understanding of 'intellection' or discursive rational analysis. It is, rather, a process of union between the knower and the known. Just as the will longs for the good, so the intellect longs for the true; and since the good and the true are identical in God, the highest form of knowing and willing (loving) coincide entirely. Much of this is brought out in Thomas's consideration of the relation between the intellect and the feelings in the contemplative life. In the opening objection, Aquinas produces Aristotle as an authority for the claim that 'the goal of contemplation is truth. And truth is entirely a matter for the intellect.

So apparently the contemplative life is wholly intellectual'.[72] While Aquinas accepts the view that the contemplative life refers to those who seek the truth, he points out that to desire the truth in the first place is an act of the will. 'This is why Gregory locates the contemplative life in the love of God, inasmuch as it is love of God which fires people to look at his beauty. And because we all enjoy obtaining what we love, the contemplative life culminates in enjoyment, which is a matter of our feelings, and this in turn makes love more intense.'[73] For Thomas, then, contemplation is an act of the intellect which fulfils the will's desire for God. Intellectus is not some kind of 'intellectualism' in our pejorative sense, but a movement which ultimately transcends the objects of sense; further it is the consideration of realities which even 'reason can neither discover nor grasp, realities, that is, which involve a high contemplation of the truth of God, and it is in this truth that contemplation finally reaches its perfection'.[74] Every act of intellectus is, for Thomas, a partial fulfilment of mind, but 'the ultimate perfection of the human intellect is the truth of God'.[75] So the perfection and fulfilment both of human knowing and loving is found in the contemplation of God. As was also true of Maximus, Aquinas believes that, at the highest level of knowing and loving, the intellect and the will are progressively *available* to God; we could say that in mystical contemplation it is not the mystic who knows and loves but rather the mystic is the one *known* and *loved* by God. All is grace, and therefore nothing is happening in the intellect or the will except what God is doing; and in God, knowing and loving are aspects of the one trinitarian act of existence.

This conception of the unity of knowing and loving is not based on an analysis of the human subject but of the divine subject; it depends on considering the issues from the teleological standpoint of divine reality. In the human subject, knowing and loving are distinct, and as directed towards other creatures they are often in conflict with each other; as directed towards God they are not just complementary but essential to their mutual fulfilment, indeed in the relationship with God they are united in each other. But a shift to a more anthropological analysis, a reading of the mystical life primarily in terms of the inner self is, not surprisingly, going to unravel the perceived unity.

By the later Middle Ages, the assumption has become in some cases nearly insurmountable that knowing is the task of theologians, while loving is a task for mystics; and instead of perceiving knowing and loving as one coinherent activity in God, they come to appear as strangers, rivals, even enemies struggling for dominance in the drama of the inner self.[76] Denys Turner argues that whereas in Dionysius the Areopagite the final stages of the *Mystical Theology* speak of the intellect surpassing *itself* in the darkness of divine presence, in later medieval affective mysticism 'intellect is negated by love, not by itself and is simply bundled away at the point at which its affirmations fail'.[77] Thus the ascending dialectics of love and knowledge in Dionysius have, by the later Middle Ages, been 'replaced with a simple bi-polarity of knowing and love. . . This is an apophaticism in which the cloud of unknowing is a metaphor not of self-transcendent intellect but of its simple abandonment. It is therefore an apophaticism which, unlike [Dionysius's], is pregnant with the possibilities of an anti-intellectualism'.[78] The impact of this shift on the relationship between mystical and academic theology in the later Middle Ages is not hard to imagine.

Simon Tugwell has noted how by the later thirteenth and fourteenth centuries the concept of prayer itself has shifted away from straightforward *petition* to God towards an *affective desire* for God, thence to the enjoyment of God, finally being understood in terms of one's heightened feelings (of self); the more the emphasis falls on certain feelings as the crucial element in prayer, the more prayer itself becomes self-consciously the pursuit of those feelings.[79] This individually self-conscious affectivity in later medieval spirituality seems in some cases to have become nearly the defining characteristic. Earlier monastic meditations on the gospel had been intended to 'stir intense emotions by way of a vivid imagining usually of the passion'.[80] But later imaginative meditations seem, in Tugwell's wry phrase, to have 'escaped largely from the control of the biblical text', so that the emphasis shifts almost imperceptibly from entering existentially into the biblical world towards a state in which the biblical world becomes, literally, the 'pretext' for the emotional drama of one's inner world.[81]

It was in such an environment that the English writer Richard Rolle (*c.*1290–1349), against the apparently arid speculations of the schools, affirmed the superiority of intense religious feelings. In the final chapter of his brief work, *The Mending of Life*, Rolle summarizes five contrasting views regarding the nature of contemplation. He describes them in ascending order of aptness.

The first view is akin to what Maximus (following Evagrius) would have called natural contemplation; it is the exercise of sufficient 'freedom from all the occupations of the world' that one is able to seek out the 'knowledge of hidden future things' or the deep meanings of 'divine writings'.[82] A second view holds that 'contemplation is the free and sharpsighted exploration of wisdom, raised with wonder'. The notion of knowledge is somewhat more 'elevated' here in comparison with the first view; it is not a penetration of *things* but an exalted, wondering 'exploration of wisdom'.

The third view mentioned by Rolle suggests a moralizing trajectory which developed very widely (as the *Devotio Moderna*) in the years shortly after Rolle's death. Instead of seeking an inner depth in the scriptures per se, Rolle suggests that in this view one seeks to interpret the book of one's own moral striving, leading to 'the penetrating observation of the soul opened wide in every direction for the discerning of virtues'. Interestingly Rolle's ordering suggests that this view, which again focuses primarily on the *inward struggles of the individual*, is preferable to the mystical reading of cosmos or scripture on one hand or to the rapt ascent of *intellectus* into the universal wisdom on the other hand.[83]

Yet even this third position is less preferable in Rolle's view than the persuasion of those who say, 'and say well' (he adds in his first hint of approbation), 'that contemplation is rejoicing in heavenly things'.[84] The obvious and intended contrast here is meant to be between a supposedly cold-hearted curiosity about 'heavenly things' and an experiencing of them in terms of one's own affectivity. The crucial role of this emotional response is even clearer in the view of those who 'say best' of all, 'that contemplation is the death of carnal affections through joy, by raising of the spirit'.[85]

The highest form of contemplation is thus played out in terms of a transition from carnal to spiritual 'affections', and as always for the hermit Rolle, it is precisely one's own affective reaction to God which must be cultivated as the surest engine of this transition. It is the raising of the spirit, the quest for joy that permits one to leave baser forms of affectivity behind. Hence Rolle's well-known preference for a language of spiritual sweetness, burning desire, and jubilation: the true contemplative must 'rejoice sweetly and ardently in interior joys' and 'is seized as if in ecstasy, by the sweetness of divine love, and then, snatched up marvelously, he is delighted'.[86] One can be sure of this state, argues Rolle, not because of the sight of the 'intellectual eye' which cannot see the spiritual light 'as it is in itself', but rather the soul must depend on another sign of its contemplative progress, its affective status: 'it feels itself to have been there [in true spiritual contemplation], when it keeps the savor and fervor within itself in limited light'.[87]

The (intellectual) light is only darkness in this life, says Rolle, yet the strength and quality of one's feelings are trustworthy. Indeed, in his most famous work, *The Fire of Love*, he clearly proposes the simultaneous presence and intensity of three such affective states (burning love, songful praise and inestimable sweetness) as a sure indicator of the soul's spiritual standing and security: 'The soul in whom the three things mentioned above run together inwardly remains impervious to the arrows of the enemy while, meditating on love with an unchanged intention, she raises herself to the heavens and stirs herself to loving.'[88] In Rolle we see fairly dramatically the transformation of the roles of the self, experience and the inner affections in later medieval mysticism. Whereas Bernard spoke of experience and love in order to use a common courtly language to speak about the impression God makes upon the soul, Rolle seems to have taken this language into a newly private world that is constituted by and depends upon the persistence of inner feelings.

Given this concern with one's own 'interior joys', it is not surprising that Rolle favours the solitary life over a communal religious life; for, in his view, one's inner music is harboured and cherished in the privacy of the eremitical life whereas too much interaction with others may represent a hindrance and interference with the cultivation of one's interior fervour. 'Sweetly flowing song delights the solitary. The tumult drags him from this delight when he is placed among many people, and it does not allow him to meditate or pray except rarely'.[89] Tugwell is surely right when he comments: 'Because it is only the intensity of religious affections which is keeping at bay the tumult of unmanageable secular affections, the religious emotions have, of course, to be continual . . . . Because of Rolle's straightforward identification between the sensation of loving God and the reality, he cannot help but make the sensation something to be deliberately aimed at and cultivated.'[90]

From such a perspective it is easy to see how the communal scriptural and liturgical matrix of mystical life could be overlooked, and a preoccupation with interior states of the self become substituted for a focus on the divine stimulus of those states. In this we can see what Turner has called a 'positivism' of mystical language, in which the metaphysical language of interiority and ecstasy (which spoke of the transcendence of all experience) is read literally as enjoining the pursuit of inner feelings.[91] So in a case like Dionysius, the language of negation gets interpreted by the later Middle Ages in terms of the so-called 'affective dionysianism' in which the supereminence of God and the consequent *negation* of experience (as found in Dionysius himself) becomes a positive *experience* of negativity, darkness and the absence of God. And this can be just as true of more cataphatic mystics like Rolle whose awareness of the superabundance of divine life (which cannot be an object of experience in itself) crystallizes in terms of a positive experience of superabundance – hence the language of jubilation, inestimable sweetness and so on. In either case this involves the transformation of language about the process of mystical knowing and the dialectics of encountering the divine other into a language of the interior self whose feelings must be stimulated, sustained and analysed.

It is intriguing that Rolle develops two 'avoidances': the fear of the other person (even to an extent the fear of community) conceived as a threat to the cultivation of the inner world, and the fear of ordinary, 'carnal' affections. Both of these are seen as jeopardizing one's spiritual life for they would both, not coincidentally, lead one out of a private inner world into the common world of the other. Rolle's reaction to these threats seems to call for a retreat into the dramatic world the self and its play of emotions, indeed, to call for the construction of self in terms of an ever-intensifying inner affectivity rather than relationality. In the next section I want to suggest how writers such as Hadewijch and Angela of Foligno, with their even more frankly erotic mysticism of bodily knowing, offer a way back out of the experiential self into a more communal understanding of the mystical life.

Bodily Knowing: Possibilities for Retrieval

Rowan Williams has pointed to the entanglement of later medieval nominalism with the divorce of scholastic and mystical theology. 'A highly sophisticated analysis of given theological propositions' is combined 'with a deep skepticism about the human mind's capacity to abstract beyond the immediate data of sense experience'.[92] In this setting, there is a curious disjunction at work whereby, on one hand, academic theology 'is conducted as a discipline analyzing the relations between concepts' and, on the other hand, 'the essence of religious experience [is seen] as private and unanalyzable piety. Christian life is lived beyond the reach of public, shared reflection, while theology refines its dialectical skills without reflecting on the foundation of the enterprise itself.'[93] In Williams's view

> Western Catholicism by 1300 was rapidly losing the means to express theologically the basic principle of its life, the *ekstasis*, emptying, displacement of self in response to the self-emptying love of God, the communion of God and humanity by the presence of each in the other. It was losing the sense of Christian experience as growth in direct encounter with God, growth, therefore, in obscurity, pain and struggle; there was less realization that the roots of theology lie in such experience and that Christian speculation is properly inseparable from engagement with the paradoxes of the cross and resurrection.[94]

The problem seems connected to two fundamental issues: the process of knowing and the constitution of the self.

An earlier writer like Maximus conceived of both issues as finding their integrity in Christ. People enter into the highest form of the *knowledge* of God not as disparate souls searching their private feelings for clues to the nature of God. Rather the believing community comes to know God precisely by being baptismally re-created and eucharistically re-membered as the Body of Christ. This is not an isolated liturgical event but a daily struggle sacramentalized in the liturgy; it is the discovery of one's *personhood* in living out the concrete manifestations of the paschal mystery in the daily details of one's existence. In this view, both the activities of being and of knowing take place as one comes to participate ecclesially in the Word's own mode of existence. All this suggests a provisional response to the questions about the constitution of the self (being) and what one comes to understand in that self-discovery (knowing). Christians come to *be* most fully who they are, precisely as they leave themselves behind in love for the other – just as Jesus' identity as the Word of God is most fully expressed and discovered in his loving of his people, even to the end. Similarly, Christians come to *know* God most fully by participation in the Word's incarnation of the trinitarian relationality which is God's life. In both cases, as Williams suggests, this would imply a profound 'engagement with the paradoxes of the cross and resurrection'.

Now the usual reading of later medieval Christian spirituality tends to see an intensifying preoccupation with the passion of Jesus in terms of emotionality, extreme ascetical practices and paranormal phenomena. More, in other words, of the self-focused affectivity we considered at the end of the last section. But I want to suggest that at the core of this developing passion mysticism there lie the seeds of exactly the kind of participatory being and knowing in the Word which might restore a public, communal, *theologically available* dimension to the mystical journey.

In a helpful essay on 'The Humanity and the Passion of Christ', Ewart Cousins has traced the development of a growing devotion to the suffering humanity of Jesus.[95] The monastic practice of *lectio divina*, the slowly ruminative reading of religious texts, came to involve a growing imaginative involvement in the biblical scenes. This naturally encouraged monks to respond 'to the scene with a variety of emotions. This led to an identification with Christ and a desire to imitate his virtues, especially his poverty and humility, along with a willingness and even a longing to suffer with Christ in his passion.'[96] In this trend we see a powerfully affective imaging of Jesus' life becoming the framework for the spiritual journey.

No single figure seems to have concretized this shift so effectually as Francis of Assisi (1181–1226). As the first known case of stigmatization, Francis's fervent joy in the infancy of Jesus and his intense sharing in Jesus' vulnerability and suffering were highly influential. Even a Neoplatonist like Bonaventure (1217–74) was drawn to follow Francis. So for example in his meditations on Christ's life, Bonaventure urges his readers to enter as fully and passionately as possible into the biblical narratives; 'there is a heightened concentration on the physical details of Christ's suffering with a subsequent evoking of compassion'.[97]

Perhaps even more intriguingly, Bonaventure's *Journey of the Mind to God* begins to re-interpret the Neoplatonic mystical framework in terms of the historical pattern of Jesus' life, death and resurrection. The Franciscan tells us that as the seventh successor to Francis as Minister General he felt a longing for peace and quiet; he travels physically to what was already becoming a sacred place, the site of Francis's stigmatization on Mount Alverno. While he is there (bodily), his mind begins 'pondering on certain spiritual ascents'.[98] One might expect a fairly standard Neoplatonic series of ascending negations, but Bonaventure's actual physical presence in the location of Francis's physical encounter with the seraphic image of the crucified Jesus seems to have altered his perspective. There is still going to be an ascent by stages to an ecstatic wisdom but now it is clear to the Franciscan that 'the road to this peace is through nothing else than a most ardent love of the Crucified', and the final stage of union with God is never rightly entered 'save through the Crucified' (Prol 3, 1–2). It is worth noting that Bonaventure does not focus this spiritual itinerary in the eternal Word per se, or even in the Incarnate Word in general, but specifically in the suffering humanity of the Word.

This human focus is highlighted in the penultimate chapter of the work. It is in the contemplation of Christ, says Bonaventure, that the mind is most perfectly illumined, for then it sees how God unites the 'first and the last, the highest and the lowest, the circumference and the center . . . the Creator and the creature' (VI.7, 36). This suggests that for Bonaventure the highest form of mystical knowledge is not an apprehension of bare deity, but precisely the awareness of the eternal *ekstasis* of deity by which the divine draws all creation into loving union in Christ.

This is confirmed in the remarkable final chapter of the work. For here the ultimate state of encounter with God involves the soul in a reciprocal ecstasy, going out of self in response to the self-emptying love of God. Yet again, however, Bonaventure makes it clear that the locus of this mutual ecstasy is not an anonymously metaphysical ascent but rather a *descent* into the passion of Jesus. So the mind must ultimately pass over into Christ's great 'passover':

> In this passing over (*transitus*), Christ is the way and the door; Christ is the ladder and the vehicle (VII.1, 37) . . . . The one who . . . beholds Christ hanging on the cross, such a one celebrates the Pasch, that is, the Passover, with Him. Thus using the rod of the cross, he may pass over (*transeat*) the Red Sea, going from Egypt into the desert, where it is given for him to taste the hidden manna, he may rest with Christ in the tomb, as one dead to the world (VII. 2, 37–8). . . . If you wish to know how these things come about, ask . . . not light, but the fire that wholly inflames and carries one into God through transporting (*excessivus*) unctions and consuming affections. God himself is this fire, and His furnace is in Jerusalem; and it is Christ who enkindles it in the white flame of His most burning Passion. This fire he alone truly perceives who says, My soul

chooses hanging, and my bones, death. He who loves this death can see God, for it is absolutely true that Man shall not see me and live. Let us die, then, and enter into this darkness. Let us silence all our cares, our desires, our imaginings. With Christ crucified, let us pass out (*transeamus*) of this world to the Father (VII.6, 39).

The divine ecstasy reaches its fulfilment in the self-emptying of the Incarnation and its consummation in the unreserved love of the Cross. The paschal mystery itself is therefore the ultimately apophatic moment: God's life is most mysteriously poured out and accessible to humanity and humanity is, reciprocally, most poured out into the divine hands. What Bonaventure has done here is to set the apophatic ascent of Neoplatonism into the context of the paschal narrative. The implication is that the highest form of mystical union entails a participation in the bodily apophasis of the Cross, where the sheer aching physicality of divine and human love is inescapable and serves, as Bonaventure puts it, as a 'vehicle' within which the believer passes over into the presence of the Father.

Unquestionably the passion mysticism that grew ever more popular in the years after Bonaventure moved to an even more graphic fascination with the physical details of Jesus' suffering and death.[99] But I want to suggest that, when interpreted with Bonaventure's model in mind, at least some of these texts are far from being the marginal popular pieties of no interest to theology which they seemed to the some of the academic theologians of their day. Could passion mysticism manage to avoid becoming yet another acquisition for the possessive self? The question is whether what is being taught is a freeing abandonment that renders the self and everything else *transparent to God*. My suggestion is that in the abandonment of Gethsemane and the dereliction of Golgotha one human being was indeed enabled to make this relinquishment into the unity and expressivity of ultimate reality – and that in the physicality of some passion mysticism, many women and men were enabled to share in this abandonment in its most potent form, namely the bodily knowing of their whole humanity. So the paradox to which I point is that the deepest fulfilment of the apophatic mystical journey may take place in the most fully bodily participation of a concrete historical event, namely the passion, death and resurrection of Jesus.

In numerous studies Carolyn Walker Bynum has articulated the view that for both medieval women and men, the physical body and especially the bodiliness of woman represented the fullness of human nature.[100] The Christian doctrine of the Incarnation suggests that it was the enactment of divine life in just this fully human physicality that constituted the redemptive *ekstasis* of divine expressivity. The full divine presence and meaning can only be known by sharing in this particular form of self-donated bodiliness – not simply because only creaturely reality is accessible to creatures but, more strongly, because it was precisely in those bodily terms that God *chose* to communicate the divine meaning.

It is no accident that Julian of Norwich, who so entirely desired to share Christ's physical suffering and isolation, could express so much more clearly than most that 'love was his meaning'. For these mystical writers, bodiliness is not, therefore, a possessively grasped creatureliness that obfuscates the divine reality, but is rather a *medium of communication*, and quite literally of communion. Herbert McCabe puts it clearly: 'We should not then see human bodies as atomic units externally linked by media of communication; to be human, to have a human body, is to be in communication, a common language is an interweaving of extensions of the human body. The body is itself the basic medium of human communication, not, however, simply the body as we are born with it but the body as we have extended it through the creation of linguistic media.'[101] My suggestion is that *the bodily language of Christ's passion becomes the communicative medium in which divine meaning and human knowing are able to converse.* So bodies, as McCabe points out, are not 'atomic units' but are intrinsically *communal* events of converse, of language and communion, and this means that bodily knowing in mystical theology is an inherently public and communal form of theological speech.

Communion is a good interpretive frame. For Hadewijch there is in fact a close connection between the physicality of her love relationship with Christ and her participation in his bodily suffering. For her, the desire for God is anguished, never-satiated and excruciating.[102] She describes the ultimate relationship as that between those who 'wander in the storms of Love,/Body and soul, heart and thought - /Lovers lost in this hell'.[103] This painful hungering and her share in Christ's suffering converges for her in the Eucharist, the bodily presence of Christ in the form of his poured out self-donation of the Cross. She describes Love as a chain that binds the lovers indissolubly together

> So that each knows the other through and through
> In the anguish or the repose or the madness of Love,
> And eats his flesh and drinks his blood;
> The heart of each devours the other's heart,
> One soul assaults the other and invades it completely,
> As he who is Love itself showed us
> When he gave us himself to eat,
> Disconcerting all the thoughts of man.[104]

The double meaning in our English usage of the word 'passion' (of desiring love and the suffering of Jesus) is the merest hint of the kind of interweaving at work in Hadewijch's poetry. Here the suffering of the cross is clearly recontextualized in the suffering of love – and vice versa – so that the mystical knowledge of God's *ekstasis* in Christ is made available in the 'passionate' converse of the Eucharist. And for Hadewijch it is not simply the believer who eats, assaults and enters into the life of Christ, but 'the heart of each devours the other', leading to the startling mutuality disclosed four lines later in poem: 'He eats us; we think we eat him'.

We see something of the same complex of meanings in Hadewijch's contemporary Beguine, Mechtild of Magdeburg (*c*.1212–*c*.1282). Speaking of the mutuality of Jesus' and Mary's roles in the work of redemption, Mechtild writes: 'They were both opened, his wounds and her breasts. The wounds poured out and the breasts flowed, so that the soul quickened and was even cured. As he poured the bright red wine into her red mouth, she was born out of the open wounds and was quickened.'[105] The play of gender, role, feeding and birth weaves together an image in which the believer passes mystically through the Eucharist into the 'lactating' and life-bearing wounds of Christ. This is a bodily language of salvific intimacy and sacrificial desire. Angela of Foligno (*c*.1248–1309) speaks similarly of Christ placing her mouth on his wounded breast and feeding her in that way; and after she is granted an apprehension of 'the acute pain which was in Christ's soul' because of 'his immense love for humanity', Angela finds that her will has been utterly conformed to Christ's salvific will and she in turn enters his tomb and, lying down with him, kisses and embraces him in his mortal state.[106] What seems like an intensely private moment of individualized affectivity is an occasion of sharing in the universal mission of salvation. Such women mystics 'use their pain not to isolate themselves further but to link themselves to the crucified, and through him to all Christians'.[107]

This theme – drawing love from the beloved in the suffering embrace of the Cross – is presented from another perspective when Hadewijch employs a language almost of twinship with Christ, so that the beloved, paired or oned with his suffering body, shares fully in all his acts. In this vision, a virtue called peacefulness announces to Hadewijch 'that she had been announced and born with him; and that her body was born from the other; and that she grew up with him and lived together with him as man in all like pains, in poverty, ignominy, and in compassion for all those with whom justice was angry; and that her body was nourished interiorly and exteriorly from the other.'[108] Bynum points out that in the bodily language of the Middle Ages 'suffering was considered an effective activity, which redeemed both individual and cosmos' so that the practice of *imitatio Christi* occurs 'as fusion with the suffering physicality of Christ'.[109] Hadewijch clearly understands mystical union with Christ to involve not merely a private 'enjoyment' of him but a full sharing in his mission to all people, a sharing in his struggle which is simultaneously to be 'nourished' by him.

Not only does this bodily knowing lead to a new communal *understanding* of Christ's redemptive work, but it also affords a new matrix for viewing the mystical journey itself. The suffering physicality of Jesus becomes the basis for the deepest apophasis, the way of the Cross becomes the ultimate way of negation. Henry Suso (*c.*1300–66) reinterprets Eckhart's apophaticism in this manner, recontextualizing the latter's concern for abandonment of the will in terms of the passion. Complaining to the Lord that what he seeks is 'your divinity, but you show me your humanity', the servant (Suso) hears Eternal Wisdom reply that 'no one can reach the heights of the divinity . . . without first being drawn through the bitterness I experienced as man. . . . My humanity is the path one takes; my suffering the gate through which one must pass'.[110] So far this sounds like a conventional admonition to imitate Christ, but then as Eternal Wisdom's speech continues it begins to sound curiously Eckhartian:

> You shall constantly carry my torment in your heart with the intense love of a mother. . . . Your divinely motivated way of life will often be scorned as foolish by the all-too-human. Your untried body will be scourged by a harsh and severe way of life. You shall be derisively crowned by the suppression of your spiritual life. After this you shall be led out with me along the desolate way of the cross, as you withdraw from your own willing, give up yourself and all creatures, and become as truly free of all creatures in things that can interfere with your eternal salvation as a dying person.[111]

The contemplative servant's spiritual journey is here cast in terms of Jesus' scorning, scourging, crowning with thorns, and way of the cross. This is the true, the mystical, meaning of the contemplative path. In other words, the way of the cross is *not* here taken to be a powerful but culturally limited symbol of the real universal of interior experience; rather, the inchoate and inexplicable interior darkness is, for Suso, a concrete manifestation of the paschal mystery. This 'bodily' mysticism, therefore, might be said to effect a crucial transposition: ultimate detachment is transposed from a metaphysical problematic into the salvation-historical terms of Jesus' suffering and death. The significance of this lies precisely in its ability to transpose the fundamental key of late medieval mystical thought – from a personal and possibly self-preoccupied spiritual journey (in which attention focuses on the states of the soul's inner accomplishments), to a more communal mystical theology in which the contemplative journey is seen in terms of participation in the common, ecclesial, mystery of Christ.

But what kind of knowledge is gained from this physicality? Is it primarily of devotional and practical value or is it also conversant with theological discourse?[112] One reading might suggest that these writers have simply misconstrued earlier metaphors that used sensual imagery to convey spiritual meaning, that they have simply taken it all literally and indulged in bodily knowing when they should have aimed for something 'higher'. Put this baldly, we can see, I hope, the essentially unchristian burden of such an argument. For surely the goal in Christianity is not to escape from bodiliness to something higher; the resurrection of Jesus does not render him somehow more purely spiritual and less bodily but on the contrary he is more bodily than ever. That is, he is more available than ever to all people, more explicitly and concretely the locus of a new communion among people. The knowledge that comes from sharing in the bodiliness of Jesus, from feeling the burden of his grief, the pain of his suffering, the scintillating joy of being given new life to forgive those who had betrayed him – this is not a case of being 'trapped' in a world of physical sensations, but rather these actual sensations are, Christians believe, the very structures of a new creation. They are the patterns of a new, emergent reality which is fully noetic and intelligible, but which cannot be 'known' apart from the practical, bodily commitment of one's whole being.

Simone Weil (1909–43) points to the example of a worker whose learning of a new trade takes place in part through sheer bodily familiarity with the correct motions and sensations of the work. She argues that our knowledge of the universe must similarly be a bodily knowing if it is to be complete: 'Each time that we have some pain to go through, we can say to ourselves quite truly that it is the universe, the order, and beauty of the world and the obedience of creation to God that are entering our body.'[113] We might say analogously that the bodily knowing of these mystical writers is a crucial dimension of mystical theology, for it is not a knowing primarily of one's own feelings and sensations, but of the ultimate mystery of God articulated in frail flesh.

The physical body of Jesus extends itself linguistically, creates a language and way of life, a new way of being in the world which we call the ecclesial body of Christ. It is communal and relational in the most fundamental ways possible. It is a body that makes possible a new way of communicating with each other, a way that does not flinch at loving but leads one to commit oneself utterly to the other in love. This linguistic communal body is precisely the expression in human terms of the divine Trinity, the linguistic relationality of speaking the other and loving the other, of being absolutely *for* the other in love and freedom which makes God who God is. Now it is this communication, this communion, which is uttered as Jesus, the Word made flesh, and so the most crucial form of knowing this divine meaning is to enter into this particular bodily way of life. The passion mysticism of writers like Hadewijch, wherein we find the apophasis of the self in the embrace of the crucified, is a discovery of this divine speech as the very source of existence, the recovery of a true sense of self only as one exists no longer as 'my' self but ourself, in the mutuality of love, the play of lover and beloved that enacts the eternal play of the trinitarian persons:

> When he takes possession of the loved soul in every way,
> Love drinks in these kisses and tastes them to the end.
> As soon as Love thus touches the soul,
> She eats its flesh and drinks its blood.
> Love that thus dissolves the loved soul
> Sweetly leads them both
> To the indivisible kiss —
> That same kiss which fully unites
> The Three Persons in one sole Being.[114]

What I am suggesting in all this is not simply the groundwork for a mystical theology of the Trinity, the Incarnation, and the self — though that is what I shall elucidate in slightly less inchoate form in the final chapters — but a basis for realizing the *theological significance and validity* of mystical texts such as these. For here we can see mystical theology re-emerging from the private drama of the inner world and self-preoccupying affectivity into the public realm of communal speech: the speech of the physical body of Jesus and of all who share his life. This is the entirely human language of the divine Word, a language named quite appropriately as 'the mystical Body of Christ'.

Notes

1 Vladimir Lossky, *The Mystical Theology of the Eastern Church* (Crestwood, New York: St Vladimir's Seminary Press, 1976), 8.
2 Ibid., 10.
3 Ibid. 10–11: 'The theological doctrines which have been elaborated in the course of these struggles [against various heresies] can be treated in the most direct relation to the vital end — that of union with God — to the attainment of which they are subservient. Thus they appear as the foundations of Christian spirituality.

It is this that we shall understand in speaking of "mystical theology".'

4   William Temple, *Nature, Man and God. The Gifford Lectures 1932–4* (London: Macmillian, 1956), 321–2.

5   Rowan Williams, 'Teaching the Truth', chapter in *Living Tradition: Affirming Catholicism in the Anglican Church*, ed. Jeffrey John (Cambridge, Massachusetts: Cowley Publications, 1992), 36.

6   Helpful literature on the issues involved includes: John J. Collins, *The Apocalyptic Imagination: An Introduction to the Jewish Matrix of Christianity* (New York: Crossroad, 1984); Christopher Rowland, *The Open Heaven: A Study of Apocalyptic in Judaism and Early Christianity* (New York: Crossroad, 1982); and, Michael Stone, *Scriptures, Sects and Visions: A Profile of Judaism from Ezra to the Jewish Revolts* (Philadelphia: Fortress Press, 1980). On Neoplatonic thought see in particular Andre Jean Festugière, *Contemplation et vie contemplative selon Platon* (Paris: Vrin, 1936); Stephen Gersh, *From Iamblichus to Eriugena: An Investigation of the Prehistory and Evolution of the Pseudo-Dionysian Tradition* (Leiden: E. J. Brill, 1978). See also, Andrew Louth, *The Origins of the Christian Mystical Tradition from Plato to Denys* (Oxford: Oxford University Press, 1981).

7   McGinn, *The Foundations of Mysticism*, vol. 1 of *The Presence of God: A History of Western Christian Mysticism* (New York: Crossroad, 1991), 71.

8   Louis Bouyer, 'Mysticism: An Essay on the History of the Word' in *Understanding Mysticism*, ed. Richard Woods (Garden City, New York: Doubleday, 1980), 42–55.

9   Ibid., 47.

10   Andrew Louth, *Denys the Areopagite, Outstanding Christian Thinkers* Series (London: Geoffrey Chapman, 1989), 28.

11   Olivier Clément, *The Roots of Christian Mysticism*, trans. Theodore Berkeley and Jeremy Hummerstone (Hyde Park, New York: New City Press, 1995), 95.

12   Jaroslav Pelikan, 'The Odyssey of Dionysian Spirituality', introduction to *Pseudo-Dionysius: The Complete Works*, trans. Colm Luibheid and Paul Rorem, *Classics of Western Spirituality* (New York: Paulist Press, 1987), 22. All English citations from Dionysius will be from this translation, giving the standard abbreviation for the work, the column references to the Greek text in J.-P. Migne ed., *Patrologia Graeca* 3 (Paris, 1857), followed by the page no. in the Luibheid-Rorem translation. DN=*The Divine Names*, MT=*The Mystical Theology*, CH=*The Celestial Hierarchy*, EH=*The Ecclesiastical Hierarchy*, and Ep.=*The Letters*. Transliterations from the original Greek text are made from the critical edition: *Corpus Dionysiacum*, 2 vols, ed. Beate Suchla, Gunter Heil, A. M. Ritter. Patristische Texte und Studien, vols 33 and 36 (Berlin: Walter de Gruyter, 1990–1).

13   See, e.g., Paul Rorem, *Biblical and Liturgical Symbols within the Pseudo-Dionysian Synthesis. Studies and Texts* 71 (Toronto: Pontifical Institute of Medieval Studies, 1984), especially 133–8; and Andrew Louth, *Denys the Areopagite*, 28–9.

14   Rorem, *Biblical and Liturgical Symbols*, 137.

15   See the powerful critique of Dionysius in Grace M. Jantzen, *Power, Gender and Christian Mysticism. Cambridge Studies in Ideology and Religion* 8 (Cambridge:

Cambridge University Press, 1995), 95–109; e.g., 'Once the mystical path was delimited in the way that Dionysius had done, there would not be many women who *could* walk it. The social construction of mysticism after Dionysius was a construction which precluded women from counting as mystics. Only when women developed a counter-construction could they also have a place, and then at the cost of arousing male defensiveness' (109).

16 McGinn, *Foundations of Mysticism*, 48.
17 Louth, *Denys the Areopagite*, 85.
18 Ibid., 85–6.
19 Ibid., 11.
20 See e.g. CH 305B which von Balthasar translates as: 'the Thearchy as it were reduces its radiance so as to uphold the oneness and unknowability of its own mystery.' (Hans Urs von Balthasar, *The Glory of the Lord: A Theological Aesthetics*, vol. II: *Studies in Theological Style: Clerical Styles*, trans. Andrew Louth, Francis McDonagh and Brian McNeil [Edinburgh: T. & T. Clark, 1984], 193.)
21 Ibid., 168.
22 Rorem, *Biblical and Liturgical Symbols*, 56.
23 Ibid., 140–2.
24 Especially useful are: Alain Riou, *Le monde et l'église selon Maxime le Confesseur* (Paris: Editions Beauchesne, 1973) and Juan Miguel Garrigues, *Maxime le Confesseur: La charité, l'avenir divin de l'homme* (Paris: Editions Beauchesne, 1976).
25 Maximus, *Four Centuries on Charity*, I.11, trans. Polycarp Sherwood, OSB, Ancient Christian Writers series (New York: Newman Press, 1955), 138. Transliterations are based on the critical edition: *Capitoli sulla carita*, ed. Aldo Ceresa-Gastaldo (Rome: Editrice Studium, 1963).
26 Ibid., I.12, p.138.
27 Ibid., II.6, p.153.
28 Ibid., I.90, p. 150.
29 Maximus, *Chapters on Knowledge*, II. 4, in *Maximus Confessor: Selected Writings*, trans. George C. Berthold. *Classics of Western Spirituality* (New York: Paulist Press, 1985), p. 148. *Patrologia Graeca* 90, 1125D–1127A.
30 Ibid., I.66, pp. 139–40. PG 90, 1108B.
31 Maximus, *Liber Ambiguorum* 7, PG 91, 1084D.
32 *Chapters on Knowledge*, I.54, p. 138. PG 90, 1104B.
33 Ibid., I.55, p. 138. PG 90, 1103C.
34 Ibid., II.18, p. 151. PG 90, 1133BC.
35 *Commentary on the Our Father*, in *Maximus Confessor*, p.118. PG 90, 905CD.
36 *The Church's Mystagogy*, in *Maximus Confessor*, p. 206. PG 91, 701C
37 *Chapters on Knowledge*, II.88, p. 167. PG 90, 1168AB.
38 Louth, *Origins of the Christian Mystical Tradition*, 200.
39 Ibid., xi.
40 Williams, *The Wound of Knowledge: Christian Spirituality from the New Testament to St. John of the Cross*, 2nd edn (Cambridge, Massachusetts: Cowley Publications, 1991), 3.

41   The following works of von Balthasar are given over entirely to the problem: 'Theologie und Heiligkeit', *Wort und Wahrheit* 3 (1948): 881–96; expanded in 'Theologie und Heiligkeit', *Verbum Caro: Skizzen zur Theologie* I (Einsiedeln: Johannes Verlag, 1960); 'Theologie und Spiritualit"t', *Gregorianum* 50 (1969): 571–87; 'Theology and Holiness', *Communio* 14 (Winter 1987): 341–50.

42   Von Balthasar, 'Spirituality', *Explorations in Theology*, vol. 1, *The Word Made Flesh* (San Francisco: Ignatius Press, 1989), 214.

43   Grace M. Jantzen, *Power, Gender and Christian Mysticism. Cambridge Studies in Ideology and Religion* 8 (Cambridge: Cambridge University Press, 1995).

44   Jantzen, *Power, Gender and Christian Mysticism*, 326.

45   Colin Morris, *The Discovery of the Individual 1050–1200* (New York: Harper & Row, 1972).

46   Ibid., 70–6.

47   Ibid., 77.

48   Ibid., 139–52.

49   Bernard of Clairvaux, *The Works of Bernard of Clairvaux*, vol. 2, *On the Song of Songs* I. *Cistercian Fathers* Series, no. 4. Trans. Kilian Walsh (Kalamazoo, Michigan: Cistercian Publications, 1981), 16. There are four volumes in the *Cistercian Fathers* Series translations of Bernard's great sequence *On the Song of Songs*. Hereafter I will make parenthetical reference to Bernard's sermon no., the volume no. in this translation of the Song of Songs sequence, and then page number. Hence this reference would be, [sermon]3, I.16 [volume and page]. The other volumes are: *On the Song of Songs* II. *Cistercian Fathers* Series, no. 7. Trans. Kilian Walsh (Kalamazoo: Cistercian Publications, 1983); *On the Song of Songs* III. *Cistercian Fathers* Series, no. 31. Trans. Kilian Walsh and Irene Edmonds (Kalamazoo: Cistercian Publications, 1979; and *On the Song of Songs* IV. *Cistercian Fathers* Series, no. 40. Trans. Irene Edmonds (Kalamazoo: Cistercian Publications, 1980). The original is from the critical edition, *Sancti Bernardi Opera*, ed. Jean Leclercq et al., 8 vols (Rome: Editiones Cistercienses, 1957–77). Here: *Sermo Super Cantica* (SSC) 3, vol. 1.14: 'Hodie legimus in libro experientiae. Convertimini ad vos ipsos, et attendat unusquisque conscientiam suam super his quae dicenda sunt.'

50   Bernard McGinn, *The Presence of God: A History of Western Christian Mysticism*, vol. 2, *The Growth of Mysticism* (New York: Crossroad, 1994), 185.

51   Jean Leclercq, *Love of Learning and the Desire for God: A Study of Monastic Culture*, trans. Catherine Misrahi (New York: Fordham University Press, 1974), 256–5.

52   Bernard Bonowitz, 'The Role of Experience in the Spiritual Life' in *La dottrina della vita spirituale nelle opere di San Bernardo di Clairvaux*, 321–5; quoted in McGinn, *Growth of Mysticism*, 497, note 158. My emphasis.

53   SCC 84, vol. 2.304: 'Inde, ni fallor, quod a Verbo visitata iam sit et quasita.'

54   SCC 1, vol.1.7: 'Istiusmodi canticum sola unctio docet, sola addiscit experientia. Experti recognoscant, inexperti inardescant desiderio, non tam cognoscendi quam experiendi.'

55   SCC 9, vol. 1.46: 'Quibus studium est orare frequenter, experti sunt quod dico.'

56 SCC 21, vol. 1.124: 'Puto quod hoc ispsum, si attenditis, vestra vobis experientia intus respondet quod ego foris loquor.'

57 SCC 1, vol. 1.8: 'Non auditur foris, nec enim in publico personat: sola quae cantat audit, et cui cantatur, id est sponsus et sponsa.'

58 SCC 69, vol. 2.205–6: '. . non ambigo Sponsum adesse. . Quod si se pariter infuderit humilis quaedam, sed pinguis, intimae aspersionis devotio, ut amor agnitae veritatis necessarium quoddam odium vanitatis in me generet et contemptum, ne forte aut scientia inflet, aut frequentia visitationum extollat me, tunc prorsus paterne sentio agi mecum, et Patrem adesse non dubito.'

59 SCC 21, vol. 1.124–5: 'Ergo cum te torpore, acedia vel teadio affici sentis trahi te obsecrans sponsae exemplo, donec denuo, suscitante gratia, factus promptior alacriorque . .'

60 Ibid., 125: 'Sic autem, quamdiu adest gratia, delectare in ea, ut non te existimes donum Dei iure hereditario possidere, ita videlicet securus de eo, quasi numquam perdere possis: ne subito, cum forte retraxerit manum et subtraxerit donum, tu animo concidas et tristior quam oportet fias.'

61 Denys Turner, The Darkness of God: Negativity in Christian Mysticism (Cambridge: Cambridge University Press, 1995), e.g., 248–51.

62 Ibid., 171–2.

63 Michel de Certeau, The Mystic Fable, vol. 1, The Sixteenth and Seventeenth Centuries, trans. Michael B. Smith (Chicago: University of Chicago Press, 1992), 178.

64 Ibid., 178–9.

65 Evelyn Underhill, Mysticism. A Study in the Nature and Development of Man's Spiritual Consciousness (New York: E. P. Dutton, 1961), 75-6.

66 De Certeau, The Mystic Fable, vol. 1, 188.

67 Ibid.

68 Ibid., 189–90.

69 Louth, Origins of the Christian Mystical Tradition, xv–xvi.

70 Andrew Louth, 'Bernard and Affective Mysticism', in The Influence of Saint Bernard, ed. Benedicta Ward, SLG (Oxford: SLG Press, 1976), 3.

71 Gregory the Great, Homilia in Evangelia 27 (Patrologia Latina 76, 1207).

72 Thomas Aquinas, Summa Theologiae II.II, Q. 180, art. 1, obj. 1; in Albert and Thomas. Selected Writings, trans. and ed. Simon Tugwell. Classics of Western Spirituality (New York: Paulist Press, 1988), 540; 'Finis contemplationis est veritas. Veritas autem pertinet ad intellectum totaliter. Ergo videtur quod vita contemplativa totaliter in intellectu consistat' (Blackfriars Edition [London: Eyre and Spottiswoode, 1966], 12).

73 Ibid., 541; 'Et propter hoc Gregorius constituit vitam contemplativam in caritate Dei, inquantum scilicet aliquis experience dilectione Dei inardescit ad ejus pulchritudinem conspiciendam. Et quia unusquisque delectatur cum adeptus fuerit id quod amat, ideo vita contemplativa terminatur ad delectationem quae est in affectu, ex qua etiam amor intenditur' (14).

74   Ibid., Q. 180, art. 4, ad. 3; 550; 'ponitur consideratio intelligibilium quae ratio nec inveniri nec capere potest, quae scilicet pertinent ad sublimem contemplationem divinae vertatis, in qua finaliter contemplatio perficitur' (28).
75   Ibid., ad. 4; 550; 'ultima perfectio humani intellectus est veritas divina' (28).
76   Further on this, see the helpful analysis of Bernard McGinn, 'Love, Knowledge and *Unio Mystica* in the Western Christian Tradition' in Moshe Idel and Bernard McGinn, *Mystical Union and Monotheistic Faith: An Ecumenical Dialogue* (New York: MacMillan, 1989), 59–86. On some of these issues in the cultural matrix of twelfth-century monastic life see Jean Leclercq, *Monks and Love in Twelfth-Century France* (Oxford: Clarendon Press, 1979); especially interesting is chapter 2, 'New Recruitment – New Psychology'.
77   Denys Turner, *Darkness of God*, 193.
78   Ibid., 193–4.
79   Simon Tugwell, OP, *Ways of Imperfection: An Exploration of Christian Spirituality* (London: Darton, Longman and Todd, 1984), 116–17.
80   Ibid., 108.
81   Ibid., 109–10.
82   Richard Rolle, *The Fire of Love* and *The Mending of Life*, trans. M. L. del Mastro (Garden City, New York: Doubleday, 1981), 85.
83   In his important article, 'Le divorce entre théologie et mystique', F. Vandenbroucke had highlighted this growing trend towards moralism in the *Devotio Moderna* as a key factor in the ultimate state of separation between spirituality and theology (*Nouvelle Revue Théologique* LXXII (1950): 372–389, see esp. 384ff.).
84   Rolle, *Mending of Life*, 85.
85   Ibid.
86   Ibid., 87.
87   Ibid.
88   Rolle, *Fire of Love*, 144.
89   Ibid., 138.
90   Tugwell, *Ways of Imperfection*, 164.
91   Turner, *The Darkness of God*, e.g., 260–5.
92   Williams, *The Wound of Knowledge*, 140.
93   Ibid., 142.
94   Ibid., 138–9.
95   Ewart Cousins, 'The Humanity and the Passion of Christ', chapter in *Christian Spirituality. High Middle Ages and Reformation*, ed. Jill Raitt. *World Spirituality: An Encyclopedic History of the Religious Quest*, vol. 17 (New York: Crossroad Publishing, 1989), 375–91.
96   Cousins, 'Humanity and Passion of Christ', 377.
97   Ibid., 385–6.
98   Bonaventure, *The Journey of the Mind to God*, trans. Philotheus Boehner, OFM (Cambridge: Hackett Publishing, 1993), 1. Hereafter I will give parenthetical references to the chapter and paragraph of the text, followed by the page no. in this translation.

99   See Richard Kieckhefer, *Unquiet Souls: Fourteenth Century Saints and Their Religious Milieu* (Chicago: University of Chicago Press, 1984), esp. chapter 4, 'Devotion to the Passion'.

100 See especially 'Woman as Body and as Food', chapter in *Holy Feast and Holy Fast: The Religious Significance of Food to Medieval Women* (Berkeley: University of California Press, 1987) and 'Religious Women in the Later Middle Ages', chapter in *Christian Spirituality: High Middle Ages and Reformation*, ed. Jill Raitt.

101 Herbert McCabe, *God Matters* (London: Geoffrey Chapman, 1987), 121.

102 See Bynum, *Holy Feast and Holy Fast*, 186.

103 Hadewijch, *Poems in Couplets*, 16, in *Hadewijch: The Complete Works*, trans. Mother Columba Hart, OSB. *Classics of Western Spirituality* (New York: Paulist Press, 1980), 358.

104 Ibid., 353.

105 Mechtild of Magdeburg, *Flowing Light of Divinity*, Book 1.22, trans. Christiane Mesch Galvani. Garland Library of Medieval Literature, vol. 72, series B (New York: Garland Publishing, 1991), 15.

106 Angela of Foligno, *Memorial*, chapters 1 and 7 in *Angela of Foligno: Complete Works*, trans. Paul Lachance, OFM. *Classics of Western Spirituality* (New York: Paulist Press, 1993), 128, 181–2.

107 Elizabeth Alvilda Petroff, *Medieval Women's Visionary Literature* (New York: Oxford University Press), 40.

108 Hadewijch, Vision 12.112, in *Hadewijch*, 295.

109 Bynum, *Holy Feast and Holy Fast*, 207.

110 Henry Suso, *The Little Book of Eternal Wisdom*, chapter 2, in *Henry Suso: The Exemplar, with two German Sermons*, trans. Frank Tobin. *Classics of Western Spirituality* (New York: Paulist Press, 1989), 214.

111 Ibid., 215.

112 For a fertile if somewhat unusual discussion of these questions see John Giles Milhaven, *Hadewijch and Her Sisters: Other Ways of Loving and Knowing* (Albany: State University of New York Press, 1993), esp. pp. 75 to the end.

113 Simone Weil, 'The Love of God and Affliction', in *Waiting for God*, trans. Emma Craufurd (New York: Harper & Row, 1973), 131–2.

114 Hadewijch, *Poems in Couplets*, 16, *Hadewijch*, 355.

Chapter 3

RECOVERING THE MYSTICAL ELEMENT OF THEOLOGY: THE TWENTIETH-CENTURY EXAMPLES OF RAHNER AND VON BALTHASAR

How do you know anything at all, let alone the mystery who is God? An entire epoch of such fundamental epistemological questioning marks the modern period of theology. And in some ways the West's journey into modernity also marked the low ebb of Christian mysticism. The possible grounds that we noted in the last chapter for a renewed dialogue between theology and spirituality went unexplored; and the tendency towards preoccupation with inner states of the soul in some medieval mystical thought guaranteed that, by the early years of the Enlightenment, theology would be profoundly allergic to 'mysticism' as matrix for theological construction. Early modern theology's dialogue with rationalism and empiricism tended to sequester explicitly mystical thought into the intense salons of the Quietists, the pious affections of the Pietists, or to exile it altogether into the obscurely echoing esoterica of a Jakob Boehme (1575–1624) or William Blake (1757–1827). The modern era in theology yet awaited the rediscovery of the mystical as an element within theology itself.

And yet the questions about *knowing* were themselves liable to point theology back to its relationship with the spiritual life. The perspectives of Descartes and Kant, Fichte, Hegel and Schleiermacher all focused theological attention afresh on the structures and limits of human knowing and on possible points of communion between human subjectivity and divine reality. And so, rather intriguingly, the famous Cartesian 'turn to the subject' – and all that followed – seemed to open a back door for mystical thought into the academic mind of modern theology. Would such a 'back door relationship' between spirituality and systematic theology constitute a healthy basis for renewed dialogue, or only a guilty conscience for each – leading to a more rigorously enforced academic division of fields?

This chapter considers two contrasting approaches to the question of a rediscovered relationship between spirituality and theology in the twentieth century. Karl Rahner represents perhaps the greatest achievement of what might be considered the mainstream approach. Like Schleiermacher, Rahner takes Kant's strictures on the limits of human knowing as an important guideline, and his response will draw the spiritual dynamic of the human person into the very heart of theology. An alternative is proposed by Hans Urs von Balthasar, who in dialogue with both his fellow Roman Catholic Rahner but also the strongly Protestant Karl Barth charts a theological path that fully integrates doctrine and the spiritual life *within* the dialogue of the divine Trinity.

Karl Rahner's Mystagogy

Kant may have persuaded modernity that we only know anything at all through the categories of our own subjective judgement of sense perception, but from the time of Schleiermacher, theology had pressed and poked at the borders of human consciousness, questing for a way beyond the Kantian critiques. Might there not be a form of experience prior to the categories of the subject and its division from every conceivable object? If theology could reflect on that consciousness which is the very condition for the possibility of any thought at all, it might be able to give its talk about God an important new basis. For if God-talk could be shown to emerge from a point in the human consciousness *prior* to the operation of the subjective categories of thought, then it might escape from the Kantian critique of much traditional Christian theology – as being only so much speculation, an illusory projection onto metaphysical and objective space of ideas inherently circumscribed by the categories of our judgement.

Needless to say, this approach has fairly unavoidable consequences for how we interpret any given religious texts, including mystical ones. It means that the particularity of theological language would tend to be discounted in favour of the more primordial religious experience on which it is based. Theology conducted in this key would be able to find little significance in the explicit theological teaching of mystical writers, except insofar as their texts, once duly excavated to expose the underlying common core of mystical experience, might count as evidence for the sheer existence of such a primordial common core, a religious consciousness that could escape the Kantian limitations on knowledge.[1] By the beginning of the twentieth century, the mystical comes to be seen as the case par excellence for this wonderfully universal pre-reflective religious experience of humanity. Indeed 'mysticism' is now to be studied as the most psychologically acute form of the religious consciousness, pointing in especially observable form to the self-transcending dynamic of human existence.

Transcendentality in Rahner

When we turn directly to the theology of Karl Rahner we can see a magisterial response to the characteristic modern questions. Schleiermacher had developed his theory of a pre-doctrinal religious consciousness at least partly through his conversations with the Pietist and Romantic movements in Germany. Rahner develops an analogous approach by drawing very markedly on the transcendental Thomism emerging early in the twentieth century from the thought of his fellow Jesuits, Pierre Rousselot and Joseph Maréchal.[2] Like Schleiermacher, Rahner will turn throughout his theology to a primordial aspect of human consciousness, namely our sense that we only know and will anything at all because we are fundamentally drawn towards an ever-transcending horizon of absolute mystery. As we consider the role of this transcendental anthropology in Rahner's treatment of mysticism, I will be asking two questions: does the great Jesuit theologian's approach lead him to persist in the usual modern notion of 'mysticism' as a variety of extreme states of human subjectivity? And how might Rahner's approach influence the reading and interpretation of mystical texts themselves?

Nothing could be clearer than that for Rahner our transcendental drive towards mystery is truly an aspect of who we are as human persons. In one of his most succinct explanations, Rahner writes:

> We shall call *transcendental experience* the subjective, unthematic, necessary and unfailing consciousness of the knowing subject that is co-present in every spiritual act of knowledge, and the subject's openness to the unlimited expanse of all possible reality. It is an *experience* because this knowledge, unthematic but ever-present, is a moment within and a condition of possibility for every concrete experience of any and every object. This experience is called *transcendental* experience because it belongs to the necessary and inalienable

structures of the knowing subject itself, and because it consists precisely in the transcendence beyond any particular group of possible objects or categories.[3]

The classic modern passage across Kantian terrain is hereby negotiated with precision. The basis for theology is *not* unwarranted speculation about objects-in-themselves. Rather theology is grounded in the unthematic experience that is the condition of possibility for any knowing at all, and, Rahner goes on to say, the *whither* of that unthematic apprehension of being is what we name God:

> There is present in this transcendental experience an unthematic and anony-mous, as it were, knowledge of God. Hence the original knowledge of God is not the kind of knowledge in which one grasps an object which happens to present itself directly or indirectly from outside. It has rather the character of a transcendental experience. Insofar as this subjective, non-objective luminosity of the subject in its transcendence is always oriented towards the holy mystery, the knowledge of God is always present unthematically and without name, and not just when we speak of it.[4]

So this ever-receding horizon of our experience is really a sign of the ultimate source and goal of our being, namely God. But this transcendental aspect of human being is only and always present as the *arousal* of response to God's eternal gracious act of self-communication. Because God desires communion with us, we *are*. In other words, what might all too easily look like *merely* a founding of theology on anthropology is never quite so simple. In Rahner's view, there never really is *just* human nature per se; for we always bear within us the echo of God's eternal self-disclosure, and this echo within us is a fundamental structure of human being which draws us ever further into consciousness of ourselves and of the mystery which calls to us.[5] Here is a significant difference between Rahner and Hans Urs von Balthasar. For Rahner we come into fully personal being through our interior transcendental apprehension of being and drive towards mystery. For von Balthasar we only really become fully the persons God has created us to be insofar as we discover our true mission through participation in the mission of Christ.

Everyday mysticism.

From Rahner's starting point in transcendental anthropology there are profound consequences for the integration of spirituality and theology in his thought. All human knowing, whether we realize it or not, takes place precisely because we are always standing before the hidden God, the *deus absconditus*, and it is this fact that encourages Rahner to describe the fundamental transcendental experience as a kind of mysticism of everyday life. It is in this sense a dimension of every human person's life, an 'orientation to boundless mystery', which one can try to ignore but only perversely; for it 'is not some extraneous spiritual luxury but *the* condition for the very possibility of everyday knowing and wanting'.[6] So in the most basic sense for Rahner, mysticism is simply this fundamental orientation and questioning that tugs at the very heart of every human being.

The explicitly or *narrowly* 'mystical' is a kind of acuteness and sensitivity. It is possibly accompanied by various unusual psychological states, enabling a given 'mystic' to grasp in a dramatically personal and transformative way the very same transcendental consciousness that is the condition for everyone's experience of reality.[7] Herein lies the theological significance of mysticism: not that it affords a particular access to the reality of God but that it *roots* the encounter with that divine reality more profoundly in the soul than more common forms of religious experience, thus lending a certain undeniable intensity or personal appeal to a mystic's life or teaching.

In Rahner's view, everything that one says conceptually about God, everything about God that is delivered into the categorical *constraints* of rational, linguistic knowing, is an always inadequate (though necessary) specification of the more primal consciousness of God. Furthermore, if ever the wordy, conceptual talk about God becomes divorced from its 'mystical' roots in transcendental experience, then it really loses its validity and authenticity as theology. Indeed Rahner's usual prescription is to re-root not only theological discourse per se but all institutional 'speaking' about God back into those moments when one realizes something of the fundamental incomprehensibility of being.

> Don't go talking about them, making up theories about them, but simply endure these basic experiences. Then in fact something like a primitive awareness of God can emerge. Then perhaps we cannot say much it; then what we 'grasp' first of all about God appears to be nothing, to be the absent, the nameless, absorbing and suppressing all that can be expressed and conceived. Consider for example the situations in which man is brought back to this basic experience of God. Somewhere, someone seems to be weeping hopelessly. . . . Someone has the basic experience of being stripped even of his very self. . . . Someone experiences joy. . . . All that man has then to say of this God can never be more than a pointer to this primitive experience of God. If someone says that this is mysticism, then it is in fact mysticism and then this very factor of mysticism belongs to God. But it is not mysticism in the specific sense: it is the obviousness of being encompassed absolutely by God at the moment of a man's whole awakening to mental existence.[8]

Already here we begin to see a crucial tendency in Rahner's thought. Because of the transcendental starting point, he consistently assumes that the infinite, the formless and non-linguistic is preeminent over the particular and the expressive, and that mysticism is inherently connected with this *in*expressibility *per se*. Note for example, in the passage above, the rather strong language: what we grasp mystically about God is always 'the nameless, absorbing and suppressing all that can be expressed and conceived'.

This is rather different from the classical Christian idea that the mystical is precisely that which is hidden and yet revealed in the very concrete imagery of the biblical text or the liturgical rite. In this earlier view, the mystery is not the divine namelessness which suppresses all expressibility as Rahner puts it; rather the glory of the mystery is exactly that the infinite should freely choose to *be expressive*, to disclose the ultimate nature of love in the humiliated constraints of finite existence – a body broken on a cross, wine to drink, oil to anoint, a psalm to sing.

Now of course Rahner is hardly an iconoclast, and he honours the expressive forms of the Christian life as much as any theologian. But he shows a notable inclination to divide the forms of mystery from the incomprehensible abyss whence they spring. It might be, of course, that the Jesuit is simply trying to clarify the distinction between knowledge as scientific mastery of categorical data and, on the other hand, knowledge 'in the primary sense' which 'is the presence of the mystery itself': this second and deeper kind of knowledge 'is being addressed by what no longer has a name, and it is relying on a reality which is not mastered but is itself the master. . . it is the last moment before the dumbness which is needed if the silence is to be heard, and God is to be worshipped in love.'[9]

It does seem to me, however, that we need to be very careful here not to confuse two different ways of distinguishing the varieties of knowing. There is a classical Christian approach, represented by Maximus the Confessor (among others) in which one distinguishes between the normal everyday knowledge of things as particulars, and, on the other hand, knowledge as the contemplative wisdom which comes from knowing *Christ as the inner principle of all things*. It is worth noting that in this contemplative knowledge one does *not* forgo knowing things as such in favour of an absorption into nameless silence; rather one knows everything by participation in the divine Word in whom and through whom all things are made. It would be anachronistic in the worst sense, I believe, to conflate this classical Christian analysis of knowing with the modern post-Kantian distinction. The modern analysis wants, in order to take account of Kant's critique, to distinguish between the categorical knowledge that a human subject has of particular given objects, on the one hand, with, on the other hand, the transcendental consciousness of the absolute that is the condition of possibility for any knowing at all.

Rahner, I think, is attempting to re-frame this modern post-Kantian distinction in terms of the earlier mystical analysis of knowing, but I wonder how successful this move can be. It seems to me to wash out of the picture entirely the role of the concrete form as mystical expression of God's reality – a finite form not jettisoned in earlier mystical theology but irradiated and invested with mystical expressivity because both it and the knower are united in the God who loves them both. The coming-into-linguistic-form of mystical consciousness is secondary in every sense for Rahner, so that the images and ideas of mystical texts are 'merely the tiny signs and idols which we erect', inevitably, in our clumsy attempt to put the mystery into words.[10] In Rahner's approach, all the highly-imaged expressions of mystical thought in, say, Catherine of Siena, inevitably seem to fade in significance before the unthematic silence of pre-categorical transcendental consciousness – which is anyway the same for Catherine as for anyone else. But this makes it rather hard to take Catherine's actual teaching, not to mention her bodily forms of spiritual knowing, as theologically very significant. She becomes yet another interesting piece of evidence, albeit a very splendid one, for the existence of the universal transcendental experience that grounds all consciousness whatsoever.

The experience/interpretation disjunction

All this gives rise to a tension in Rahner's thought: on the one hand he recognizes the significant contributions mystical thought has made to theology, but on the other hand we always have to realize that these contributions are only the secondary reality, the conceptual interpretation given to the more basic and fundamental transcendental consciousness which is common to all people anyway. In his view the primordial and really theologically significant experience can never wholly be 'a matter for reflection or be verbally objectified'.[11] Therefore we find a distinction in spiritual literature, says Rahner, between those writers who simply consign their primordial experience to the categories of their preconceived theological systems and those (obviously more praiseworthy in his eyes) 'in which the mystical element thrusts through to expression, time and again, as the ultimate source of this literature's authenticity and vitality, even though here we have only occasional effective testimony to the author's mystical experience'.[12] Note that the great *desideratum* here is the author's experience itself; what is significant theologically is the 'authenticity and vitality' it lends to the writing, *not* the actual ideas or concepts in which this golden universal experience has inevitably been haltingly uttered. The extended mystical process of conceptualization and textualization has little theological patina in this view.

Here Rahner is only joining what had been something of a twentieth-century consensus about the universality of primordial religious experience and its sad differentiation and division into the varieties of local and particular thought forms. There is a hint here of that quintessential modern longing for a universal human religious sensibility, uniting peoples in such a way as to liberate them from the peculiarities of their own histories, languages and customs. Needless to say, this is an ideal with only attenuated appreciation for the intrinsic value of the particular or the bodily, the historical or the linguistic, as expressions of divine reality. Rahner sighs regretfully that all spiritual texts inevitably 'carry with them the relativity of the religious, cultural, historical milieu of the person providing the description' of their 'original experience itself'.[13] Once again, I would want to suggest that this approach to understanding mystical thought inevitably tends to devalue the theological vision of spiritual texts, conducing to an approach which utilizes them as archaeological sites for the unearthing of precious shards of the prior underlying experiences of the authors.

And yet there is something in Rahner which never quite leaves him comfortable with this view *tout court*. He allows that even after the primal religious consciousness has been brought into conceptual interpretation there still may be some value in it: 'Christianity is far from regarding such a conceptually articulated teaching in the last resort as a superfluous, merely accidental, and arbitrary phenomenon within the totality of Christianity.'[14] My hunch is that the inherently incarnational logic of Christianity has such a deep hold in Rahner's thought that it leads him to resist the modernist impulse towards ever greater abstraction: 'The actual *experience* of love is indeed absolutely basic and absolutely indispensable. But despite this fact the experience itself as such can in itself be accepted more profoundly, more purely, and with greater freedom when we achieve a knowledge of its true nature and its implications at the explicitly conscious level.'[15] The tension is clear in this passage between the (supposed) priority of transcendental experience and the value of historical, categorical articulation. Is there any sense in which Rahner could think of the divine infinity and the unthematic consciousness it arouses in us as fundamentally *not* silence and formlessness but radiant form-*fullness*? Such a perspective would enfranchise the concrete particularity of mystical theology, not in terms of fanciful visions or hypertrophied experiences, but in terms of the textual aspect of its encounter with God. It would mean, in other words, not just that thinking out our unthematic transcendental experience into conceptual terms is a useful exercise (as Rahner seems to suggest in the passage just above), but that there is no 'experience' which is ever really quite so unthematic; for every encounter with God is an encounter with infinitely radiant self-disclosure.

The recovery of a christological apophaticism?

To do justice to Rahner's thought I need to conclude this section by considering an important trajectory in which, arguably at least, he might be seen to provide a much more christological basis for his construal of mystical thought, akin to the perspective I hinted at just above. If this were so, it would open the lines of dialogue between him and von Balthasar (and even Barth) in some very important ways. It would mean that human transcendentality does not simply ascend apophatically into infinite silence but is truly *confronted* by an Other.

I have tried to indicate all along that it would be a grave mistake to think of Rahner's account of human transcendentality as a description of a merely human phenomenon. It is fully an aspect of who we are as human persons, to be sure, but it is for all that a momentum – which constitutes us as human – set loose in us by the divine self-communication. The problem is that, because the divine ground of this momentum-towards-mystery is so deeply a dimension of who we are in every moment of our lives, it is easy enough (though fatal) to equate it with the limited state of our being-in-the-world – and thus not realize that it really is pulling us beyond ourselves.[16]

Rahner suggests that what has 'burst' open this self-enclosed world is the historical appearing of Jesus Christ, because 'in this way, God confronts man directly with a demand and a call which throws man out of the course prescribed for him by nature, a course which would have spent itself within the horizons of the world.'[17]

The impact of this historical appearing, this distinctly *categorical* call to humanity, is that the transcendental ascent of consciousness itself is tinged with an equivalent sense of confrontation, of cross, of inability to arrive at an answer. It is for this reason that the 'eternal temptation' to settle for an answer 'within the horizons of the world' is so self-defeating, for the true end and bliss of human existence is the enjoyment of God's incomprehensibility. Rahner emphasizes that this is *not* simply an indication of the finiteness of human knowing. Rather, the inexhaustibility of God's life 'is precisely that which [human knowing] wants to reach. If this is correct, then indeed the essence of knowledge itself changes, it becomes something else, for which the incomprehensibility of God is no longer a forbidding boundary but is that

which is sought.'[18] So the transcendentality of humanity is oriented towards
the infinite reality of God, a reality which cannot simply be known, a reality
which calls for a renunciation of knowing according to our human ability to
know. 'Hence man must let himself fall into this incomprehensibility as into
his true fulfillment and happiness, let himself be taken up by this unanswered
question. This unintelligible risk, which sweeps away all questions, is usually
called worshipful love of God.'[19]

In this essay from which we have quoted, Rahner goes on to speak of this
coming to 'knowledge' by means of an abandonment to love, by growing in
'the practice of love and not by a theory of the desire to know.' The stage is set
for the ultimate expression of this true apophaticism: a journey into the darkness
not of ever more refined philosophical abstraction but of Jesus' self-surrender
in love and freedom to the Father. For Rahner clearly argues in numerous places
that 'the mystical occurrence of surrender to God, as he is in and for himself,
ultimately succeeds only through Jesus' redemptive death as it renders itself
historically manifest'.[20] Thus Jesus' commitment to the mission given him by
the Father leads him more and more deeply into a full and loving surrender to
the incomprehensible mystery of God, and this leads him into the only knowing
of that mystery which is possible for a creature: participation in God's own self-
disclosure. The mystical journey towards divine incomprehensibility can
ultimately find fulfilment only insofar as it takes place by sharing in this self-
abandonment of Jesus. So Rahner, in a stupendously significant footnote,
argues with great clarity that any form of apophatic journey 'must also conceive
itself as a participation in Christ's "kenosis", for he alone experiences the true
mystical "emptying" through the cross, death and the tomb. . . . Finally it must
realize that in earthly man this emptying of self will not be accomplished by
practising pure inwardness, but by the real activity which is called humility,
service, love of our neighbour, the cross and death.'[21] Now one has to make a
crucial decision in reading Rahner. Option one is to say that Jesus' historical act
of self-surrender to mystery is important because it raises to consciousness in us
the universal dynamic of human transcendentality, which must inevitably make
a journey of self-abandonment in love if it is not to stagnate in terminal self-
preoccupation. Once one has awakened to the innate necessity of this self-
surrender, then the actual historical event of Jesus is of indifferent importance,
possibly even deleterious if one clings to it instead of making its lesson one's
own. Option two is to say, no, Rahner really is *not* thinking of Jesus here as a
handy visual aid (option one) but as the saviour who concretely and historically
inaugurates a new way of life and community which makes this self-abandonment in love *possible*. I think the latter choice is truer to Rahner's intentions.[22]

The question then becomes, what are the hermeneutical implications of reading Rahner this way. Just after the passage quoted above, the Jesuit adds somewhat disconcertingly: 'This basic incarnational structure of the unconfused unity of God and his creatures gives us to understand that we can apprehend God in the sign (or in the form of a vision) only if we do not cling to the sign (*"noli me tangere"*) as if it were the ultimate reality, God himself. The sign must be welcomed and passed by, grasped and relinquished.'[23] But while, as Rahner's allusion suggests, Mary Magdalene was indeed admonished not to cling to the bodily sign of the risen Jesus, there *does* continue to be (in the resurrection) a bodiliness to Jesus. Indeed, surely the glorified Body of Jesus is not etherealized but is, so to speak, more bodily than ever, more real, more self-communicating; for that concrete expression in human bodily terms is simply part of who Jesus is as the divine Word, and it has been wrought to perfection in the death and resurrection of Jesus. So the language of passing by and relinquishing that Rahner uses here is perhaps unfortunate. His own conviction that the ultimate form of apophaticism is the paschal mystery suggests that the journey into divine incomprehensibility is *not* all about the *relinquishing* of historical expressivity but rather about its being *rendered transparent* to the super-expressivity of the trinitarian life. What emerges from this is not the absolute silence of a formless pure consciousness (the 'alone with the Alone'), but the radiantly super-abundant love which is inherently other-directed and ecclesial. The apophatic journey does not end in the pious hush of the tomb but breaks forth into the startling jubilation of Pentecost; apophasis thus leads into that super-expressivity which marks the presence of trinitarian speaking in and through the new corporate body of Christ. What I am trying to suggest in all this is that Rahner's approach – at least insofar as it is truly centred christologically – is open to a positive construal of mystical thought not just as an interesting phenomenon of human consciousness but as legitimate theological expression. Because if the paschal mystery is the truest form of mystical apophasis, then the aim of the apophatic journey is not to succumb to a final speechlessness but to become free enough from self-preoccupied speech so as to be available for that infinite dialogue which catches up our language into its supernal converse, namely the communion of the trinitarian Persons.

Whether Rahner himself would be comfortable moving in this direction is not always easy to tell. Does divine incomprehensibility remain for him the incomprehensibility which is defined by an infinite formlessness or is God ultimately incomprehensible precisely because of an infinite trinitarian expressivity which undergirds and transfigures all forms? If we turn now to Hans Urs von Balthasar, we see something like the latter notion: an approach which emphasizes that God is incomprehensible exactly in the infinite mutuality of the Three Persons. It is this infinitely *expressive* triune self-giving that ultimately leads Jesus into the utter self-abandonment of the Cross. The mystical journey (which takes place in Christ) is thus the rendering of human consciousness and speech available to the outbreak of adoring wonder at Easter and the pure freedom of divine speaking at Pentecost. This means that the theology inherent in mystical texts, in all its pluriformity and variety, its severe silences and its exuberant imagery, is – if it takes place within the mission of Christ – an aspect of the super-expressivity of God.

Von Balthasar and the Trinitarian Encounter

Let me try to highlight one possible source of the differences between Rahner and von Balthasar – whether in manner only or matter too remains to be seen. Von Balthasar pointed to a fundamental distinction between Christian mysticism which has truly emerged from the paschal mystery (and leads back to it) and, on the other hand, Christian mysticism which has not quite freed itself from the common Neoplatonic inheritance of the ancient Mediterranean world. A mysticism of the second kind, in which the soul is urged to transcend itself in order to rediscover its unity with the One in an eternal silence of union without distinction is quite different, in his view, from a more inherently trinitarian mysticism. For the mystical journey which takes place in union with Jesus in his prayer to the Father in their Spirit is finally a mysticism of communion and dialogue. Such a trinitarian mysticism tends inherently towards the expressivity of concrete form – whether in the obedience of a particular state of life or in the mystagogical structures of a spiritual text.[24]

What especially concerns von Balthasar is that journeys towards an Absolute One, because there is not much one can say about the One except how one is doing on the way, tend to become self-preoccupied with analyses of the mystic's inner states. This is only avoidable if the apophatic journey is grounded more deeply within the paschal mystery itself. That is especially significant for our purposes, because it means that christologically-grounded mysticism is likely, in von Balthasar's view, to be more expressive of the objective realities of God's own self-disclosure rather than focused on states of inner experience.

The christological basis of the mystical

Von Balthasar liked to speak of the life, death and resurrection of Jesus as a kind of dramatic stage (*Spielraum*) upon which all human beings are able to discover their truest and most authentic calling in life; here all people may each discover the 'role' whose enactment will mean the fulfilment of their existence.[25] This is perhaps a good place for us to start, because it helps to make sense of von Balthasar's notion that the destiny of every human being is inalienably bound up with Jesus' mission.

In von Balthasar's view (following Maximus), the whole creation is given its existence through the work of the divine Word, the eternal expression of the Father's self-giving love. This means that every creature bears within itself, as part of the very structures of its existence, a profound correlation with the pattern of the Word's own act of existence. And the Word's act of existence consists ultimately in the historical mission to bestow love by being human as the historical figure Jesus of Nazareth. Jesus Christ is, in other words, the real meaning and enactment of the very patterns of existence by which every creature is given life and unfolds life. The intrinsic patterns of meaning in our life are not part of an abstract metaphysical scheme but the contours of a historical human being's struggle to love, to be available for God and neighbour. Christ, says von Balthasar, is 'the origin and ground in which our whole being with all its roots is fixed, from which it draws its sustenance and derives all its best and characteristic features.'[26]

So on the one hand, every human person is predisposed to discover the truth of reality by coming to share – practically, concretely, spiritually – in the life-pattern of Jesus. On the other hand, Jesus, as the incarnation of the very same pattern of self-giving love by which all things came to be, is himself predisposed to a kind of existential openness to everyone. His life is eminently 'participable' or shareable; indeed he seems to live by giving himself away. Drawing on the mystical theology of Pierre de Bérulle (1575–1629), von Balthasar suggests that Jesus' inherent openness to others reaches the deepest level of human consciousness to include a kind of sharing in Jesus' own experiences of life.[27] No situation of Jesus' life is a closed or finite thing; rather Jesus makes it available for participation and it becomes a new framework for the re-creation of human consciousness.

In this christological vision of cosmos and personal being, it is the saints and mystics whom von Balthasar believes have been the most obvious examples of being thus drawn into an inner participation and understanding of Jesus' existence. 'Their charisma consisted in the ability to re-immerse themselves, beyond everything that convention might dictate, in a "contemporaneity" with the Gospel.'[28] For von Balthasar in other words, and this is really the key, *mystical consciousness is the receptive and perceptive impression made in people as they are drawn hiddenly (mystically) to share in Christ's own life and consciousness.* This inclusive capacity of Jesus does not lead necessarily to mystical delights, for there is no state of Jesus' existence when he is more given-away, more shareable, than his passion. Indeed von Balthasar sees in the saints and mystics of Christianity signs

> which are quite inexplicable except as participations in Christ's states. These constitute the vast, limitless field of the 'dark nights'. . . . To my knowledge, no theology has seriously undertaken the task of seeing them as a whole and evaluating them from the point of view of dogma. . . . The important thing is not the 'mystical phenomenon' . . . but the fact that something of the passion is, through the grace of the Head, constantly being made present in the body, and that the body needs to understand what is happening there by relating it to the Head as its source and end.[29]

Here we can see von Balthasar's conception of mysticism as an ecclesial process in which the members of Christ's body come to understand the mysteries of ultimate reality precisely by sharing in the life of the Word made flesh. 'The saints are not given to us to admire for their heroic powers, but that we should be enlightened by them on the inner reality of Christ, both for our better understanding of the faith and for our living thereby in charity.'[30] And from the vantage point of mystical participation in Christ, argues von Balthasar, the believing community comes to an ever new and transformative understanding of all the mysteries of faith.

How might this perspective shape our understanding of the relationship between spirituality and theology? Surely the most immediate point to be noted is that von Balthasar's perspective implies a very practical and ecclesial notion of mysticism. The preparation for, consciousness of, and reflection upon God's intimate presence all take place in the concrete daily work of membership in Christ's body. There is no particular form of life (monastic enclosure, for example) which would be a requirement for mysticism in this view. Mystical consciousness emerges in people as they seek to discover, by sharing in the pattern of Christ's self-giving love, the true meaning of their own lives. Through this way of life, Jesus' own consciousness becomes an interpretive framework by which believers experience everything – they come to see reality more and more through the eyes of the risen Christ. Because the mysteries of Christ's life, death, resurrection and eternal life as the Son of God are seen as the lenses of mystical vision, mysticism is understood as essentially a personal appropriation of revelation. It is not a new revelation in the sense of something different or possibly at variance with the canonical witness of the Scriptures, but is rather an existential participation in that witness. And because it takes place in the lives of very different people in very different times and places, this mystical vision affords an embodied representation of the scriptural witness in ever new forms and voices – albeit under the critical norm of the Gospel.

This would seem to imply a very direct link between spirituality and theology. Mystical participation, for example, in Jesus' sense of compassion and experience of suffering are not simply states of intense feeling but the very threshold of the mystery of salvation. Similarly, mystical sharing in Jesus' consciousness of the One he called 'Abba' in the power of their Spirit would be seen as an intimate, unfathomable, initiation into the trinitarian life of God. In this view, preparation for, consciousness of, and reflection upon the immediate presence of God is *inherently theological*; not in the sense that it is a subdivision of theology or is ruled by theological dogmas or methods, but in the sense that the mystic has been invited by a free act of God into a vision of God's activity in the world – viewed from within the incarnate heart of that activity. This model is intrinsically contextual and relational. That is, it situates mysticism concretely within the historical struggle of real people to live out together the meaning of their life in God.

Von Balthasar's model also assumes that mystical consciousness flows within an encounter between the human subject and the divine Other mediated directly by the human other, Jesus. It is a notion of mysticism that is oriented directly to conversation and away from any hint of solipsistic self-absorption; it emphasizes, in von Balthasar's view, the gospel social and relational concern in place of what he saw as a tendency towards transcendental self-analysis latent in Rahner's approach. Whether von Balthasar's diagnoses of Rahner and vice versa were always very accurate is another matter.[31]

Because the relationship of theology and spirituality was so frequently an explicit theme in von Balthasar's work, the best elucidation of his approach may be simply to offer a demonstration of it in practice. But can he mine living, vital theology from the mystical encounter without simply jettisoning the extremely personal matrix in which it grew? In other words, can he take account of the 'subjective turn' in modern theology as Rahner did, without sacrificing what he sees as the inherently objective expressivity of divine self-disclosure in Christ as that is mediated in human consciousness?

Within the wide range of von Balthasar's studies I shall take as a discrete grouping his treatment of three Carmelites: John of the Cross,[32] Thérèse of Lisieux,[33] and Elizabeth of Dijon.[34] Together these figures present von Balthasar with common themes and comparable problems.[35] Among other things, they will highlight his concern about a subjective turn in mystical theology. The aim will be to see how von Balthasar is able to unfold from their works many features of a doctrine of God. This will afford some further

comparison with the role of God's incomprehensibility in Rahner's view of
the relation between mysticism and theology.[36]

Experiential justification

Von Balthasar offers a very straightforward justification for taking the saints as
living doctrinal inscriptions: both the saints themselves and those who
consider their lives and teaching have experienced a deepening understanding
of the great mysteries of Christian faith. We could say that von Balthasar's
approach is not so much theoretical as experiential. He draws his readers into
the project with him, and, as it were, asks us to try taking up a position next
to the saint in question and then to follow their gaze and see if we do not see
something illuminating.

In this way von Balthasar builds a helpful bridge between the modern turn
to the subject and the more objective doctrinal reality he longs to express. For
von Balthasar does not shy away from the highly subjective inner states of his
subjects; he asks us to share as much as we are able in the inner world of the
saint, and *then* to notice how that inner vision is evoked by a startling divine
reality, a reality which leads human experience *far beyond what it might have
perceived for itself.* We could for a moment translate this from hagiographical
terms into metaphysical ones comparable to Rahner's thought. For example
in speaking of God's relation to created being, von Balthasar writes: 'If it is true
that God in his dealings with his creation cannot abuse its transcendental laws
of being, it is likewise true that the free opening of the heart of the innermost
mystery of God cannot be anticipated on the basis of this transcendental
lawfulness.'[37] Translated back again: human experience as such could never
direct us (as Rahner seems sometimes to suggest) to the worshipful reality of
God, and yet certain particular human patterns of life (i.e., those of the saints)
have been *drawn* into this reality and can remain a medium for its impression.

There are some saints, remarks von Balthasar, who kindle a special response
among believers: 'Each of us discovers in them some quality which particularly
attracts us so that we penetrate more deeply into the meaning of holiness.'[38]
Von Balthasar cannily links this special attractive power of certain saints to
something else, namely, the power with which they express something of
God's own mission in the world. They share 'the divine quality of being
perfectly concrete, yet beyond comprehension. Comparable in this respect to
God's nature, they are absolutely determinate . . . whilst harbouring boundless
interior riches.'[39] So apart from whatever they may teach *about* God, these
saints, precisely in their particular form 'saintliness', suggest something about
God: a quality, perhaps, of supreme definiteness and particularity which is not

for all that envisaged as any limitation of God, but on the contrary as 'boundless interior riches'.

But von Balthasar speaks of the saints' aptness for divine expressivity in other ways as well. The saints are those in the world who have been given a taste of heaven, who burn for it, and yet who do not abandon their earthly mission. 'Rather they live a life of intense longing and move the world by the strength of that heaven which has first been granted to them and then closed to them. They hang crucified between this world and the beyond; exiles from earth but not yet in their heavenly home, their position serves as a kind of pulpit and their whole life is a sermon.'[40] Here is an excellent example of the perspective which will allow von Balthasar to derive doctrinal fruit precisely in and through the 'subjective' human life-patterns. For what we see, he suggests, is not heaven itself open above the saint, allowing us to leave her or him behind for the objective beyond. Rather we see the impact of heaven upon those who have tasted its life. The theologian's job then would be not only to describe the state of the mystics but to estimate the force and nature of that divine reality which could have so aroused the saints' desire as to suspend them 'between this world and the beyond'. It is a process of working backwards, not from the concrete to the abstract, but from the concrete to the ever more concrete – from the saints to God.

The knowledge of God and the dark night

Crucial to understanding von Balthasar on this theme is his belief that a virtual sea change in spirituality was set loose by Ignatius of Loyola. The patristic and medieval spiritual journey, he argues, was largely directed towards the eternal vision of God as the given supernatural end of humankind. This meant that human aspiration itself, duly purified of course, could serve as a sort of spiritual compass towards the final goal: 'man only needs to gaze upon his own "restless heart" in order to realize where his path lies to "eternal rest in God".'[41] But then Ignatius subordinates everything, even one's own happiness, to the praise and service of God.

> Human nature, even when it is elevated by grace, cannot act as the guide for man in his praise, reverence, and service of God; ultimately such guidance can only come from God and revelation of his will. Therefore Ignatius builds his whole spirituality upon the concept of choice; that is, upon God's choice, accomplished in eternal freedom, which is offered to man to choose for himself. This new 'identity' and 'fusion' between the Creator's choice and that of his creature begins ever more surely to replace the classical ideal of identifying their essences, the ideal of 'deification'.[42]

What von Balthasar sees taking place here is a recasting of the classic spiritual itinerary from an essentialist to a voluntarist frame of reference. In other words, what would before have been spoken of as an elevation of the believer's *nature* now comes to be seen in terms of the believer's growing *obedience* to the will of God. And the key in this shift, for von Balthasar, is that while the former essentialist approach provided a basis for a kind of natural theology of the *cor inquietum* variety (not without significant echoes in the Rahnerian transcendentality), the new emphasis on obedience to the divine will instead directs attention to the history of salvation and the believer's participation therein. The theological emphasis is less on epistemology and more on the inter-personal struggles of the spiritual journey.

Of course no one is more aware than von Balthasar of the deep and subtle influence of Dionysius, the master apophaticist, upon John of the Cross. Yet he does see some striking new features in John. Broadly put, we might say that in John, the Dionysian stripping away of divine attributes becomes a journey through the terrible personal absence of the Beloved, a descent into hell. Von Balthasar reads John's itinerary as leading the soul into a knowledge of God via a *suffering* of the 'absolute distinction between the sinful creature and the absolute God in his purity.'[43] And this means that the soul comes to know God through the mode of dispossession and the absence of God, even as an awful separation from God. Von Balthasar is quite graphic about all this. For him John's poetry of the soul's renunciation of everything in its search for the Beloved speaks of the soul's piercing and division by the remorseless Gospel: 'To bear witness to this, [John's] poetry must therefore begin inside the division, as the scream of the vivisected soul in the middle of the night, in order to end in the song of praise of the soul, even more fully alive at a deeper level, wounded in the fire of glory.'[44] If the soul's journey to God is conceived not so much as a transcendental ascent but as a journey through sin, death and hell, we will not be surprised to find von Balthasar thinking in christological terms. The soul is dying with love for the absent Bridegroom, 'but Christ has died and withdrawn himself from the Bride, and she must seek him in real death by dying with him.'[45] The soul has to learn to know God in a way which transcends all subject–object distinctions, but von Balthasar interprets this more metaphysical side of the journey in John in terms of the soul's following after Christ in his descent to a hell of nothingness. In other words von Balthasar takes the passion-of-love imagery not as a dispensable metaphor for the real inner metaphysical ascent but as the very means of that ascent – an ascent by way of descent.[46]

Given that the soul comes to know God in this way, what must God be like? It would seem that God's otherness from all created reality, God's transcendence of all conceptualities, is itself encompassed within the yet more terrible distance between the sinner and the holy God. Von Balthasar sees *that* as the otherness which gives the greatest clue to the nature of God. It is an otherness which can only be surpassed if the loving soul seeks after the Beloved no longer on its own powers, 'but jumps and is caught by the open arms of the love of God'.[47] God, in other words, is whoever it is that can reach the sinner by means of 'a love stronger than Hell, a life stronger than death'.[48]

Elizabeth of Dijon presents her own experience of the otherness of God. The first thing to grasp is that her experience of the Infinity of God was *not* 'the experience of a void and nothingness beyond the trustworthy concrete world'.[49] She speaks of letting herself go into the abyss and yet encountering precisely in the Infinity of God his intimacy, almost tangibility. For Elizabeth, Christ literally crossed the threshold of finite and Infinite and so opened the way for creatures:

> There comes a moment when the creature not only sees present in faith the Infinite made finite, but when, raised above its limitations, it has to enter the yawning depths of infinity, without being itself engulfed or annihilated. Nor may the moment when this frontier is crossed be put off till death. On the contrary, the creature must, by his faith in the Incarnate Infinity, train himself, still in the finite sphere, to become a citizen of the Infinite.[50]

This is no 'Infinity' which justifies its infinity simply by remaining inaccessible, 'a spurious divine boundlessness' von Balthasar calls it (not without a certain critique of the transcendental reduction of all to infinite mystery in Rahner).[51] Elizabeth does not offer an apophasis which moves into infinity by the endless negation of finite names. Rather she points to an infinity which *exemplifies* its very infinity precisely in the love enacted by Jesus, 'a love immediately present, infinite and absolute, like a consuming fire in its purity'.[52]

It becomes clear that the real definition of the Infinite is given first and last in a love which knows no limits. There is a fairly strong fragrance of paradox hanging about here, for von Balthasar wants above all to avoid any idea of God's otherness or infinity as being somehow shapeless, without form or self-definition. Elizabeth is a Godsend for him because she experiences this infinity *as* infinity precisely in God's capacity to give himself tangibly, intimately, even finitely, in Christ. 'Infinity is, for Elizabeth, no abstract idea but a superabundant presence – the presence of Christ, of the Triune God, of the saints, who, through their wonderful love, stir up in us a feeling of what infinity is. The real infinite is love.'[53] The key here is surely his phrase, 'superabundant presence'. The infinite God is infinite not by being equally absent or present everywhere all the time, but rather by being infinitely present exactly according to the concrete christological pattern of superabundant love.

This seems obvious in many ways and yet I sense it is a hard won point in von Balthasar. Over against the purest philosophical understandings of infinity as being equally everywhere and nowhere, von Balthasar is drawn by a gripping experience in these saints of something different. This is not something he wishes only to pay lip service to as a biblical rubric, (God was in Christ . . . , God is love, etc.). Rather he senses from the saints that the philosophically coherent versions of infinity and omnipresence are somehow badly askew. Maybe what is really infinite is *not* everywhere always already the case but is a very *particular* kind of eternal event with a very concrete though universal contour. On this view, God's infinity is expressed above all by the extension of love between the Father and the Son, an extension which is revealed in the capacity of that love to encompass within itself even the creature's separation from God. Thus we might say that what is *really* infinite is the relation between the Father and the Son in the Spirit, and that *this* infinity is even greater than the separation between God and the creature since, as infinite love, it can and does establish communion across this distance without simply abolishing it.

God as Trinity

We have seen how von Balthasar brings his readers to the vantage point of the saints who are his subjects. He intends that the reader may catch from there at least a glimpse of what illumines the saint, but, if not, the saint's own spiritual stance, positioning, even predicament, has become tolerably apparent. From this awareness von Balthasar attempts to locate the 'gravitational force' which so operates upon the saint in any given case, and then to give it a theological identity and elucidation. This procedure comes into its own when we turn to the trinitarian naming of God. For here, above all, the mystic's entrance into communion points towards a divine partner characterized *in se* by 'partnership', by communion itself.

In his treatment of John of the Cross, von Balthasar is keen to make sure John's emphasis on *nada* does not leave the reader with any sense of having passed *beyond* a trinitarian structure. He sees John struggling to avoid either a kind of pantheism or a merely accidental, occasional, relation between God and the creature.[54] Out of his own journey to God, John begins to sense a particular pattern. The soul-Bride is infused by the wind-Spirit with the perfumes of the Beloved: 'here already the mystery of the Holy Spirit shared by Bride and Bridegroom is glimpsed as the mystery of the infusing love of the Spirit common to Father and Son, creaturely love, through grace, becomes a participation in the divine *spiratio* itself.'[55] What von Balthasar is uncovering here is a trinitarian structure, not within the mystic's own being, but in the new relationship experienced as the mystic comes to live more and more in communion with Another. The theme of separation and distance which we noted before is crucial here: the creature lives in a kind of distance from God, within which, quite wondrously, the most intimate communion can happen – *without* the distance being overthrown and the creature annihilated into identity with God.

It is this pattern of encounter which von Balthasar sees as pointing to the fundamentally trinitarian character of God. For it is the relational 'distance' of the divine persons one to another which permits the human soul's entrance into this limitlessness of eternal love without thereby being dissolved as person: 'We are a long way here from seeing man's relation to God as either one of opposition or immersion. Within the formless itself we can see once more something like a form emerging out of the trinitarian distance of persons.'[56] In other words, the boundless *nada* of ever-more self-dispossessive love is never finally a featurelessly monistic incomprehensibility, because that love is ultimately accomplished and perfected ('It is finished.' [Jn 19.30]) in the eternal self-giving of the divine persons one to another. Their distance or otherness from each other is what permits their relationality and of course also allows the creature to share in this relationality (in Christ) secure from any threat of submersion into total identity.

In passing on to Thérèse we also regress a trifle, for as von Balthasar is not hesitant to point out, Thérèse's explicitly self-referential experience is less apt for the unfolding of certain theological mysteries. 'The fact that Thérèse did not see further into the interior life of the Trinity and its reflection in the economy of salvation is to be explained by her peculiar approach to theology . . . . She has to demonstrate it all in her own person, and even her life cannot demonstrate such an objective, massive doctrine as that of the Trinity.'[57] Nevertheless Thérèse does approach a trinitarian paradigm in her exploration of the graced will. Thérèse finds in the interplay of self-renouncing love a spontaneous adoption of the will of the other as one's own. A command or obligation becomes 'simply the external expression of one's deepest desires'.[58] Here von Balthasar sees at least the embryo of a trinitarian encounter: the will of the other remains distinct from one's own and yet becomes the very heart of one's own willing, just as Jesus plunges into the will of the Father, accepting it as his own meat and drink.

It is however with Elizabeth of the Trinity, not surprisingly, that von Balthasar finds the most sustained possibilities for trinitarian extrapolation. At the heart of Elizabeth's thought as we saw above is a strong *attrait* for the divine depths. For her this was known above all in the act of adoration. She writes: 'I can only describe it [adoration] as the ecstasy of love. Adoration is love overwhelmed and engulfed by the beauty, the power, the infinite greatness of the Beloved. It means sinking into the depths of silence . . . this silence is the wonderful hymn of praise that resounds eternally in the communion of the silent Trinity.'[59] Already with that final phrase we can see that Elizabeth understands this ineffable adoration as itself a participation in an eternal intra-trinitarian worship – it is a silence which is far from an absence of speech, but rather an infinite dialogue beyond the opposition of speech and silence. On the one hand, the adoration is too profound to have for its object anyone or anything other than God, and on the other hand it is an adoration too fulfilled and too perfect to be the act of anyone other than God (and in this case, the creature *in* God) – a worship therefore of God by God in the power of God.

As von Balthasar ultimately formulates it, Elizabeth's teaching on adoration is the 'submission in self surrender of human love, enforced by the infinite love which gives itself. . . . It implies a mode of participation. Communion with the Son has been shown to be a *participation* in his communion with the Father. Elizabeth points out that the primary act of adoration is that of the incarnate Son before the Father, that act which is the initial source of all the acts of transcending by faith.'[60] As ever for von Balthasar, it is because of the mystic's participation in Christ that mystical encounter may legitimately be read as an experiential unfolding of the whole range of Christian doctrine. As the Triune 'event' of adoration, God alone can ground the mystic's peculiar consciousness – sharing in worship of the Father precisely by participating more deeply in the self-surrendering life of the Son.

As a concluding example of von Balthasar's hagio-theological extrapolation we find him returning with Elizabeth to his favoured theme of distance between the creature and God as secured and yet enfolded within the distance between the divine persons. So he says that Elizabeth understands the soul's transformation in God as a 'close unity in abiding distinction, a still closer unity in that ever further withdrawal which is adoration'.[61] The soul realizes its true and abiding distance from God not by transcendental negation, but only as this very distance is bridged-over by the self-giving intimacy of the soul's Beloved. It is God's embrace of the soul, in all its separateness, which at last reveals how unfathomable that distance between God and creature really is – and yet also reveals it as a possibility for communion. 'This distance is ever again dissembled and forgotten in the fact that the Son of God clothes himself with it, divinizes it, makes it the expression of the internal distinction of the divine persons in their unity of nature. What distinguishes the creature from God becomes precisely what makes it resemble him, otherness in unity.'[62]

Perhaps the key to the realm of mystical theology is found in this life-stance of the mystic: participation in Christ reveals humanity's otherness to God not as an insuperable barrier to the knowledge of God but as itself 'the expression of the internal distinction of the divine persons'. It is this paradox that gives rise to the saints' disconcerting experience of being ceaselessly overwhelmed both by the painful absence and the joyful intimacy of their Beloved. And it is in this experience of unity-in-adoring-otherness that von Balthasar believes theology must search for buried treasure.[63]

Modernity and Mystical Thought

Our comparison of Rahner and von Balthasar has raised some central issues about how best to construe mystical thought in the modern era. Let me try briefly to formulate here some of the implications of what we have seen, most of which will have to be developed in the next chapter on hermeneutics. I want to suggest, for purposes of discussion at least, that the issues seem to run between two poles of concern. On one side are the questions relating to modern epistemology and on the other, those relating to our notion of God.

Say we accept Kant's strictures on the nature of human knowing, the constitutive role of the categories of the human mind in every act of thought and the irreducible division between the knower and every known object; it has then been generally assumed in modernity that the mystical, insofar as it represents some kind of immediate encounter with God (who can hardly be an object susceptible to categorical knowing) must take place either at the fringes of human consciousness (William James) or as the very condition for the possibility of knowing anything at all (Maréchal and Rahner).

The other pole of concern inevitably relates, as we have already seen, to the understanding of God who is in some sense present in mystical consciousness. Because this divine presence (as non-categorical) must be the transcendental mystery of all human knowing and willing, such divinity must indeed give rise to experiences which are utterly incomprehensible, ineffable, inexpressible, and thus safely beyond the borders of all categorical thought. Otherwise one cannot account for even the possibility of mystical thought at all. That at least has been the general outline of the majority view in the modern era. It seizes upon ineffability language in mystical texts as evidence for the transcendental, unthematic, non-categorical nature of all mystical experience. In such a view, the concrete details of any given mystical text are only the culturally-necessitated language in which the original unthematic mystical experience has been clothed, and the task of modern mystical theology is to uncover this more primal experience and reflect upon it.

We have seen some reasons both for the development of this approach but also for its questioning by another, more christological and trinitarian perspective. Indeed it seems to me that mystical 'experience' is never really unthematic, that the divine 'object' in mystical encounter is never silent, and that the theological expressivity of mystical texts, therefore, is never simply to be discarded in favour of a supposedly more original 'experience' lying behind the language of the text.

This is no place to engage in the massively-fraught argument over whether there can *be* any pre-categorical experience at all. But even supposing a fundamental human transcendentality as in Rahner, such a primordial human dynamic – as the great Jesuit himself points out – is itself the momentum aroused within human consciousness by the self-communication of God. Here is exactly where von Balthasar complements Rahner so strongly. For it is von Balthasar's contention that all human consciousness is irreducibly inter-personal, that is, I am aware of myself and of anything at all because 'I' have been addressed by another. From the earliest stages of human life in infancy we come to be who we are precisely because we are drawn into a network of relationships and responses to those around us.[61] And this is not less but infinitely *more* the case in respect of our transcendental consciousness; we are called into being not because we are 'addressed' by a divine silence but by superabundant speech and expressivity, the very eternal relationality of the trinitarian life.

Now it is true that classical Christian mysticism speaks of the inexpressibility of God, but we ought not to assume this means that *God* is somehow *less* expressive than human beings, indeed the mystics regularly assert that the ineffability of God is the result of God's 'ever-greater' reality: God's existence speaks *more* than we know how to say and in that sense *we* are reduced to silence. So in its fundamental basis, the mystical encounter in this perspective would be one which is *eminently* 'thematic' and linguistic, for it is a language of love which always drives not towards the ever more abstractly conceptual but towards the *concrete good* of the other. Of course since God is infinite, mystical encounter obviously does not yield an 'object' among other categorical objects of our perception; but far from needing therefore to be located at a supposititious borderland beyond the fringes of categorical consciousness, mystical encounter might almost be said to *constitute* the categories of human knowing, embracing all knowing according to the categories of inter-personal encounter – *divinely* trinitarian at basis, *humanly* relational in terms of our experience. That is, the patterns by which I come to 'know' anything at all are ultimately congruent with the trinitarian relations of infinitely giving love.

This means that I will only know insofar as I am ready to love the other, learning in other words to know as God knows Godself.

The move from mystical encounter to mystical text need not, therefore, be seen as a move from 'pure experience' to mere secondary interpretation. And this on two counts. First, the God whom one encounters is always the trinitarian event of expressive love and is thus in infinite act towards the concrete, embodied good of the other. This infinitely expressive procession of the trinitarian Persons includes and embraces (as we saw in von Balthasar) the finite good of human others, and thus the concrete forms of human expressivity. Second, if the structures of human consciousness are themselves structured in response to the inter-personal relationality of trinitarian life, then the understanding of concrete forms such as one finds in mystical texts is not primarily a process of abstraction; the goal is not to find a meaning somehow confided *outside* the categories of thought but rather to enter into the process of personal encounter, transformation and transfiguration which the concrete 'other' of the mystical text now represents.

That is, we understand a mystical text not by 'transcending' its imagery and symbols but by seeing how they themselves, like the resurrection body of Jesus, disclose their meaning by drawing the believing community into new transforming patterns of life, of relationship to each other. Perhaps we could say that the 'meaning' of a mystical text is discovered in the patterns of life and thought which it gives birth to in the community that receives it.

Notes

1   For an illuminating assessment of the influence of Schleiermacher's position on such trend-setting modern interpeters of mysticism as William James and Evelyn Underhill, see Jantzen, *Power, Gender and Christian Mysticism. Cambridge Studies in Ideology and Religion* 8 (Cambridge: Cambridge University Press, 1995) 304–21.

2   On the ideas of these thinkers and their relation to Rahner see Gerald A. McCool, SJ, *From Unity to Pluralism: The Internal Evolution of Thomism* (New York: Fordham University Press, 1989). For a very helpful introduction to Rahner's thought see Anne Carr, *The Theological Method of Karl Rahner* (Missoula, Montana: Scholars Press, 1977).

3   Karl Rahner, *Foundations of Christian Faith: An Introduction to the Idea of Christianity*, trans. William V. Dych (New York: Crossroad, 1982), 20.

4   Ibid., 21.

5   Cf. ibid., 34: 'Whenever man in his transcendence experiences himself as questioning, as disquieted by the appearance of being, as open to something

ineffable, he cannot understand himself as subject in the sense of an *absolute subject*, but only in the sense of one who receives being, ultimately only in the sense of grace. In this context "grace" means the freedom of the ground of being [God] which gives being to man, a freedom which man experiences in his finiteness and contingency. . . . *Insofar as man is a transcendent being, he is confronted by himself, is responsible for himself, and hence is person and subject.*' (My emphasis.) For a helpful and highly stimulating analysis of these issues in Rahner and more broadly see R. R. Reno, *The Ordinary Transformed: Karl Rahner and the Christian Vision of Transcendence* (Grand Rapids: Eerdmans, 1995).

6   Idem., *The Practice of Faith. A Handbook of Contemporary Spirituality*, ed. Karl Lehmann and Albert Raffelt (New York: Crossroad, 1992), 78. This anthology is a very useful gathering of many sources from throughout Rahner's oeuvre dealing with the relationship between spirituality and theology.

7   Ibid., 73–6.

8   Ibid., 63–4.

9   Ibid., 66.

10   Ibid., 78.

11   Ibid., 22.

12   Ibid., 71.

13   Idem., 'Experience of Transcendence from the Standpoint of Catholic Dogmatics' in *Theological Investigations*, vol. XVIII, trans. Edward Quinn (New York: Crossroad, 1983), 173–88, here 177.

14   Ibid., 178.

15   Idem., 'The Experience of God Today' in *Theological Investigations*, vol. XI, trans. David Bourke (New York: Seabury, 1974), 152.

16   'Will man be able to bear this *ecstasis* of his being, this waiting to see whether God wants perhaps to come? Will he not succumb rather to the eternal temptation of taking the world as the final revelation of God and thus of making God the meaning of the world in such a way that the world becomes the meaning of God? . . . Every form of idolatry is nothing but the concrete expression of man's existential attitude which builds on the decision not to let God be anything more than the original unity of the forces governing this world and the destinies of men.' (Rahner, 'The Passion and Asceticsim', *Theological Investigations*, vol. III, trans Karl-H. and Boniface Kruger [London: Darton, Longman & Todd, 1967], 77. Rahner goes on to say that even the thought of Hegel and Heidegger is idolatrous in this respect.

17   Ibid., 77–8.

18   Idem., 'Thomas Aquinas on the Incomprehensibility of God' in *Celebrating the Medieval Heritage: A Colloquy on the Thought of Aquinas and Bonaventure*, ed. David Tracy. *The Journal of Religion* Supplement 58 (1978): S107–S125, here S122.

19   Ibid., S123.

20   Idem., *Practice of Faith*, 74. See also Rahner, 'Experience of Transcendence', 180–1: 'a Christian theology would insist that such a mystical experience of a decline of all "normal" mediation would be a participation in the death of Jesus who in

his actual death as absolute decline came to the final dawning of God himself.'

21   Idem., *Visions and Prophecies. Questiones Disputatae* (New York: Herder and Herder, 1963), 14, note 12.

22   See, e.g., his important essay, 'The Concept of Mystery in Catholic Theology' (*Theological Investigations*, vol. IV, trans. Kevin Smith [London: Darton, Longman & Todd, 1966], esp. 68ff., where Rahner emphasizes the trinitarian ground of all transcendental consciousness: the beatific vision, for example, which Rahner takes to be the goal towardss which human transcendentality is moving, is only possible 'insofar as it is mediated by the hypostatic union of the human nature of Jesus with the Logos of God' (68). See also his apologia for the certainly highly expressive thought of Teresa of Avila (in contrast to the radical 'absence of images' in John of the Cross) in *Opportunities for Faith: Elements of a Modern Spirituality*, trans. Edward Quinn (New York: Seabury Press, 1974), 126: 'If we consider that the loss of imagery today is to be counted precisely *as* a loss and not as a gain, if we see that our relationship to God today must either be mediated perhaps more explicitly than ever through our relationship to the concrete Jesus of Nazareth, to his life and death and his relationship to his fellow men, or it will not exist at all, then it is perhaps not so obvious that for us today Teresa of Avila must rank behind John of the Cross.'

23   *Visions and Prophecies*, 14, note 12.

24   See, e.g., von Balthasar's uneasiness with the Neoplatonic pattern of apophatic ascent in *Mysterium Paschale*, trans. Aidan Nichols, O.P. (Edinburgh: T. & T. Clark, 1990), 39–40, 76, 125 among other places. Further on his views regarding speech and silence in religion see the very fruitful work of Raymond Gawronski, S. J., *Word and Silence: Hans Urs von Balthasar and the Spiritual Encounter between East and West* (Edinburgh: T. & T. Clark, 1995).

25   Further on the relation of spirituality and theology in von Balthasar see Mark A. McIntosh, *Christology from Within: Spirituality and the Incarnation in Hans Urs Von Balthasar. Studies in Spirituality and Theology*, vol. 3 (Notre Dame: University of Notre Dame Press, 1996).

26   Hans Urs von Balthasar, *Prayer*, trans. A.V. Littledale (New York: Paulist Press, 1967), 49.

27   Idem., *The Glory of the Lord: A Theological Aesthetics*, vol. 5, *The Realm of Metaphysics in the Modern Age*, trans. Oliver Davies, Andrew Louth, Brian McNeil C.R.V., John Saward, and Rowan Williams (Edinburgh: T. & T. Clark, 1991), 123: 'One can see here how Bérulle gives a metaphysical foundation to the Pauline concept of the indwelling in Christ by faith . . . . Existence in Christ, integrated by the integration of his human states in his fundamental state as the God-Man, is an existence which explains our spiritual capacity (*capacité* in the sense of the possibility of existing spiritually in another, the world or God) in terms of Christ's capacity for us.'

28   Idem., *Mysterium Paschale*, trans. Aidan Nichols, O. P. (Edinburgh: T. & T. Clark, 1990), 38.

29   Idem., 'Theology and Sanctity', 199–200.

30   Ibid., 204.

31   A highly illuminating work comparing the two thinkers and considering their mutual criticism is Rowan Williams, 'Balthasar and Rahner' in *The Analogy of Beauty: The Theology of Hans Urs von Balthasar*, ed. John Riches (Edinburgh: T. & T. Clark, 1986).

32   John of the Cross is the subject of the second chapter of *The Glory of the Lord, III: Studies in Theological Style: Lay Styles*, trans. Andrew Louth, John Saward, Martin Simon, Rowan Williams. (Edinburgh: T & T Clark, 1986). German edn, 1984.

33   *Thérèse of Lisieux: The Story of a Mission*, trans. Donald Nichol (New York: Sheed and Ward, 1954). German edn, 1950.

34   *Elizabeth of Dijon: An Interpretation of her Spiritual Mission*, trans. A.V. Littledale (New York: Pantheon Books, 1956). German edn, 1952.

35   For insightful analysis of von Balthasar's dialogue with three other figures see the essays of Cyril O'Regan: *Newman and von Balthasar: The Christological Contexting of the Numinous, Église et Théologie* 26 (1995): 165–202; *Balthasar and Eckhart: Theological Principles and Catholicity, The Thomist* 60 (April 2 1996):203–39; and *Von Balthasar and Thick Retrieval: Post-Chalcedonian Symphonic Theology, Gregorianum* 77/2 (1996): 227–60 (on von Balthasar's conversation with Maximus). O'Regan's mastery of Hegel makes his forthcoming work on von Balthasar all the more worthy of attention.

36   Further on the theme of divine incomprehensibility in von Balthasar and Rahner, see the very fine University of Chicago dissertation of John Kevern.

37   *The Glory of the Lord*, vol. IV, *The Realm of Metaphysics in Antiquity*, trans. Brian McNeil, Andrew Louth, John Saward, Rowan Williams, and Oliver Davies (Edinburgh: T & T Clark, 1989), 25.

38   *Thérèse*, Introduction, xvi.

39   Ibid.

40   Ibid., 149.

41   *Thérèse*, 225.

42   Ibid., 225–6.

43   *Glory*, III, 110.

44   Ibid., 127.

45   Ibid., 119.

46   This theme of the descent into hell comes to play a crucial role in the mystical experiences and writings of von Balthasar's spiritual colleague, the Basel physician Adrienne von Speyr, and through her in his own work as well. For his comments on this phenomenon see von Balthasar, *First Glance at Adrienne von Speyr*, San Francisco, 1981. For his most concentrated exposition of the theme see von Balthasar, *Mysterium Paschale*.

47   Ibid.

48   Ibid.

49   *Elizabeth*, 54.

50   Ibid., 54–5.

51   Ibid., 63.

52   Ibid., 64.
53   Ibid., 68–9.
54   *Glory*, III, 141.
55   Ibid., 141–2.
56   Ibid., 143.
57   *Thérèse*, 223.
58   Ibid., 210.
59   Elizabeth of Dijon, quoted in *Elizabeth*, 71.
60   *Elizabeth*, 93–4.
61   Ibid., 108.
62   Ibid., 109.
63   An earlier form of the preceding sections was published as McIntosh, 'A Hagio-Theological Doctrine of God: Hans Urs von Balthasar on Three Carmelites', *The Irish Theological Quarterly*, 59.2 (1993): 128–42.
64   See, for example, the important essay 'Movement Towards God' in *Explorations in Theology*, vol. III, *Creator Spirit*, trans. Brian McNeil, CRV (San Francisco: Ignatius Press, 1993), 15–55.

Chapter 4

THEOLOGICAL HERMENEUTICS AND SPIRITUAL TEXTS

For some time now I have been using a novel by the American writer Ron Hansen in a course I teach to undergraduates. *Mariette in Ecstasy* is about a young woman who joins a convent in upstate New York in 1906. During the course of the novel Mariette undergoes a number of intense mystical encounters. These are described with enough sensitivity and ambiguity that the whole novel begins to take on the character of a spiritual text. My students, like Mariette's fellow nuns, are quickly caught up trying to interpret what is going on in Mariette and in the priory as a result of her presence there. But it soon becomes clear that multiple interpretations are possible, that the perspective of the interpreters is more than slightly significant, and that the meaning of the novel as a text itself extends far beyond whatever Mariette may or may not have experienced.

One of the brilliantly realistic features of Hansen's work is his depiction of the nuns' hungry, almost greedy, fascination with what Mariette is *experiencing*. They become obsessed with asking her what she is feeling, seeing, hearing and so on. This is, in fact, painfully emblematic of the state of hermeneutics in respect to mysticism – quite beyond the world of the novel. Philosophical and anthropological approaches to the study of mysticism have tended to focus their attention almost wholly on what may be postulated about a mystic's *experiences,* which are somehow deemed to be available to the interpreter by reading behind the lines of the mystic's actual written text or life story. While the nuns do their best to define and explicate Mariette's experiences, she is pouring out her impressions and new awarenesses in a series of letters to the priory's father confessor; these written texts – mystical theology in the making – are, however, secretly (and unknown to Mariette) continually confiscated by the prioress, who neither reads them herself nor wishes anyone else to read them. The mystical text is suppressed.

Later in this chapter I wish to consider this fraught relationship between experience, interpretation and text in the realm of Christian mystical theology. Hansen's novel is a salutary advance warning that if we insist on thinking that we can in some fashion get past the text, leaving it behind in a quest for 'what actually happened', we may be pursuing a putative experience that is *not* in itself the real locus of mystical meaning. As Mariette came to learn, the deepest and most meaningful understanding of her encounters was only possible when she herself was able to relinquish her own need for experiential phenomena and pyrotechnics.

At the end of the novel, Mariette is asked to leave the priory. The conflict of interpretations has become too divisive! She spends the rest of her days keeping the substance of her religious vows in the very unexceptional and ordinary circumstances of life in the world. Thirty years after the time of her dramatic experiences as a postulant, she writes a letter to one of her remaining friends at the priory:

> I still pray the hours and honor the vows and go to a sunrise Mass. (Each day I thank God for the Chrysler automobile, though I hate the noise.) I tidy the house and tend the garden and have dinner with the radio on. Even now I look out at a cat huddled down in the adder's fern, at a fresh wind nagging the sheets on the line, at hills like a green sea in the east and just beyond them the priory, and the magnificent puzzle is, for a moment, solved, and God is there before me in the being of all that is not him.[1]

Where do we search for the meaning in the spiritual text which is Mariette's life? Is it only to be found in the extraordinary experiences of her youth – which have long since ceased? Or is there a deep mystical theology in Mariette's own reflections on the enormous transitions and shifts in her life? Clearly she has now come to read the world mystically, that is, to see the mysterious trace of God precisely in the withdrawal of all the early phenomena. That is the 'magnificent puzzle' which is, 'for a moment, solved' – the hidden reality of God, present by means of absence, 'there before me in the being of all that is not him.'

At the end of the novel, we are still not entirely sure what Mariette did in fact experience. We *do* have access to her letters, her theological reflections. Are the validity and value of these perceptions dependent on knowing with certainty and accuracy the quality of her prior inner states? Would it make a difference, for example, if we knew for sure whether Mariette's experiences were self-induced or were purely events of grace – and how could one tell that the one possibility was really distinct from the other? Our post-Enlightenment approach to history-like texts has been to assume that their locus of meaning lies in whatever we can recover of the experiences that took place 'behind' the text, as its pre-history. But as Hans Frei has notably taught us to ask with regard to this approach to scripture, is that really what such a text is all about – a clumsy and pre-scientific attempt to report a sequence of events?[2] And of course in the case of mystical texts, while we may have more secondary historical information about a given writer, it remains a fallacy that we can ever 'know' his or her interior experiences. What we have is simply that which the mystics themselves laboured over and bequeathed to us: their texts.

There is a more sophisticated hermeneutical move, however, that still very easily eclipses the language of the mystical texts themselves. Again, the development of biblical criticism provides an illuminating analogy. Rudolf Bultmann is famous for his efforts to understand the peculiar power of scriptural language.[3] Bultmann, of course, understood that not all biblical language was designed to give a historical account (a good one in the view of conservative scholars; a flawed or even tendentious one in the view of liberal and radical critics). Such a misconstrual of the text only led, in Bultmann's view, to a blindness and false objectification in respect of the text. It is the power of *myth* which pervades biblical language. In order to interpret such texts properly, one must accordingly know how to read back out of the mythological language the meaning for our own era which correlates with its meaning for the era of its authors.

Bultmann had a range of conceptions of myth, some quite different from one another. So in Enlightenment terms, a myth might be thought of as a pre-rational attempt to describe the world from a primitive view of the cosmos. In more existentialist terms, a myth is an attempt to express a valuation of inner states of human existence, but it is able to do so only in a kind of alienating picture language about things 'out there'. Bultmann came to see that the Enlightenment view of myth led rather abruptly to the wholesale reduction of biblical language to tidy ethical formulas. But since, in Bultmann's judgement, mythology pervades the whole pattern of the gospels, such a remedy was too drastic. Rather, 'the inner meaning of New Testament mythology had to be preserved even while its external form was overcome'.[4] And so came about Bultmann's programme of 'demythologizing': freeing the gospel call to existential crisis, with which the biblical text intends to confront us, from the falsely objectifying tendency of its imagery. So, for example, we have the famous instance of Bultmann's interpretation of the resurrection narratives as all about the new rising of faith in the lives of the formerly dispirited disciples.

Once again, however, the language of the text is left behind in favour of a supposedly more authentic meaning which, beguilingly, is all about our inner quest for the really real. In my view, such an approach suffers from at least three liabilities. First, it leads to the assumption that one can express the inner meaning of a mystical text better than the text's own author. Second, it fosters the view that the concrete rhetoric of the text is somehow an obstacle, a lingering cultural accretion standing in the way of a more universal meaning. And third, it legitimates the privatizing perspective that what is most meaningful is an inner experiential state – rather than the public struggle to negotiate communal meaning in the presence of a shared mystery. In short, I want to argue for an interpretive approach to mystical texts that gives maximal value to the texts themselves, with all their particularities of imagery, structure and language.

After this introduction to some of the hermeneutical skirmishing implicit in dealing with spiritual texts, perhaps the most prudent thing would be to resort to several general hermeneutical theorists whose sage modelling of the issues could then frame our discussion. So for example, Hans-Georg Gadamer's well-known concern for the fusion of horizons between text and reader might be deployed to adjudicate questions regarding the locus of meaning – for Gadamer, in the conversation between text and reader rather than 'behind' the text in a supposedly recoverable pre-history. Paul Ricoeur's hermeneutical spiral could help us discover some much needed critical distance in dealing with these texts; we would need to move from his initial reading through a range of possible critical stances to a new theological appropriation of the text in a 'second naivete'. These and other general theories of hermeneutics can be immensely helpful and some have already been adopted by other scholars.[5]

Perhaps perversely, I feel somewhat constrained by these strategies, and would propose instead that we begin simply by considering the hermeneutical clues, the interpretive 'directions', implicit in the *activity of mystical theology* itself. If we think for a moment of the Christian Neoplatonism of Dionysius, or Eriugena (*c*.810–*c*.877), Bonaventure, Eckhart (*c*.1260–1327), or Jan van Ruusbroec (1293–1381) – all quite various in formulation – there is a familiar and unmistakable pattern involved: the procession of all things from their eternal being in God into created existence, and the return of all into blissful unity with God. For each of these writers (Thomas Aquinas as well), this cosmic structure of *reality* is also the proper pattern of *theology*. It begins by tracing the sounding forth (the cataphasis) of God's glory in divine self-expression – from the eternal trinitarian life to the creation of the universe. Then it moves towards consummation by a series of 'ascending' dialectical negations (the apophasis) into the eternally fruitful darkness of unknowing, which is the only real knowing a creature can have of God. For these authors the fullest understanding of this cataphatic–apophatic structure is to take the spiritual journey along that way oneself. This means that the medium in which the *structure* of reality and our *knowledge* of reality are held together is mystical theology. And as was especially clear in Bonaventure (chapter 2), and in Rahner and von Balthasar (chapter 3), the pivotal turning point in this cataphatic–apophatic dynamic is a concrete historical event: the life, death and resurrection of Jesus.

How does this help us to search for clues to the interpretation of spiritual texts? I suggest we begin with the apophatic quality of mystical discourse, tracing it back 'downwards' into its pivotal phase as the trinitarian speech of the Incarnation and Cross. This should make clearer the theological *meaning-fulness* of that strange phenomenon, the mystical text itself.

Apophasis: Mystical Speech as Superabundance of Meaning

In his essay, "The Experience of God Today', Karl Rahner argues that the apparent absence of God from the quotidian consciousness of our era is not such a bad thing, for it means that we may have finally escaped from the idea of a particular deity who is one item among all the others.[6] It may be possible for our era, which has experienced the absence of God so painfully, to begin to recover a true sense of what Rahner calls the transcendental dynamic of reality – the irreducible mystery of everything. As we saw in the last chapter, for Rahner this transcendence is an apophatic momentum at the heart of intelligible life; we only know and love in so far as whatever we know and love is placed in an ever greater context. This movement towards ultimacy (which of course demands the continual and painful relativization of everything – apophasis) is the foundation of meaningfulness, for without it nothing would have a larger context in which to be recognized and loved.

We begin then simply with the idea that the silence, absence or apparent withdrawal of God may serve to liberate us from idols, from the idea of revelation as, in Ricoeur's words, a 'massive opacity' which might be the manipulable possession of any human institution.[7] In our era's dispossession of 'God', we may at last be free to discover the mystical presence of the true and living God.

Yet apophatic mysticism ought not to be thought of as something undertaken by people who are absorbed by the unutterable *remoteness* of God. On the contrary, apophasis happens because, like Moses and the burning bush, persons have been drawn so *close* to the mystery that they have begun to realize how beautifully, appallingly, heart-breakingly mysterious God really is. In other words, the *absence* to which apophasis conducts one is an absence of any particular thing or item that could satisfy one any longer; apophasis is the intensifying of desire to such a point that one is left hungering only for the living God – who is of course, as Aquinas so clearly reminds us, never available as one of the *things* that we are capable of grasping, sensing or knowing in any normal sense. Hence absence; for what is so powerfully attractive about the true God is that one only journeys into deeper encounter with God by entering into the desert of liberation. This is the fertile wilderness where one is freed from ideas and ways of life that are unmasked at last as traps and snares, subtle slaveries of spirit.

Another point worth bearing in mind is that apophatic speech is *not* a case of there simply not being much to say. You run out of things to say about a square or a plastic cup in the end because there is not 'enough' of them to capture the imagination for long; you run out of things to say about God because the more you know and the more you speak, the more you realize how inadequate words are. If, as Turner rightly says, apophatic theology is 'speech about God which is the failure of speech', it is failure in the sense of speech slowing to a halt in awed wonder before the presence of what is always more than one can say.[8] Thus apophatic speech might take the form of a quieting down, a stilling into hushed silence. But it might also take the form of an explosion of speech, a carnival of self-subverting discourse, language tripping over itself in paradox or fantastical repetition as it comes undone in the whirlwind of divine superabundance.

So the 'temperature' of the mystical text needs to be taken. Do we read a bracing icy stillness of negation, mesmerized into silence before the unutterable, or a feverish piling up of contrasting images in language that pants deliriously after the One whom it can never grasp? The key point is that in *either* case, the writer's 'experiences' may be entirely the same. What the *language* of apophasis is aiming at is not the writer's *feelings*, which are in fact likely to be all too easily described, but the impossibly overwhelming *reality of God*. In other words, I would argue, it would be a hermeneutical fault to read mystical language in a positivistic fashion, reducing it to a direct report of 'things' that 'happened' – whether in external events or interior sensations – or as enjoining would-be mystics to cultivate particular feelings, attitudes or spiritual stances. Mystical language is, rather, more like lenses for viewing what cannot be seen; it is describing in a simple or direct sense neither God nor the mystic's experiences but evoking an *interpretive framework* within which the readers of the text may come to recognize and participate in their own encounters with God.

If a text *is* descriptive, this is by way of provocation and performance, of drawing the reader into a new event. Take for example the ecstatically erotic language of some of the Beguine writers; whatever may have been Hadewijch's experiences, her poetry has consumed those experiences and drawn them into a new polyvalent textuality – and *that* is what she now offers to her fellow Beguines. It is an abyss of meaningfulness in which one cannot simply stop to admire a given feeling or experience as a reified object, but is rather plunged into a new world of yearning which has no name. Of course there are mystical texts which are more theoretical or didactic in nature and operate less allusively, less performatively. But for that very reason they are more easily recognized as proposing a new framework for living, lenses for perceiving experience anew. It is the texts that 'teach' without seeming to do so which are more easily misconstrued as being merely reportorial accounts of some thing.

Another way of putting all this would be to say that the reading of apophatic texts is most satisfactory when it mirrors the *momentum* of the texts; in other words, a proper hermeneutic of mystical texts would, like the texts themselves, relinquish the acquisition of fixed objective referents. What Michael Sells says so well of this language of 'unsaying' is thus true also of the attempt to follow such language: 'It demands a willingness to let go, at a particular moment, of the grasping for guarantees and for knowledge as a possession. It demands a moment of vulnerability.'[9] So the theological interpretation of mystical texts must resist the urge to trivialize the apophatic by rendering its language of paradox and play into a more 'stable' statement of propositional truths or a putative account of pre-textual experience. 'Apophatic texts have suffered in a particularly acute manner from the urge to paraphrase the meaning in non-apophatic language or to fill in the open referent – to say what the text really meant to say, but didn't.'[10]

On the other hand, theology that is willing to risk 'a moment of vulnerability' may be able to bring the richness of mystical thought to bear on contemporary theological problems. It could do this by refusing to domesticate mystical language; instead it would allow the strange aporias and intense silences of mystical speech to reconfigure theological discourse *around* themselves, re-shaping the usual patterns of thought and argument in theology.

But, it might be objected, is this not to risk mere mystification, a cloak for unclarity of thought and a debilitation of theological progress? The only answer to this type of inquiry, really, is to remind ourselves of the goal of theology. If this goal is discourse about a deity who is yet another object of human thought, albeit defined negatively as the God who is greater than the capacity of our thoughts, then truly mystical theology will be a threat to any theology so conceived. But if theology wishes to speak truthfully of a God who is *not* simply the highest item of existence (who happens also to be invisible), then ultimately it can only achieve its goal by helping the community to that moment in its encounter with God when divine superabundance finally transcends all our faculties and leaves us in a silence so complete that neither wonder, adoration, nor despair can any longer be distinguished.

Is such a moment really alien to Christian theology? I want to suggest that the meeting place for mystical perceptivity and Christian theology is marked out by the journey from Gethsemane through Golgotha.

The Trinitarian Basis of Mystical Speech

In Augustine's famous hermeneutical distinction (from *On Christian Doctrine*), all reality may be discussed as either *res* (thing) or *signum* (sign). Our usual creaturely tendency is to interpret the world around us as a collection of things that we, willy nilly, appropriate for our own enjoyment. For Augustine, of course, what we live in the midst of are only *provisional* realities; they are best read not as opaque *objects* but as *signs* pointing us to God who is the source of all reality and hence the only true *res* in the fullest sense. Christianity as a hermeneutical practice enjoins us to cease the manipulative possession of the world around us. We are called to realize that the only true satisfaction of our desire lies in ceasing to 'reify' our world and instead to let its sign-quality (or transparence to God) guide our 'reading' of life. But how exactly are we to make this crucial hermeneutical transvaluation of the world?

Rowan Williams gives a thought-provoking response in his reading of *De Doctrina*.[11] In Augustine's view there is only one worldly *res* that constantly pushes us to discover its true depth as *sign*: the life, death and resurrection of Jesus. There are two crucial elements to this notion of Jesus as a hermeneutical 'event'. First, the Incarnation of the Word in historical human life 'reveals what the spiritual eye ought to perceive generally – that the whole creation is uttered and "meant" by God, and therefore has no meaning in itself'.[12] Because every act and word of Jesus is handed over to God and is in fact the 'speaking' of God, it never allows an interpreter to possess its meaning or prematurely foreclose the process of journeying participatively into a deeper understanding. When reality is viewed within the translucent framework of the Incarnation we discover that 'we live in a world of restless fluidities in meaning: all terms and all the objects they name are capable of opening out beyond themselves, coming to speak of a wider context, and so refusing to stay still under our attempts to comprehend or systematize or (for these go together) idolize'.[13]

But the Incarnation has a momentum to it, namely, Jesus' self-bestowal as divine speech, and so there comes to be a second crucial hermeneutical moment: the death of Jesus. Here is consummated that handing over of creation in love to be the speech of the Other; it is the charter for creation's freedom *not* to be manipulatively objectified – to remain instead richly and disclosively open to the One who causes it to be in the very act of speaking it. This transparency and openness are won at a cost, for they require the painful undoing of all our attempts at fixity and foreclosure; only thus can God's transcendent reality be glimpsed – when we are no longer able to grasp God as the most sublime object of our thoughts:

> How is God present in the world? In a death, in weakness, inactivity, negation.
> . . . It is the 'void' – in worldly terms – Christ incarnate and crucified that
> establishes the *difference* of God; it is this emptiness of meaning and power that
> makes Christ supremely *signum*. He is God's speech *because* he is worldly
> 'silence'; he is what cannot be enjoyed or rested in. . . . We can only allow it
> to detach us from self-sufficient satisfaction, from image and expectation. The
> unbridgeable distance between the eternal *res* and all earthly representation
> opens up through this 'anti-representation' that is the Cross; yet in the
> recognition of distance is also buried the apprehension of gift or revelation.[14]

My argument is not, of course, that all mystical texts are 'really' trying to talk about the Incarnation and the Cross, but that reading this *christological* event as a *hermeneutical* event suggests something important about the provenance of mystical speech. The apophatic momentum of Christian mystical texts, their resistance to easy foreclosure of meaning and their push towards meaning beyond manipulable objectivity – these qualities bear the marks of that ultimate apophasis enacted by Jesus. Reading mystical texts within that matrix or, at least, as drawing their apophatic power from that source, recovers something of the inherent integrity of spirituality and theology.

Such a proposal is not without warrant among the mystical writers themselves. We might consider, for example, Eckhart's interpretation of the spiritual journey in terms of the birth of the Word in the soul and the breakthrough into the divine ground. Throughout the great Dominican's works, we find the Neoplatonic scheme of procession and return presented in terms of trinitarian speech and silence.[15] The coming forth of all creation is the extension into time of the eternal speaking (Word) of the Father; and the fullness of rational creaturehood is likewise achieved as the soul recognizes itself as that very same eternal speech of God: 'The Father gives his Son birth in the soul in the same way as he gives him birth in eternity, and not otherwise. He must do it whether he likes it or not. The Father gives birth to his Son without ceasing; and I say more: He gives me birth, me, his Son and the same Son.'[16] The awakening to mystical awareness is thus conceived as an event of trinitarian speech; the soul, in Eckhart's extravagant language, begins its spiritual journey by discovering its mystical (hidden) identity as God's self-expression.

As we might well imagine, however, nothing stops there for Eckhart. Because this moment of mystical awakening is itself an event of eternal divine self-expression, it is carried along in the momentum of the divine life. The mystical journey of famously Eckhartian detachment is the necessary correlate of the divine speaking; for just as God knows Godself by the outpouring of self-expression, so the soul must participate in this, its ground, by a reciprocal ecstasy of the self – and that means leaving behind all possessions, desires and aspirations which obscure the soul's mystical identity as a form of divine speech. 'Now God wants no more from you than that you should in creaturely fashion go out of yourself, and let God be God in you. . . . Go completely out of yourself for God's love, and God comes completely out of himself for love of you. And when these two have gone out, what remains is a simplified One. In this One the Father brings his Son to birth in the innermost source.'[17] In this mutual *ekstasis*, a true standing outside of self, the created distinction between God and the soul is overcome and God is able to 'speak' the soul as God's own Word. But as we have seen this entails an apophasis for the soul. And just as the origin of mystical consciousness lies in the trinitarian momentum towards Incarnation, so also the consummation of that mystical journey is situated in a trinitarian event.

Eckhart speaks of God creating the soul 'so that it might be a bride of the Only-Begotten Son', and the Son desiring 'to come forth from the secret treasure chamber of the eternal Fatherhood' in order to woo the beloved soul and 'bring her back again into the exaltation from whence she came'.[18] But the Son's pursuit of the soul and return with her is not described as an apophasis of abstract metaphysics; the Son's love for the soul and his desire to free her to journey with him back into 'exaltation' involve him in a certain trauma:

> This is why he came out, and came leaping like a young hart (Sg. 2.9), and *suffered his torments for love*, and he did not go out without wishing to go in again into his chamber with his bride. This chamber is the silent darkness of the hidden Fatherhood. When he went out from the highest place of all, he wanted to go

in again with his bride to the purest place of all, and wanted to reveal to her the hidden secret of his hidden divinity, where he takes his rest with himself and with all created things.[19]

Here the apophatic ascent into the mystical presence of God is clearly darkened by suffering; as with numerous Beguine texts, the suffering of the Cross is interpreted in terms of the ardent suffering of yearning love. This journey describes what in other places Eckhart refers to as the 'breakthrough' of the soul into the divine ground. It is the impulse with which the inner spark 'wants to go into the simple ground, into the quiet desert, into which distinction never gazed'.[20] This final breakthrough has been described by Donald Duclow as marking the hermeneutical moment *par excellence*, for it is the occasion when the soul's continual penetration into deeper (mystical) meaning and understanding reaches a climax: 'If Eckhart conceives the procession into created being as verbal symbolic expression, then breakthrough is the *interpretation* which traces this expression to its source – a mystical *Quellenforschung*, if you will. This violent hermeneutical motion penetrates to the origin of discourse, to the *principium* where "the Word subsists in the silence of the Father's intellect".'[21]

The point here is that, for Eckhart, not only is the mystical journey situated within the moments of the eternal trinitarian existence, but the formulation of mystical understanding – we could even say the process of mystical 'textualization' – is itself an event of trinitarian speech. Mystical speech might thus be conceived as being drawn into full expression (as text) in two stages: first as the speaking and hearing of the ineffable Word; and, second, as the mystical text shares in the momentum of the divine Word, which pulls the text towards consummate expression in that apophasis embodied by the self-surrendered silence of the Cross. Mystical texts by their very apophasis are in motion towards a hermeneutical breakthrough into divine meaningfulness; and if this ultimate interpretive moment is a passage into silence, it is for all that a silence of trinitarian fecundity and profound theological significance.

So I want to suggest that there is reasonable justification for seeing the trinitarian speech of the Incarnation and Cross as the matrix of mystical speech. This would mean that mystical texts in some real sense participate in the primary event of God's veiling by unveiling; they are – precisely as texts – events of meaning themselves, which draw their readers into a new world of understanding and perception, a world that is inherently theological in its ramifications.

Mystical Speech as Event: Texts as Calls to Encounter

Jean Leclercq once remarked of Bernard that the Cistercian abbot felt so strongly about the ministry of the word that he was compelled to offer all his thoughts to God as vehicles of divine expression: 'Every thought that comes to him is intended for God's service. If he chose to keep it for himself, it would lose all its value; it belongs to the Spirit whose nature it is to communicate Himself. Bernard, in expressing it, is in a certain way prolonging the Incarnation of the Word.'[22] I have been developing this notion of mystical speech, both in its expression and the interpretation it evokes, as an extension of the trinitarian 'speech event', namely the life, death, and resurrection of Jesus. Now it is time to consider what this notion of mystical texts as events of meaning might yield.

The concept of a meaning event

Drawing on various forms of Anglo-American philosophy and the hermeneutics of Paul Ricoeur, Michael Sells has proposed that we think of mystical texts as 'meaning events'. In the first place we have no access to the experience of the text's author, and even if we did, the author's act of discourse has constituted a new public world of meaning that is not bound by the author's experience. As Ricoeur puts it: 'My experience cannot directly become your experience. . . . Yet, nevertheless, something passes from me to you. . . . Something passes from one sphere of life to another. This something is not the experience as experienced, but its meaning. Here is the miracle. The experience as experienced, as lived, remains private, but its sense, its meaning, becomes public. Communication in this way is the overcoming of *the radical non-communicability of the lived experience* as lived.'[23] The text as an event of meaning is, therefore, not simply an afterthought in relation to the more important underlying experience. The text is a continual unfolding of meaning precisely because it affords readers their own place of encounter and transformation. In this sense, I would argue, a mystical text is analogous to a scriptural text in its functioning: just as the biblical witness can be God's chosen 'site' for a new encounter between believers and the Incarnate Word, so a mystical text functions, non-canonically of course, as another location for the Word's encounter with believers.

The advantage of Sells's approach to this possibility is that he is able to provide a distinct explanatory basis for such a view grounded in interpretation theory. For Sells, the meaning event of the mystical text can be described as the product of its own semantic structures; and that helps us to see how we might make sense of my notion of mystical discourse as an extension of the discourse of trinitarian life. Sells, analysing the structures by which the fundamental apophasis in mystical texts takes place, is able to propose the following:

> The meaning event is the semantic analogue to the experience of mystical union. It does not describe or refer to mystical union but effects a semantic union that re-creates or mimics the mystical union. . . . Rather than pointing to an object, apophatic language attempts to evoke in the reader an event that is – in its movement beyond the structures of self and other, subject and object – structurally analogous to the event of mystical union.[24]

The patterns of the mystical text draw its readers into a play of meaning that re-structures the readers' perceptions. So for example, the shock of paradox, leaps of logic, and provocative imagery in an Eckhart sermon all engage with my reading of such a text. They undo my usual self-image as defined over against a divine Other, reconstituting the encounter with God within a new matrix. This is why Sells argues that 'the meaning event is a reenactment (within grammar, syntax, and metaphor) of the fusion of self and other within mystical union'.[25]

None of this is exactly unheard of in hermeneutical theory. Work on reader-response theory has often pointed to the manner in which the interaction of text and reader accomplishes a new work or world in which both participants are transformed. The text invites the reader into this new moment precisely by its gaps and negations, features especially prominent in mystical texts. A leading theorist of this approach, Wolfgang Iser, remarks:

> What is concealed spurs the reader into action, but this action is also controlled by what is revealed; the explicit in its turn is transformed when the implicit has been brought to light. Whenever the reader bridges the gaps, communication begins. The gaps function as a kind of pivot on which the whole text–reader relationship revolves. Hence, the structured blanks of the text stimulate the process of ideation to be performed.[26]

So we might say that a given writer's possible mystical experience is only a part of an ongoing event of meaning which moves *through* (a) textualization to (b) the interaction of text and reader and so on to a new *enacted* 'textualization' in (c) the transformed practices and perceptions of the reader. It would seem

an overly narrow construal to insist that only one phase or another of this
process is 'mystical' per se.

Ricoeur's discussion of the poetics of biblical texts provides further
clarifying analogies here. The process of understanding in which a reader is
engaged moves *beyond* both the author's presumed experiences or intentions,
and also beyond the structures of the texts just in themselves. The goal is rather
the 'the world the text unfolds before itself'.[27] How does the text open this
world between itself and the reader? Ricoeur suggests that the most significant
element in this process is a biblical text's poetic function. In his view this poesis
lifts the reader beyond the standard patterns of descriptive, objective reference
towards 'a more primitive, more originary referential function.'[28] What this
means is that in the interaction of text and reader, the reader's process of
understanding is drawn out of its usual opposition of self and other and the
analysis of the other as a manipulable object for the controlling self. Rather,
'poetic' language (and mystical language, whether poetry or prose, would fall
very clearly in this category) pushes the reader towards a far more participatory
and existential kind of 'knowing'. The language of such texts 'restores to us
that participation-in or belonging-to an order of things which precedes our
capacity to oppose ourselves to things taken as objects opposed to a subject'.[29]

Especially noteworthy in this regard is Ricoeur's impression that all this is
possible exactly because the poetic text works a kind of apophasis on the
reader, detaching one from the process of knowing by objectifying and
moving one towards a process of knowing by self-bestowal and participation.
The process of reading a text endowed with this poetic function sounds very
like an analogue of the mystical journey. What opens up 'across the ruins of
the intraworldly objects of everyday existence' is a new world in which the
self discovers a new pattern of life.[30] The drive towards understanding, in this
view, would not entail the delineation of items of thought but rather, as in
Duclow's reading of Eckhart, a breakthrough into participative knowing, a
knowing which shares more and more in the pattern of life of the 'known'
(who is now discovered to be as much the *knower* as the known).

The trinitarian basis for this interpretive process is worth bearing in mind.
The process of mystical understanding, I suggest, operates at least analogously
to the process by which Jesus comes to recognize his identity as Word and
make himself ever more available for the mission of being this Word. I have
been arguing that this 'interpretive' journey that Jesus undergoes might well
be seen as the matrix and categorical framework for the unfolding event of
Christian mystical speech – including the drive towards meaning and
understanding.

Christians believe that Jesus is God's Word spoken humanly and historically; thus we might say that Jesus' life and activity represent an ongoing performance of 'interpreting' his true identity and mission, precisely by attempting to enact them. So Jesus' life might be seen as an attempt to hear and understand his hidden (mystical) depths of identity as the eternal Word. Jesus knows himself entirely in terms of his relationships – with his people and the One whom he calls 'Abba'. He enacts the identity and mission of the Word of this Father and discovers who he is in doing so, a full and complete human being. But as Jesus moves towards the Cross, his sense of identity as God's beloved becomes complicated, darkened. As he is drawn into further participation in the Father's will, so the infinity and absoluteness of the Father become overwhelming to him: to enact, to *be*, the Word of this One is necessarily to go beyond the perceived limits of human knowing and loving (precisely because our broken version of what it means to be human is cut short by sin). To speak this Word in a life lived out in the language of *our* world is to be reduced to silence. To interpret his identity as Word in the full depths of its mystery leads Jesus into the darkening apophasis of his final hours

As Herbert McCabe points out, 'the fact that to be human means to be crucified is not something that the Father has directly planned but what we have arranged. We have made a world in which there is no way of being human that does not involve suffering.'[31] It is in this radical, fundamentally critical sense – as the uncompromised and therefore crucified speaking of what our world refuses to speak or to hear – that the interpretive phases of Christian mysticism take place. It is in this sense that the reader is drawn towards a new perceptivity by the gaps, silences and negations of the text. It is in this sense that the interpreter is drawn into a new world of meaning by participating in the fundamental momentum of mystical texts towards the infinite being of God – not by ceasing to be embodied, human and historical, but precisely by living out the full possibilities of what human being was created to be.

Meaning as call to encounter

Ricoeur has long insisted that event and meaning not be simply conflated, but that they be seen as a dialectic in which the reader of the text moves from reading as an event – a moment of confrontation and transformation – to reading as the birth of meaning in the reader's new way of thinking and living.[32] But what category can we use to describe this new existential perceptivity? It is not simply a matter of having new experiences or new concepts. Because these would yet again become the cherished (spiritual!) possessions of the self. This is why Eckhart, for example, was most concerned of all about those who rest secure in the knowledge that they have forsaken material gratification for a supposedly 'higher calling'.[33] The process of mystical understanding would seem to push towards a less manipulable goal – a focus like the journey of Jesus towards the Cross, which is defined by its stepping over into a beyond-without-limits.

Throughout this book I have alluded to spirituality as an encounter with the other, both divine and human. It is now time to draw directly on the source of this formulation in the fertile thought of the twentieth-century Jewish thinker Emmanuel Levinas. We have already seen how texts, perhaps mystical texts especially, foster an interaction with readers. For Levinas, scripture as revelation proffers an undeniable 'invitation to seek, to decipher' which 'already marks the reader's participation in the Revelation'.[34] Indeed Levinas suggests that revelation (in its totality) is only heard as the polyphony of each person's act of listening; 'the Revelation has a particular way of producing meaning, which lies in its calling upon the unique within me'.[35] This is significant, for, in Levinas's thought, hermeneutics is in the first place a response to a divine calling, a process of understanding that takes place precisely as one is called in one's uniqueness into obligation towards the Other. We could say, preliminarily, that living in care for the other is the stance in which meaning becomes luminous; a mystical text accrues meaningfulness only as it becomes a kind of performance guide towards compassionate living – for it is just *this* ethical ecstasy that prevents one from appropriating spiritual insights as personal possessions, from lapsing into self-sufficiency.[36]

But how exactly does hermeneutics as call or command work against this continual impulse to settle down in a finite yet totalizing reading or existence?

> Could we account for intelligibility in terms of a traumatic upheaval in experience, which confronts intelligence with something far beyond its capacity, and thereby causes it to break? Surely not. Unless, perhaps, we consider the possibility of a command, a 'you must', which takes no account of what 'you can'. In this case, the exceeding of one's capacity does make sense. In other words, the type of reason corresponding to the fracture we have spoken of is practical reason.[37]

For Levinas this process of responding to an unfulfillable demand is what revelation initiates in the hearer or reader. It is a questioning, an awakening – of the finite by the Infinite – and an invitation towards the kind of understanding which is discovered in love for neighbour and God. As Levinas suggests, this would connect the activity of biblical interpretation with practical reason, and I want to propose that *mutatis mutandis* the interpretation of mystical texts is likewise a practical process.

Levinas, it seems to me, helps us to see the profound link between intelligibility and contemplative discipline or discipleship. The meaningfulness of mystical texts is, in other words, less like the meaningfulness of propositions and more like the call to take up one's cross and follow Jesus into the apophasis of Gethsemane and Golgotha. The textuality of mystical discourse should no more prevent us from seeing this practical dimension to interpretation than does the textuality of the gospels themselves. 'There is meaning testified to in interjections and outcries, before being disclosed in propositions, a meaning that signifies as a command.'[38] All this points us to a crucial hermeneutical insight, namely that mystical texts are more adequately understood not as descriptions of experiences but calls towards a new framework for having any experiences whatsoever. It has been suggested, to take a fairly obvious example, that the best reading of the *Spiritual Exercises* of Ignatius is not as a prescription for working up a series of particular experiences, but as a matrix of symbols which serves to re-contextualize one's experiences entirely.[39]

The meaningfulness of mystical texts, on this view, would clearly not subsist in whatever experiences might lie behind the text or might even be evoked in the reader, but rather in the shape of that new interpretive framework posed for the reader by the text. Denys Turner has most perceptively noted this in connection with Eckhart's texts; the latter's calls for detachment and interiority are not proposed as preferable, 'higher' experiences as opposed to other types of experiences, 'but as form to content, as shapers to experience shaped. As categories, detachment and interiority are, for Eckhart, experientially empty. Detachment is not itself an experience alongside all the rest, no more is interiority. . . . [they] are, for Eckhart, not so much the names of experiences as *practices for the transformation of experience*'.[40] It is in this sense that we might understand Levinas's idea of the practice of interpretation as akin to responding to a call from the other. To enter into the meaning of a mystical text is to allow one's own categories for understanding and experiencing reality to be given over – perhaps broken – certainly to be transformed, by the reality of the other who is always beyond oneself. The mystical text as an address of trinitarian speech to the reader is most fully 'heard' as one is drawn into the same trinitarian dynamic – a pattern inherently self-dispossessive and yet self-constitutive in its dispossession-for-the-other.

Throughout this chapter I have argued that Christian mystical texts are a part of the Christian community's participation in that 'speech event' which constitutes the community – the trinitarian speech of God in creation, the calling of Israel, the Incarnation, death and resurrection. The patterns of mystical speech themselves suggest a hermeneutic rooted in the paschal mystery. If the event of mystical *textualization* is analogous to the Incarnation, and the struggle of the *interpretive process* is a kind of sharing in the apophasis of the Cross, so also the ongoing *realization of mystical meaning* draws one into those new patterns of life and consciousness which have their consummation in the resurrection and Pentecost. The point of drawing these hermeneutical analogies is not once again to straightjacket spirituality within dogmatic confines, for on any adequate reading it is precisely the paschal mystery at the heart of Christianity that always bursts and supersedes all conceptualizations. Rather my aim has been to suggest the inherent integrity of Christian spirituality and theology, and the degree to which the mystical journey underlies and even generates whatever is most truthful in theological perceptivity.

Experience, Interpretation and Texts

Now it is time to turn, at least briefly, to some vital implications for the theological interpretation of Christian spirituality. Broadly speaking we can divide these into three areas. The first has to do with the vexing and controversial question of experience and its relationship to mystical texts. The second question is how, if we are moving towards constructive theology, we are to deal with the breathtakingly unsystematic concreteness and imagery of spiritual texts. And the final question regards what procedures we might consider for the critical tasks of appraising and appropriating spiritual 'texts' (including the lives and missions of holy people) in theological reflection.

Mystical experience and mystical texts

Throughout the book I have noted the crucial shift in the history of Christian spirituality from an emphasis on the ineffability of the *divine mystery* to an emphasis on the ineffability of the *mystic's experiences*. The first emphasis implies the notion, first clearly articulated by Gregory of Nyssa, of God's unboundedness and infinity. The second implies that what counts as 'mysticism' chiefly is pre-linguistic and unthematized experience, or a 'pure consciousness event'. So for example, in his introduction to *The Problem of Pure Consciousness*, Robert Forman defines the mystical so as to rule out from the very start any spirituality that is expressed 'in terms of sensory experience or mental images'.[41] My reading of the history of Christian spirituality leads me to think that this approach rests on a mistaken interpretation. The preeminence of ineffability and nothingness language (in writers like Eckhart) has led modern interpreters, who are already conditioned to focus on mysticism as primarily an *experiential* phenomenon, to assume that this language is a report about a particular type of experience, namely an experience of nothingness or 'pure consciousness'. But as Turner puts it, we have 'psychologized' the metaphors of mystical speech: 'Whereas our employment of the metaphors of "inwardness" and "ascent" appears to be tied in with the achievement and cultivation of a certain kind of experience . . . the medieval employment of them was tied in with a "critique" of such religious experiences and practices.'[42] Where Forman and his fellow essayists are working to find an experience of pre-linguistic or 'pure' consciousness, the Christian mystics themselves are trying to persuade their readers against seeking any 'experiences' whatsoever. It is not, in other words, an experience of nothingness that Eckhart advocates, but the nothingness of experience, the letting-go of all experiences even, perhaps especially, those that seem most 'pure' and ascetical.

What difference does all this make? A tremendous difference to theology; because if mysticism is inherently about inner experiences, and these are most characteristic when *contentless* and are universally the same across all religions, then it is rather hard to see how mystical texts themselves could have much theological import. They are simply later interpretations, encrusted with the locally-conditioned dogmas of the mystics' traditions; whereas the really significant thing is the pre-theological experience itself, the universal common core, the marvellous perennial philosophy. Along with Grace Jantzen, I note with some suspicion the (undoubtedly unwitting) power play of modern academics who insist on the pure experientialism and ineffability of mystical experience, and the putative existence of a common core of mystical experience that can be liberated from any particular doctrinal trappings.

> It plays directly into the hands of modern bourgeois political and gender assumptions. It keeps God (and women) safely out of politics and the public realm; it allows mysticism to flourish as a secret inner life, while those who nurture such an inner life can generally be counted on to prop up rather than to challenge the status quo of their workplaces, their gender roles, and the political systems by which they are governed, since their anxieties and angers will be allayed in the privacy of their own hearts' search for peace and tranquillity.[43]

To Jantzen's critique I would add that as long as the real significance of mystical speech is divorced in this way from public ecclesial life and thought, this interpretation of mysticism as primarily inner experience works covertly to disenfranchise religious communities in favour of the academic arbiters of religion.

Forman and others who pursue variations on the common core approach to mysticism have been responding to what they see as an ill-founded application of Kantian principles of everyday consciousness to the very much more special case of mystical consciousness (as they define it).[44] But their privileging of an experience that is putatively innocent of theological reference has a long history of Enlightenment and Romantic era thought behind it. Summarizing a lengthy and persuasive history of the modern notion of pre-linguistic religious experience, Jantzen argues that in reaction to Kant's strictures on the human subject's experience of God, Schleiermacher (and later in a more pragmatic vein, William James), turned, as we saw in the last chapter, to the edges of consciousness to get *behind* the linguistic and categorical structures of the mind.

> While God could not be discovered in thought, it is possible to experience God in pure preconceptual consciousness. This intense, pre-linguistic experience is available only to those who will enter into themselves and recognise their own innermost feelings. Any attempt to put the divine experience into words inevitably detracts from it; furthermore, any such effort can necessarily be made only in terms of the words and concepts available in the subject's language and culture. It is in this way that various religions and creeds are born; but the basic, pre-linguistic experience is what really counts, and it is this which is shared across the divides of language, creed, and culture.[45]

The great attractiveness of this view, especially in Western academic cultures, should not be discounted. But its premise of a theologically mute, self-transcending subject is more than a little questionable today. As I have been arguing all along, it is more plausible, both biblically and philosophically, to conceive of mystical speech as an event of trinitarian speech. And if in certain phases of the mystical event there is, not just an *experience* of nothingness, but an actual loss of all experiencing and sensing, then this may argue for a very different interpretation than is usually proffered by the advocates of the common core approach. For if mystical consciousness is elicited by the address of God's *speech*, the Word, then the silence or absence that the mystic encounters may be appropriately interpreted not as the contentless pure consciousness of the subject, but precisely as the superabundance of the originary theo-logical event, namely the eternal begetting of the Word – and its expression in the crucified 'inarticulacy' of our humanity in Christ.

Those who advocate the importance of the experience of pure consciousness seem still to be debating the Kantian interpretation of religion on its own terms, searching out possible forms of consciousness that seem to supersede the usual Kantian categories. Hence the apparent concern of the common core advocates that, unless their position is adopted, the reliability and trustworthiness, not to say reality, of mystical experience will be under threat. Unless a way around the Kantian limits on consciousness can be found, it would seem, mystical experience is seen either as an impossibility in the first place (since one cannot, for Kant, have any direct experiences of God) or else as inevitably (and presumably prejudicially) skewed by its construction in terms of particular, historically limited religions. The Enlightenment thirst for the sacred chalice of a universal, Archimedean rationality remains, apparently, unquenched. But the testimony of Christian mystical writers seems not to be taken into account here; for their impression is not that they have been able to achieve a special state of experience prior to all the normal categories of thought, language, or their faith, but precisely that God has spoken to them by the very means of those categories, in complete analogy with (perhaps even extension of) the event of incarnation.

It is worth pondering the implications of all this for the theological construal of mystical texts. If one assumes that the theological language and trajectory is for the most part a secondary accretion, not central to the most significant moment (i.e., the experience of pure consciousness), then of course that theological language — however important it may have been to the mystical writer — is suddenly rated of only limited religious significance. The abiding quest in that case will be to discover the experience *behind* the doctrinal accretions and to locate that experience in relation to the picture Western academics have been forming of the common core experience of pure consciousness. This seems to me perilously akin to telling a poet that I wish she hadn't used so much imagery in her poetry as it all gets in the way of me deciphering the powerful experience she must have had to have written such an interesting poem. Such would nearly seem to be the case with those who, in Peter Moore's words, 'treat the doctrinal elements in an account as factors irrelevant, if not actually obstructive, to the phenomenological analysis of the experience in question.'[46] Indeed it would seem that far from short-circuiting the deeper functioning of the religious consciousness by overburdening it with doctrines, Christian mystical writers have generally found their theological understanding to be of the very essence of their mystical journey.

> The lack of doctrinal presuppositions might prevent the mystic not only from understanding and describing his mystical states but even from experiencing the fullness of these states in the first place. The possession of what could be called a 'doctrinal vocabulary' might indeed serve to precipitate features of experience which would otherwise remain at the margin of consciousness if not actually beneath it. [47]

When the search for a prior, theologically mute, experience behind the mystical text becomes the interpretive mode, much seems de-valued. It would seem odd, for example, if Hadewijch's understanding of the Trinity and the Incarnation were regarded as matters of indifference.

Of course, such interpreters are usually careful to work with texts which, in their view, describe precisely a contentless experience. Yet as we have seen, even in the case of Eckhart (often pointed to as affording good examples of 'pure consciousness'), the state of nothingness entered into by the believer is not a new and higher form of experience, but the transcending of *any* experience in the breakthrough of the Word back into the super-conceptual meaningfulness of God. Eckhart's trinitarianism is sometimes seen by common core advocates as the doctrinal perspective which we are bidden to leave behind for the experience of pure consciousness. But Oliver Davies argues that Eckhart's trinitarianism is fundamental to his conception of God as the eternal activity of 'understanding': 'an identity of the subject which knows, the object which is known and the act of knowing which is its own substance. . . . [a] sense of fertile diversity being perfectly contained within a single unified act'.[48] And as Jantzen remarks of that abiding source of negativity language, Dionysius, what one arrives at is

> the silence of the *ek-static* intellect, the intellect 'standing outside of itself', transcending itself in its insight into what God is/not. Here indeed is ineffability; but the ineffability is of *God* and of God's unspeakable wonder. It is important to be clear about this, because the ineffability of *God* should not be confused with the alleged ineffability of *subjective experience* with which contemporary philosophers are preoccupied. . . . That transcendence must also be understood, for them [Dionysius and Augustine], as inexhaustible fecundity, the very opposite of frustrated speechlessness.[49]

Again the point of all this is coming to recognize that the mystical texts themselves speak of a silence that is rich with meaning and is ultimately *not related* to their own subjective experience but to the reality of the One encountered. Not to recognize this is to muzzle the theological power of the mystics and to de-legitimate their theological perceptions.

The difficulty will always remain, of course, that the mystics often do speak of the encounter with God in terms of human consciousness rather than, say, reports about human history or politics. That is why Levinas is such a helpful reminder not to allow the language of consciousness to be misconstrued solipsistically, but to recognize that the shifting patterns of self-understanding are themselves always the result of an ongoing awakening, troubling, by the call of the other. Our modern tendency, abetted as we have seen by some later medieval focus on interiority and affectivity, is to equate the mystical with the experiential in ways that misread the renewal of the self *opaquely* rather than as the mysterious but *transparent sign of the divine other*. Rowan Williams gives an extremely illuminating reading of the final books Augustine's *de Trinitate* with these concerns in mind:

> What Augustine here discusses is the re-creation of the subject, the *mens*, as a whole in the divine image: as God becomes the term and object of all the mind's activities, the mind increasingly, in knowing itself, obliquely knows God. Its desire, its intentionality, is re-ordered from self to not-self, to its ground and context. There is no mention here of determinate 'experiences', nor would they contribute anything material to the discussion; Augustine seeks to define the condition of an historical self growing into fulfilment and learning to interpret theologically the whole process of its changing self-understanding. This can properly be described as 'mystical theology', I think, though there is not a word of the phenomenology of 'mysticism'.[30]

For Augustine, as for Aquinas, God and the self are not somehow competing for logical or experiential space – as if the more one grew in the knowledge of God, the less one could know oneself. On the contrary, the handing over of self to God results in the only kind of knowledge of God possible, and also the discovery of the deepest identity and ground of the self. So when mystical writers discuss shifts in self-consciousness, this should not be read as merely a discourse of interior experiences, but as inherently theological speech. What is significant is not particular sensations, even a special sensation of quiescence, but the reality of divine activity in the life of believer.

The particularity of mystical language

This brings us to the rather practical issues involved in any actual constructive dialogue between theology and spirituality. Schleiermacher's conviction was that theology proceeds best precisely by systematizing, abstracting from particular 'devotional' imagery towards the more trans-temporal and cross-cultural meaning which such language bears. And in the early part of this chapter I pointed to Bultmann as a more recent exponent of a similar move. By now I hope it is clear that I doubt very much whether theology can do any useful task by walking away from the concrete particularity of mystical language.

As Paul Ricoeur argues with respect to the particularity of biblical genres and imagery:

> The mistaken assumption here would be to take these forms of discourse as
> simply literary genres which ought to be neutralized so that we can extract their
> theological content. . . . To uproot this prejudice we must convince ourselves
> that the literary genres of the Bible do not constitute a rhetorical facade which
> it would be possible to pull down to reveal some thought content that is
> indifferent to its literary vehicle.[51]

The example of monastic mystical texts such as commentaries on the Song of
Songs may be helpful. As Leclercq has frequently pointed out, the intense
imagery of such texts, their refusal to follow a systematic order, are all part of
their *performance* as mystical texts; that is they 'work' precisely by means of this
metaphorical language which cannot simply be abstracted. Their work as
mystical texts, and their theological meaningfulness, is not isolated in a
'finished' product of definitions or formulas but in the 'unfinished' activity of
orienting the believer towards God. In a sense they *mean* as texts by letting God
supply the theological meaning in direct encounter with the readers of the
texts. Hence the language of much mystical speech, unlike the discourse of a
theology text book, is left open and unconcluded. Similarly the multiple
reversals of gender in imagery for God among Beguine writers like Hadewijch
or Mechtild is not to be flattened out in favour of either a singular positive
proposition or a supposedly ungendered unthematized experience. These
writers employ the dialectical play of gender language *in order to* convey the
transgressive, excessive reality of God; and hence to leave the particularity of
this language behind is to close off access to meaning. Mystical texts such as
these are linguistic performances, and it is the very patterning of their language
which allows them to draw the reader into a new perceptivity.[52]

Mystical texts of a more theoretical character are less likely to be misread,
though even in such cases the temptation is strong for our era to deal with the
text chiefly by speculating on the nature of the experiences that must underlie
such a theory of the mystical journey. But whether mystical texts are abstract
in tone or more experiential in imagery, their intentionality as *mystical* texts
is towards the hidden reality of God's encounter with humanity. The
movement of interpretation, therefore, is not backwards towards a putative
experience behind the text, but forwards into reflection on the structure of
that new world of divine–human encounter that is being opened up between
the text and the reader.

This suggests that constructive theological consultation of spirituality will
need to develop a capacious and sensitive form of discourse. The shape and
dynamic of a saint's life, for example, is equally a kind of text, and equally a
text that operates by inviting its 'readers' into their own encounter with the

reality that empowers the saint. The theological appropriation of mystical meaning, in such a case, is akin to aesthetic judgement. It requires a patient attention to the particular patterns that mark a given life, and to the trajectory of the saint's mission. The significance that such texts might have for theology (no matter whether they are written or lived), depends on how well the theologian is able to think imaginatively. A theologian will need to allow the dynamics of the text (for example the weight and aim of yearning, self-surrender, paradox, negation, etc.) to become a new interpretive framework for the theological task. Once one has learned not to take the patterns of the text as a description, then the text can function as a new theological *gestalt*, a hermeneutical field within which everything is seen in a new light and is charged with a new resonance. It would be as if the elements of a theological problem were suddenly charged with a new polarity and placed in a magnetic field.

The critical turn: questions of truth and intelligibility

Clearly the burden of this chapter has been to analyse how, exactly, mystical texts 'mean' and how, therefore, the theological interpreter might best go about the task of elucidating their theological meaningfulness. But since theology is all about the meaningfulness of *truth*, we must as least note briefly some of the possibilities for evaluating the truthfulness and intelligibility inherent in Christian spirituality. To retrieve mystical texts and spiritual practices as central to theological reflection is necessarily to retrieve them critically; for they themselves, ideally at least, embody the most critical questioning; they call for the most stringent stripping away of all illusions. Not to appropriate them critically would be to skew their own trajectory.

The 'problem' comes from the peculiar way that all such texts mean, namely by *testimony* to a new way of being in the world. This means that the referents of such texts are not, ultimately, objects per se. For God could never be an 'object' strictly speaking at all, and to turn whatever experience lies behind the text into the text's object is also problematic for the reasons I have discussed above. So we cannot be assessing the truth of mystical speech and spiritual lives by criteria drawn from other modes of discourse, say, the biological sciences. As Paul Ricoeur remarks: 'In terms of the modality of judgment, the interpretation of testimony is only probable, but it only appears as such when compared to a scientific ideal which governs only one of the different requirements of thought, which reigns in only one of the centers of reflection, namely knowledge of objects.'[53] Both Ricoeur and David Tracy have proposed the model of truth as *manifestation* and *response* in cases such as we are facing.[54] The truth of spirituality, like that of art, is disclosed through the presentation of meaning in ways that simultaneously veil and unveil, evoking a response in the observer who finally can only appropriate this truth by, in some sense, participating in it, adopting it as a reference for living.

In such a case one can only really evaluate the truth of spirituality by an assessment of the kind of life it leads one to embrace, the kind of reality it leads one to encounter. There are several traditions in the history of Christian spirituality that in fact serve this function, though we usually know them by their technical name: rules for the discernment of spirits. From the first desert hermits to Cassian's reformulations and on to Ignatius of Loyola and beyond, every era of Christian spirituality has developed critical tools for gauging the truthfulness of the spiritual stances proposed in given texts and saintly lives. The development of a broad and penetrating *theological* application of these rules for spiritual discernment would be an important step in regularizing the interaction of theology and spirituality. Just by way of a preliminary example of this approach, we might look at the critical tools adopted by Hans Urs von Balthasar in his reflection on spiritual texts.

In essence, von Balthasar adapts the insights of a variety of discernment traditions, chiefly the tradition of Ignatian spirituality, to the needs of theological reflection. What aspects of these traditions, he asks, can help us assess with greatest acuity the truthfulness of a given spiritual stance – and therefore its appropriateness as a matrix for theological reflection? Perhaps the most central discriminating factor proposed by von Balthasar is the assessment of a spirituality's ecclesial orientation. The ability of a spiritual text to bear witness to the truth is, for von Balthasar, intimately connected to its service to the *whole* church, and especially to the church's mission to embody Christ concretely in the world. Thus any wide-eyed embrace of 'every alleged or authentic vision, audition, stigmatisation, and so on' is to be strictly eschewed, for such phenomena are matters of indifference in themselves and must justify their validity by showing an 'integral connection with the total Church'.[55]

Von Balthasar's concern is that any spirituality which begins to focus primarily on the stages and development of its own relationship with God will come to rely more and more on the *experiential signs of its progress*, gradually losing sight of the ecclesial life for the sake of which – it may be – these mystical charisms were given. So the test becomes the service to which saints or mystics put their spirituality. Is it a gift cherished for its own sake or is it always handed over freely to the needs of others, in obedience to the self-giving love of Christ? On these grounds, von Balthasar states his 'determinative maxim': 'it is not *experience* of a union with God which represents the yardstick of perfection or the highest stage of ascent, but rather *obedience*, which can be quite as tightly bound to the experience of abandonment by God as to the experience of union with God'.[56] If Jesus is the truth of God made flesh, then for von Balthasar the crucial rule for the discernment of a spirituality's theological fruitfulness is precisely its *transparency* to Christ and its freedom from self-preoccupation.

Since spiritual texts are, as we have seen, not ultimately descriptions of objects but invitations to particular ways of life, it seems appropriate to assess their truthfulness in this fashion. In a sense it is discerning their truthfulness by observing in what direction their spiritual gravity seems to be pulling them. What kind of spiritual reality, in other words, would account for the particular shape of a given spirituality? If the pattern of Christ's life is an indication of the 'gravitational' pull that God exerts on human life, does a given spirituality seem to be in orbit around this centre or some other (ultimately idolatrous) reality? Of course von Balthasar's formulation of such an approach to discernment is merely an example. Other quite powerful tools for the discernment of a given spirituality's truthfulness could be developed and tested very concretely. The point is that it is this *kind* of measure of truth that must be adopted here.

Finally, there remain the issues of intelligibility; how conceivable are the patterns of life engendered by a spirituality – in terms of their rough coherence both with what we generally believe to be the case about reality and with what is called for by the demands of justice. 'The danger', as Tracy points out, 'is that this set of criteria (under rubrics, e.g., like strict verification and falsification) will so quickly take over that the notion of truth as manifestation will quickly become a distant memory'.[57] It is not only legitimate but vital to ask *whose* standards of rationality are being held as the plumbline, and with *whose* gender and political location these standards are coherent. Liberation theologians have proposed the location of the oppressed as the test case for judging what counts as 'intelligible', for in such a case it would seem likely, at least, that standards of rationality and coherence would not be adopted which perpetuate or 'rationalize' the plight of suffering people.

This seems an altogether salutary proposal, especially when one considers how easily contemporary spirituality is subborned into the role of enabler for popular, media-driven, consumerist culture. Furthermore, the history of Christian mysticism is itself replete not only with committed social reformers and activists, but with the oppressive tendencies of academic, ecclesiastical and popular cultures to marginalize spiritual teachers and mystics. The coherence of mystical speech and its attendant capacity to frame the work of theological construction will need to be judged to a large extent in terms of practical effects. Spirituality that builds *justice* has a powerfully valid claim on the attention of the theologian.

Notes

1 Ron Hansen, *Mariette in Ecstasy* (New York: HarperCollins, 1991), 179.

2 See especially Frei's ground-breaking work, *The Eclipse of Biblical Narrative: A Study of Eighteenth and Nineteenth Century Hermeneutics* (New Haven: Yale University Press, 1974).

3 See, e.g., Rudolf Bultmann, 'New Testament and Mythology' in Hans Werner Bartsch, ed., *Kerygma and Myth*, 2 vols. (London: SPCK, 1962 and 1964).

4 Roger A. Johnson, *The Origins of Demythologization: Philosophy and Historiography in the Theology of Rudolf Bultmann. Studies in the History of Religions*, XXVIII (Leiden: E. J. Brill, 1974), 254.

5 See, e.g., Philip Sheldrake, *Spirituality and History: Questions of Interpretation and Method* (New York: Crossroad, 1992); especially chapter 7, 'Interpreting Spiritual Texts'. Also, William M. Thompson, *Fire and Light: The Saints and Theology* (New York: Paulist Press, 1987), and *Christology and Spirituality* (New York: Crossroad, 1991).

6 Karl Rahner, 'The Experience of God Today', in *Theological Investigations*, vol. XI, trans. David Bourke (New York: The Seabury Press, 1974), 149–65; here 160–1.

7 Paul Ricoeur, 'Towards a Hermeneutic of the Idea of Revelation' in *Essays on Biblical Interpretation*, ed. Lewis S. Mudge (Philadelphia: Fortress Press, 1980), 73–118; here, 95.

8 Denys Turner, *The Darkness of God: Negativity in Christian Mysticism* (Cambridge: Cambridge University Press, 1995), 20.

9 Michael A. Sells, *Mystical Languages of Unsaying* (Chicago: University of Chicago Press, 1994), 217.

10 Ibid., 4.

11 Rowan Williams, 'Language, Reality and Desire in Augustine's *De Doctrina*', *Journal of Literature & Theology*, vol. 3, no. 2 (July 1989):138–50.

12 Ibid., 141.

13 Ibid.

14 Ibid., 144.

15 There are a number of useful surveys of Eckhartian thought; see particularly Bernard McGinn, 'Theological Summary' in the Introduction to *Meister Eckhart: The Essential Sermons, Commentaries, Treatises, and Defense*, trans. Edmund Colledge and Bernard McGinn. *Classics of Western Spirituality* (New York: Paulist Press, 1981).

16 Eckhart, *German Sermons* no. 6, in *Meister Eckhart: Essential Sermons*, 187.

17 Idem., *German Sermons* no. 5b, in *Meister Eckhart: Essential Sermons*, 184.

18 Idem., *German Sermons* no. 22, in *Meister Eckhart: Essential Sermons*, 196.

19 Ibid. My emphasis.

20 Idem., *German Sermons* No. 48, in *Meister Eckhart: Essential Sermons*, 198.

21 Donald F. Duclow, 'Hermeneutics and Meister Eckhart', *Philosophy Today*, vol. 28, 1/4 (Spring 1984):36–43, here 40.

22 Jean Leclercq, *The Love of Learning and the Desire for God: A Study of Monastic Culture*, trans. Catherine Misrahi (New York: Fordham University Press, 1974), 320–1.

23 Paul Ricoeur, *Interpretation Theory: Discourse and the Surplus of Meaning* (Fort Worth, Texas: Texas Christian University Press, 1976), 16. My emphasis.

24 Sells, *Mystical Languages of Unsaying*, 9–10.

25 Ibid., 209. I would not necessarily agree with Sells that the event of meaning in reading mystical texts is always limited to the constitution of 'mystical union' – there is a very wide range of mystical encounters that mystical texts seem to mimic or evoke – yet certainly mystical union can stand as a paradigmatic case.

26 Wolfgang Iser, 'Interaction between Text and Reader' in *The Reader in the Text: Essays on Audience and Interpretation*, ed. Susan R. Suleiman and Inge Crosman (Princeton: Princeton University Press, 1980), 106–19, here 111–12.

27 Paul Ricoeur, 'Towards a Hermeneutic of the Idea of Revelation' in *Essays on Biblical Interpretation*, ed. Lewis S. Mudge (Philadelphia: Fortress Press, 1980), 73–118, here 100.

28 Ibid., 101.

29 Ibid.

30 Ibid., 104.

31 Herbert McCabe, OP, *God Matters*, (London: Geoffrey Chapman, 1987), 93.

32 Ricoeur, *Interpretation Theory*, 11–12.

33 'So long as a man has this as his will, that he wants to fulfill God's dearest will, he has not the poverty about which we want to talk. Such a person has a will with which he wants to fulfill God's will, and that is not true poverty' (Eckhart, *German Sermons* no. 52, *Eckhart: Essential Sermons*, 200).

34 Emmanuel Levinas, 'Revelation in the Jewish Tradition', in *The Levinas Reader*, ed. Seán Hand (Oxford: Blackwell Publishers, 1989), 190–210, here 194.

35 Ibid., 195.

36 Nicholas Lash has very helpful things to say about the 'performative' element inherent in the interpretation of some kinds of texts. See 'Performing the Scriptures' in *Theology on the Way to Emmaus* (London: SCM Press, 1986) and more recently on 'Doctrine as Protocol' in *Easter in Ordinary* (Notre Dame: University of Notre Dame Press, 1990).

37 Levinas, 'Revelation in the Jewish Tradition', 205.

38 Idem., 'God and Philosophy', in *Levinas Reader*, 186.

39 See Philip Endean, 'The Ignatian Prayer of the Senses', *Heythrop Journal* XXXI (1990): 391–418.

40 Turner, *Darkness of God*, 178–9. Emphasis is original.

41 Robert K. C. Forman, ed., *The Problem of Pure Consciousness. Mysticism and Philosophy* (Oxford: Oxford University Press, 1990), 7.

42 Turner, *Darkness of God*, 4; and also see 245–53.

43 Grace Jantzen, *Power, Gender and Christian Mysticism*, Cambridge Studies in Ideology and Religion 8 (Cambridge: Cambridge University Press, 1995), 346.

44 Forman and others have been responding to the essays of Steven Katz and those

of others he has edited in three books: Steven Katz, ed. *Mysticism and Philosophical Analysis* (Oxford: Oxford University Press, 1978); idem., ed., *Mysticism and Religious Traditions* (Oxford: Oxford University Press, 1983); and idem., ed. *Mysticism and Language* (Oxford: Oxford University Press, 1992). Katz et al. have in turn been responding to the dominant common core approach to mystical experience in this century, deriving especially from the philosophy of religion of Schleiermancher and William James; for extensive bibliography and concise survey of all the questions at issue see Bernard McGinn, *The Presence of God: A History of Western Christian Mysticism*, vol. 1, *The Foundations of Mysticism*, 291–43.

45   Jantzen, *Power, Gender and Mysticism*, 344; see also by Jantzen, 'Mysticism and Experience', *Religious Studies* 25 (1989):295-315 and idem., 'Could There be a Mystical Core of Religion?', *Religious Studies* 26 (1990): 59-71.

46   Peter Moore, 'Mystical Experience, Mystical Doctrine, Mystical Technique' in Katz, *Mysticism and Philosophical Analysis*, 110. For a good example of this see the 'common core' approach of J. F. Staal for whom the experience alone is significant and the 'added on' doctrinal super-structure is worthless or meaningless: *Exploring Mysticism* (Los Angeles: University of California Press, 1978).

47   Ibid., 112.

48   Oliver Davies, *Meister Eckhart: Mystical Theologian* (London: S.P.C.K., 1991), 206.

49   Jantzen, *Power, Gender and Christian Mysticism*, 283-4.

50   Rowan Williams, 'Butler's *Western Mysticism*', *The Downside Review*, vol. 102 (1984), 197-215, here 204.

51   Paul Ricoeur, 'Towards a Hermeneutic of the Idea of Revelation', 90-1.

52   For an analogy regarding scriptural texts, see the very fine essay by Hans Frei, 'Of the Resurrection of Christ', chapter in *Theology and Narrative. Selected Essays*, ed., George Hunsinger and William C. Placher (Oxford: Oxford University Press, 1993).

53   Paul Ricoeur, 'The Hermeneutics of Testimony', 150.

54   See, e.g., David Tracy, 'The Uneasy Alliance Reconceived: Catholic Theological Method, Modernity, and Postmodernity', *Theological Studies* 50 (1989): 548-70, esp. 564ff.

55   Hans Urs von Balthasar, *The Glory of the Lord: A Theological Aesthetics*, vol. 1, *Seeing the Form*, trans. Erasmo Leiva-Merikaki (Edinburgh: T. & T. Clark, 1982), 411.

56   Idem., 'Zur Ortsbestimmung Christlicher Mystik', in *Grundfragen der Mystik*, with Werner Beierwaltes and Alois M. Haas (Einsiedeln: Johannes Verlag, 1974), 59. See also von Balthasar's essay, 'The Gospel as Norm and Critique of All Spirituality in the Church' in his *Explorations in Theology*, vol. 3, *Creator Spirit*.

57   Tracy, 'The Uneasy Alliance Reconsidered', 565-6.

Part II

MYSTICAL THEOLOGY IN PRACTICE

Chapter 5

TRINITARIAN SELF-ABANDON AND THE PROBLEM OF DIVINE SUFFERING

With this chapter we turn at last from history and theory to the practice of theology. The real test of the idea that spirituality and theology are meant to work in concert surely lies in the fruits of such a conversation. So let me begin at the source whence both Christian spirituality and theology begin to flow.

Being drawn into an encounter, being led to make a response – these lie at the heart of Christianity. The unfolding of the Christian mystery in the life of the community has always made this clear. For whenever the church's worship has been authentic it has drawn people into an encounter. Not a bare encounter of the creature with the Creator, but the intimate encounter and response of Jesus with the One he called Father. The shape of the Christian community is patterned on this relationship, and for that reason its rhythms are baptismal and eucharistic. In baptism, Christians understand themselves to be marking sacramentally the indwelling power of the Holy Spirit, who evokes in the community a life of response to Jesus. And it is this Spirit who therefore incorporates persons into the communal Body of Christ. As John Zizioulas, speaking of early Christian life, has rightly said: 'The new identity given "in the Spirit" was constituted through incorporation into the body of Christ, the church, through a new set of relationships. These relationships were identical to the relationship of Christ to the Father.'[1] The response to Jesus that the Spirit evokes, in other words, is not a neutral acknowledgement but a willingness to follow Jesus, to be taken, blessed, broken and given over to the purposes of God – it is, in other words, to enter into 'the relationship of Christ to the Father'. For this reason so many Christian eucharistic prayers call upon the Spirit to draw bread and wine into the offering of Jesus, making it to be his very life poured out for others, just as Christians experience the Spirit as the one who calls and transforms *them* into that same self-outpouring which is Christ.[2] In the Gospel according to Luke, it is this same Spirit who draws Mary's availability and faithfulness into the purposes of God, thus drawing forth from her a human reply to God's speaking – a human responsivity that could become the very body of that speaking, the Incarnation of that Word.

Thus Christians have come to think about their life together: its *embodiment* of the structure of Jesus' earthly life in relationship to the One he called 'Abba' in their Spirit. And so, ultimately, Christians have come to think about the identity of God, an identity glimpsed and hinted at in this three-fold pattern of encounter and relationship. Throughout this book I have been suggesting that specifically *Christian* spirituality is never about a silent absorption in a putative 'inner self' but is rather the activity of being drawn into an encounter with the other. In fact I want to suggest that it is this relationship with the other that 'makes' us who we are at all, for it is in responding to the drawing near of the other that we become real 'persons' with unique and cherishable identities.

In saying this I am, I fear, trying to say a great deal all at once. For I am saying, first, that Christian spirituality is at heart the bapstismal and eucharistic journey itself: being drawn by the Spirit into the encounter of Jesus with the Father. And this means I'm saying, second, that the very structure of Christian spirituality points to all that Christians are trying to say about God when they confess the doctrine of the Trinity. Namely, that God in God's own eternal activity of being God is no more an isolated, monadic, 'inner self' than we are. Instead, I want to suggest, God's existence is that very relational encounter which structures the events concerning Jesus and his ongoing Body, the church. God, that is to say, is an eternal activity of outpouring, embodying, and responding love. David Cunningham's book in this series addresses the theology of God's triunity in creative detail. Here we are concerned to see simply that what we call Christian 'spirituality' is really the communal pattern of life by which Jesus' followers are drawn ever more deeply into his own 'encounter with the other'; *spirituality*, in other words, *is the activity of being led by the Spirit into Christ's relationship with the Father.* I will show in the next chapter how this helps us to understand the doctrine of the Incarnation, and in the final chapter its implications for our understanding of what it means to be human persons. But now we want to consider simply the Christian doctrine of God, the Trinity, in the light of this recognition – that Christian spirituality, and theological reflection upon it, both spring from and lead back directly into this relational encounter of Jesus and the Father in their Spirit.

Divine Suffering and Mythological Gods

As we turn to the constructive dialogue between Christian spirituality and doctrinal thought, we notice that issues which can easily become isolated from each other in systematic theology are often reconnected in helpful ways.

In this case we are dealing with issues in contemporary trinitarian thought that are usually seen as quite separate problems. The first issue regards the manner in which some contemporary theologians (e.g., Jürgen Moltmann, Eberhard Jüngel) have envisioned a very dramatic 'opposition' between the Father and the Son, so that the historical dereliction of Jesus on the cross is seen as *constitutive* of God's own existence. Other theologians have criticized this view as implicating the divine life in temporal suffering, or even as implying that involvement in time and space are somehow necessary for God to be God.

So John Thompson criticizes such authors for making God subject to some external necessity by acting in time, rather than understanding all God's temporal activity as God's radically free choice.[3] Behind such concerns is the idea that if God can only be God through messy involvement in the suffering and confusion of temporal existence, then God is not really so stable, trustworthy and ultimately powerful a being after all. Karl Rahner, for another example, though convinced that the eternal life of God must indeed be thought of in terms of the history of Jesus, was equally appalled at the idea that God is simply 'the fellow sufferer who understands' (in the classic phrase of the Process thinker Alfred North Whitehead). Rahner commented: 'To put it crudely, it does not help me to escape from my mess and mix-up and despair if God is in the same predicament. . . . From the beginning I am locked into its horribleness while God — if this word continues to have any meaning — is in a true and authentic and consoling sense the God who does not suffer, the immutable.'[4] So in Rahner's view, while it is crucial for Christian thought to reconnect its doctrine of God with the historical struggle of Jesus, it would be wrong to do so in any way that seems to involve God in change, or to make God subject to our human sufferings. While few theologians today would want to argue strictly for the ancient idea of divine immutability, there are many who would join Rahner in worrying that to jettison this sense of God's unchangeableness may also threaten to reduce God to a tragic super-creature. God would thus be seen as enmeshed in the suffering of time like the creature, and therefore would be unable to save the creature from this trauma because God is mired 'in the same predicament' (as Rahner put it just above). Can God suffer, even 'freely' (whatever that might mean), and still be the God of salvation, living and true?

This is the question Christian theologians are having to confront today in new ways.

The other issue I want to raise here is usually discussed as a distinct problem, though it is in fact closely linked to the first. And that is the concern that the new Western interest in stressing the radical *relationality* of the Father, the Son and the Holy Spirit may be tending to slip disconcertingly towards a delusionally mythological picture: three distinct deities attempting to maintain some kind of unity among themselves while trapped in the cosmic struggle of time and human suffering. For some while now, important new trinitarian proposals from writers such as Colin Gunton and Catherine Mowry LaCugna have been raising highly critical questions regarding what they perceive as a Western theological focus (usually attributed to Augustine) on the unity of the divine essence at the apparent expense of the reality of the three Divine Persons.[5]

But when many of these new emphases on the trinitarian relationality of God are read against the background of radically cross-oriented theologies such as Moltmann's, what seems to develop are problematic 'forms of trinitarian pluralism that threaten to become mythological – the divine life as interactive drama. . . . a highly anthropomorphic plurality of agencies'.[6] Consider this famous passage from Moltmann's 1973 work, *The Crucified God*:

> In the forsakenness of the Son the Father also forsakes himself. In the surrender of the Son the Father also surrenders himself, though not in the same way. . . . The Son suffers dying, the Father suffers the death of the Son. The grief of the Father is here just as important as the death of the Son. The Fatherlessness of the Son is matched by the Sonlessness of the Father, and if God has constituted himself as the Father of Jesus Christ, then he also suffers the death of his Fatherhood in the death of the Son.[7]

Here the concept of the divine Persons seems to have donned the apparel of modern Cartesian subjectivity. It is remarkably as if the *relational structure* of the divine life has been metamorphosed into divided *autonomous selves*, trapped in their private griefs and sorrows even while they may struggle along in the drama of relationship with each other. It is one thing to say, following the Cappadocians, that the infinitely relational communion of the divine Persons is identical with the divine being, but it is quite another to suggest that this relationality is analogous to the struggle towards relationship of separate human selves. So how can we talk robustly about the trinitarian relationality of God without veering off towards the very tritheism to which the doctrine of the Trinity was formulated as an antidote? That is another trinitarian question that theologians are facing today.

So the problem is whether we can find a way of talking together about God which rightly sees the events concerning Jesus as constitutive of our encounter with God, but does *not* do so in a way that creates God in our own image. There is the question, to put it bluntly, about God's reliability as a salvific deity: if God is God precisely in and through the triune trauma of the Cross, through the 'grief of the Father' and the 'death of the Son' (in Moltmann's phrase), is such a God going to be too grief-stricken and victimized to be of much use to the universe? And then we have the connected question of whether such a powerful exposition of the trinitarian relationality (not to say opposition) of God tends to reduce Christian talk of the divine Persons to something bordering on mythology.[8]

The Holy Spirit as Matrix for Trinitarian Thought

Our task now is to set this complex of questions within the framework of the Christian spiritual life. Thus we shall be able to see not only the *connection* between the question of divine kenosis and radical trinitarian relationality, but also a new way of thinking about them altogether. We can arrive at this perspective, I believe, by way of the one element most dramatically absent from most of the modern Western discussion: reflection on the Holy Spirit.

Christians believe that as the incarnate Word of God, Jesus does not simply placard some useful information about God before the eyes of the world. If that were the case, one could respond to God's Word with a kind of polite neutrality. Instead, however, Jesus seems to confront persons with a very definite invitation and call for decision. In that sense it is a bit like a marriage proposal; the one receiving the proposal can reject it, but if the proposal is accepted, then an affirmative response that is real and full requires more than a benignly neutral assent – it requires entering into a new state of life. Analogously, a real *response* to Jesus, if it is affirmative at all, inevitably involves being united with Christ in his death and resurrection. And how is this possible?

Christians believe that the Holy Spirit who confronts them with this offer in the historical particularity of Jesus' existence is *also* present in men and women of every era, race and nation, enabling them to hear and respond to this Word. Christians understand this presence of God, Holy Spirit, as eliciting from them the only real response that one can make to God's self-communication in Jesus, namely a willingness to participate in Jesus' own life and mission. So the strain of distance between Jesus and the One he calls Father is something Christians are drawn into by the Spirit, and therefore the radical relationality of the three divine Persons becomes the very milieu of the spiritual journey.

St Paul understood the Spirit as the power of God which initiates the vindication of Jesus as Son of God by raising him from the dead (Rom 1.4). The Holy Spirit is God presenting God's Word to the community and within the community, thus initiating the whole creation's response to this Word spoken in the events concerning Jesus. In this way, the despair and apparent dereliction of Jesus on the Cross are continually unfolding with new meaning in the life of the community. Early Christians connected Jesus' resurrection with the sending of the Spirit who would lead them into the truth of Jesus' words and deeds (Jn 14.26; 16.12–14); thus the community is initiated into the hidden depths of his relationship with the Father, and from that perspective they begin to think in new ways about Jesus' death. The painful distance that sin seemed to have pried open between the Father and the Beloved Son comes to be seen in a new light, as the outpouring in history of the eternal divine self-giving. The coming of the Spirit within the Christian community makes it possible, even necessary, for the community to participate in the mystery of Jesus' dying and rising, and so to interpret his relationship with the Father *from within* – precisely by becoming, as the Body of Christ, the living sign of God's embrace of all creation within the love of the Father and the Son in their Spirit.

William Temple (1881–1944) emphasized the importance of this aspect of God's activity: 'The Holy Spirit, as made known to us in our experience, is the power whereby the created universe – which the Father creates by the agency of the Son, His self-revealing Word – is brought into harmonious response to the love which originated it. . . . Love creates; Love by self-sacrifice reveals itself to the created thing; Love thereby calls out from the created thing the Love which belongs to it as Love's creature, so making it what Love created it to be.'[9] God as love, in Temple's view, does not remain in a starkly dialectical opposition between an eternal One and a historically self-manifested One. In fact it is the emphasis on the bareness of this opposition between Father and Son that leads to the misconstrual of trinitarian language in terms of an anthropocentric drama between conflicting selves. If we speak of the suffering of the Son in the extremity of the Father's self-emptying self-disclosure, it is only because the Spirit is the crucial eternal affirmation and acceptance of this Word. And because this Word comes to be spoken into the broken history of humanity, the same One who speaks to us in Jesus also speaks within us as the Holy Spirit, calling forth from us the acceptance of this Word.

All this is to say that God's self-expression is not just a bare announcement but a saving event. God the Word speaks the mystery of God into history, and because God's life is ultimately giving and sharable life, God's Word is only fully realized insofar as it is heard, understood, accepted. In the *eternal* life of God, this self-outpouring (Son) and self-understanding (Spirit) take place in the infinite glory of God's perfect intelligibility (that is, God is utterly intelligible in God's own being). But, Christians believe, God chooses in love and freedom to include the creation of a universe in the expression of God's own being; and so the divine activity of understanding and interpreting this Word takes place not only in the joy of heaven but also in the struggle and confusion of broken human history. And 'Holy Spirit' is the name Christians give to the activity of God by which the community is led into that ongoing process of hearing and interpreting Jesus – a process of reception which, in the world we have made, must be a continuing work of reconciliation.[10]

Thus the Christian community is led by the Spirit to hear and respond to God's Word, and that response takes the form of a new Body of reconciliation, offering the power of Christ in the heart of the world. This leads the community to new reflection on the meaning of God's Word addressed to the world. So if the Christian spiritual journey is the process of coming to hear and enact God's Word to our world, to be, together, the Body of Christ, this should lead Christian thought to a new framework for understanding God's triunity. Theology might begin to see the 'opposition' between the Father and the Son not so much in terms of a traumatic dialectic inexorably drawing God into the warp of history, but rather in terms of an overflowing of divine creative energy: the power of Love giving voice to itself even in the lostness of human existence.

If we bear in mind God's constant activity as Spirit, fostering creation's reception and understanding of the Word, then the 'disappearance' of the Son into the plight of history might be construed less as a diastasis introduced into the very heart of the divine and more as a divine faithfulness to God's own being and thus to God's creation; for it reveals an unwillingness to allow the meaning of God's creative love to go unheard – no matter how deafening the noise of human alienation. God the Holy Spirit 'drives' Jesus the Word into the wilderness of human lostness, precisely so that even there God may be encountered.

I am proposing, then, that Christian theology might best reflect on the dramatic expression of trinitarian relationality in the story of Jesus by thinking about the fact that humanity has been invited *into* this relationship between the Father and the Son. Indeed, the role of God the Holy Spirit in the story of this relationship has been to draw the Word further and further into creation, into what is 'not-God', precisely so that creation might be reconciled and drawn into fellowship with God.

Some Pneumatological Grammar

There are two elements that I especially wish to highlight in this kind of Christian talk about the Holy Spirit. If we can be clear about these, then it will be easier to facilitate the dialogue between mystical thought and constructive theology on the doctrine of the Trinity. The first point is the idea of the Spirit as God-in-the-other. And the second is that we come to *know* this immanent presence primarily as *the love which arouses us to full personhood* by inciting in us a response to (and a participation in) *the personhood of Jesus the Word incarnate*. Let me now say a bit about both of these points.

First some thoughts about the Holy Spirit as God-in-the-other. We can begin by thinking of the Word as the Father's 'otherness' to himself, the Word as the expression of the Father's ecstatic love which causes there to be an 'other' in God. Now the same ecstatic love which leads to the eternal begetting of the Son from the Father also leads to the eternal filial response of the Son towards the Father. Just as the Father is identified, perhaps we could even say 'constituted' by his eternal desire to pour out the divine life for the Other-in-God (the Son), so the Son is identified as Word because he desires eternally to speak forth the Father's giving life. Christians believe that this eternal giving life is identified in its true glory and majesty because it does not choose to be God for Godself alone, but to be God for others. God, that is, in an eternally free act of love, chooses to mirror the divine 'othering' (which takes place eternally *within* the divine life) by bringing into being a *created* other. It is an expression of the eternal fecundity of the Source, the Abyss of God's personal being, that its richness can pour out infinitely, not only begetting and sustaining rich mutuality within itself but also bringing into existence that which had no being at all. Put another way, the Father chooses to speak himself, to utter the Word, by bringing into being and fellowship with himself a universe. In that sense all things come to be through the Word and in the Word.

It is an expression of the divine richness to bring what was not into being; and so also it is an expression of the Word's ecstatic love for the giving Source to resound to the praise of that Source not only within the Abyss of divine love itself, but from within all the creatures, all that is 'other' than God. And so finally the Word reflects the divine glory by speaking the promise of this reconciling and giving love in the very midst of that which is not only 'other' than God but also opposed and alienated from God. The Word speaks God by being incarnate, by being made to be sin, by giving himself up to death. Never did the Father's Word more perfectly resound with the infinity of the divine love than when it was made perfect in the obedience of that earthly mission, for there the Word speaks even in the final silence of the Cross.

In all this God is God precisely because God chooses to *be* God by giving Godself away – a free self-donation which by its very infinity speaks not of the impoverishment but the *fecundity* of God's love. And this ecstatic love which 'beguiles' God out of heaven is no alien force, no automatic instinct of a Neoplatonic essence of goodness, but it is rather the very personal being of God, the Holy Spirit. Christos Yannaras makes this point by drawing on the distinction between nature (*ousia*) and person (*hypostasis*) which had been formulated by the Cappadocians and refined by Maximus. God, argues Yannaras, is not to be thought of as some divine nature which is driven by the exigencies of its own essence into self-diffusion; rather, the life of God is characterized by the pure loving freedom of the divine Persons.

> God is not obliged by his Essence to be God; he is not subject to the necessity of his existence. God exists, since he is the Father, the one who affirms freely his will to exist, giving birth to the Son and sending forth the Spirit. He exists, since he loves and love is only an event of freedom. Freely and from love, the Father . . . hypostasizes his Being in a Triad of Persons, constitutes the principle and mode of his Existence as a community of personal freedom and love.[11]

We might almost say that it is because there is a divine Father who loves in freedom that there is God per se. The eternal event of God being God is the event of the Father's freedom to love which gives birth to the Son and sends forth the Spirit. But because there is no kind of temporal subordination in God, only in our speech about God, we might also say that the Father *is* the Father precisely because of his Spirit, his ecstatic love which identifies him as the One who is and who will be because this One eternally chooses to be *for Another*.[12]

So God the Holy Spirit, thought of as analogous to ecstatic love, might almost be said not only to *be* a divine Person but to be the Person-constituting activity of God. For my suggestion has been that it is the Spirit as *ekstasis* who works within the divine Abyss the free decision to pour out divine life as 'Other', as Word – and it is this very begetting which constitutes the Father as Father. Again it is the same Spirit as ecstatic love who constitutes the Word as Word by filling him with the desire to respond to the Father, to celebrate the fruitfulness of the divine Source by giving voice to it in the creation of a universe and the re-creation of it in the covenant of divine fellowship.

Thus God the Holy Spirit, I am suggesting, might be thought of as the Love who in this sense is not simply a 'bond' of love between the Father and the Son but who truly marks the Father and Son as who they are, as Persons, by drawing them into this reciprocal ecstasy. The Romanian theologian Dumitru Staniloae remarks that the Holy Spirit 'is the hypostatic [personal] form of the eternal actualizing and conveying of the Father's love for the Son and the Son's response to this same love.'[13] And since God is not a composite of psychological moments each of which are somehow slightly less than God in Godself, the Father's 'love' and Son's 'response' (as Staniloae puts it) can be nothing less than God again, God the Holy Spirit.

There is an early indication of this idea in Augustine on *The Trinity*. As we know, Augustine is not in this work simply looking for edifying analogies between the operations of the human mind and the trinitarian being of God. For what Augustine will unveil in the later books is that epiphanic moment when the mind's activities, turned at last directly to the divine life in itself, become transparent to that life, energized and indwelt by God's own knowing and loving of Godself. Near the end of Book IX, the Bishop of Hippo is exploring the mysterious role of the will in the process of human understanding. Of course Augustine holds, as is often noted, that in understanding we not only come to *knowledge* but we also *affirm* what we know, that is, we relate to the object of our understanding by means of our will. I think of brussels sprouts and at the same moment I feel my repulsion at the very thought. But even in this case of a negative relationship of will to knowing, there is this intrinsic relationship between willing and knowing. For quite beyond any mere 'feelings' I may have about what I know, it is concomitant with the very activity of knowing that I also behold, respond to, or interpret whatever emerges for reflection.

Yet Augustine is not satisfied with this reading; perhaps his personal knowledge of the passionate and often recalcitrant nature of human beings led him to wonder about a far more originary and constitutive role for the will in the activity of human understanding. 'Knowledge is a thing discovered', he writes, 'and the discovery is often preceded by a search which aims at resting in its object. Search is a *striving* (*appetitus*) for discovery.'[14] Augustine points to an inherent tension in this process, for the striving remains 'in a kind of suspense' as the seeker hungers and yearns for the desired object. And while this is unfolding, the 'striving' and 'suspense' might be said to be constitutive of the seeker, for this yearning is what energizes and draws the seeker towards the other, the object of knowledge. The Bishop continues:

> We may say that the mind's 'bringing forth' is preceded by a kind of striving, by which, in the seeking and finding of what we desire to know, knowledge is born as offspring. It follows that this striving, whereby knowledge is conceived and brought forth, cannot properly be called 'brought forth'

or 'offspring'. This same striving, or eager pursuit of the thing yet to be known, becomes love (*amor*) of the thing known, when it holds in its embrace the offspring, the knowledge, in which it delights, and joins it to the begetter.[15]

We can see here how Augustine illuminates the element of desirous appetite in this process, for he highlights the sense of 'eager pursuit' leading to 'embrace' and unitive 'delight'. This language foreshadows his later conceptualization of the Holy Spirit as the energy of love which constitutes the relationship of the Word and its Source. Here we simply wish to note the originary role of this erotic striving: on one hand it defines the mind as intrinsically relational, in search of its object (knowledge), and on the other hand it defines the desired object of thought as that which is begotten by desire and destined for delighted embrace. Finally this striving, having marked and identified the Seeker and the Sought, is itself fully identified and realized as love; for now the Seeker and the Sought are constituted in relationship to each other and so the striving originary dynamic of their relationship is recognized and consummated as Love.

Now we can turn more briefly to the basis for this Christian talk about the Spirit, namely what happens to individuals as they are drawn into the personal relationship between the Source and the Word. Christians come to know the Holy Spirit as the person-constituting love of the divine life precisely because in an analogous way the Spirit awakens human individuals to fully personal existence. The Spirit does this by arousing human beings, stirring them to a new form of existence which discovers itself by giving itself away in love and freedom to others. The Spirit does this, Christians believe, by drawing individuals into the new relational existence opened to them in Christ, enabling them to discover true personal being in the mutual love of Father and Son in their Spirit.

Christians exist as those who have been given a new identity by virtue of what Christ has done. The earliest community understands Jesus as someone who has died for them and now also confronts them in a new and living way with the decision of his own life, confronts them with his own self-giving for them, their abandonment of him, and his living offer of reconciliation and new life in him: 'I have been crucified with Christ; it is no longer I who live, but Christ who lives in me; and the life I now live in the flesh I live by faith in the Son of God, who loved me and gave himself for me' (Gal 2.20). Plunged by the Holy Spirit into the death and resurrection of Jesus, Christians find they can live no longer for themselves or from themselves but only for and from Christ.

The result of this is what a number of Eastern Orthodox writers have called a shift from purely *biological* life as an individual to *ecclesial* life as a person.[16] The brokenness of human nature lies in the privatizing attempt to fulfil our nature, to *be* ourselves, in *opposition* to others instead of in loving relationship; in this way humanity degenerates into individualism, a kind of perverted counterfeit of the true personhoonhood humans are offered by virtue of being created in God's image. Yannaras puts it thus:

> What constitutes man as an hypostasis [or person], what gives him an ego and identity is not psychosomatic functions, but his relationship with God, the fact that God loves him with an erotic singularity that calls into existence what does not exist (Rm 4.17), establishing and founding the personal otherness of man. Man is a person, an image of God, since he exists as a possibility of responding to the erotic call of God.[17]

Insofar as humans turn away from the 'personalizing' (or person-constitut-ing) call of God they fall prey to the self-preserving preoccupations of mortal human nature. In Christ human nature has been concretized or personalized in the Person of the eternal Son, restoring to human nature its capacity for imaging the divine likeness by living in relationship with God. Jesus, in other words, lives his human nature into authentic personhood precisely by being the Beloved of the Father and speaking the eternal Word of the divine Source in the very mundane details of his human life and death. In Jesus the finite and broken fragments of human existence are taken up into the healing and person-constituting fellowship of the divine Persons. Christians are those who by the work of the Holy Spirit are drawn into this personal relationship of the Son with the Father precisely by being grafted into the Body of Christ.

Just as the Spirit overshadows Mary, drawing her humanity into union with the personal mission of the Word, so the Spirit overshadows the Church at Pentecost and draws a new relational, ecclesial humanity into being as the mystical expression of the Word, the mystical Body of Christ. As men and women are drawn into this relational existence, their provisional personhood is brought to full actuality; the same Spirit who draws the Father's love forth erotically in the othering of the Son as a distinct Person, the same Spirit who returns to the Father with the ever new ecstatic love of the Son, this same Spirit pours into the believing community this person-constituting relationality. Now it would be easy at this point to suspect a creeping form of theo-panism at work. This is the idea that *everything* is simply the divine activity, that the whole spiritual journey of our humanity from individualistic self-protection towards the free and loving relationship with the other (ultimately through mystical participation in the person of Christ), which marks us as personal beings, is only a kind of earthly dumbshow of the secret workings of God behind the scenes.

But here we need to remember that God the Holy Spirit is the personal presence of God-in-the-other. The ecstatic love that constitutes the Father and the Son by means of their yearning and delight in each other is not an inexorable force of the divine essence, inevitably working itself out behind the scenes of the merely pretended personal reality of the Father and Son. No, the person-constituting love of God is God again, God the Holy Spirit, whose activity is marked by that generosity towards the other which does not supplant the other, but which rather becomes the very energy and life of the other, arousing and empowering it to become authentically who it is, to *be personal* by being freely in relationship with another. Staniloae comments in this regard:

> The Son is not a passive object of the Father's love, as in fact we ourselves are not passive objects when the Holy Spirit is poured out upon us. The fact that it is through the Spirit that the Son loves the Father does not mean however that it is not he himself who loves the Father, and similarly, the fact that it is through the Spirit that we love the Father does not imply that it is not we ourselves who love him. The Spirit of the Father penetrating within us as the paternal love kindles our own loving filial subjectivity in which, at the same time, the Spirit is also made manifest.[18]

As God-in-the-other, the Holy Spirit is the very source of the other's freedom to love and so to be a person. Far from taking the place of either the divine or the human other, the Holy Spirit makes others who they are, enabling the ecstatic self-giving of true communion – which is the person-constituting life of God and humankind.

Why is all this important? Let's remind ourselves of the train of thought so far. One of the dilemmas facing contemporary trinitarian theology is the struggle to understand the eternal life of God in terms fully congruent with the life, death and resurrection of Jesus – including the darkness and dereliction of Gethsemane and Golgotha. But this laudable endeavour seems to implicate the trinitarian life of God in the trauma of historical process so univocally as almost to suggest a kind of mythological tragedy working itself out inexorably between two alienated gods. I have been suggesting that by setting trinitarian thought in the framework of the Christian spiritual journey, we might restore to contemporary theology a sensibility capable of seeing more deeply into the heart of the matter.

Sketching this framework has directed our attention to the role of God the

Holy Spirit: first, as the love who arouses the Father to love the other and the Son to return this love, unto and from the very alienated depths of human existence; and second, as God *loving-in-the-other* ecstatically. In this latter regard I have been emphasizing the person-constituting and freedom-bestowing qualities of this kenotic *erōs*. What I think we might begin to see here is the idea, with the activity of the Spirit in mind, that each of the divine Persons is most fully who they are, is a Person, by their mutual activity of going out in love and freedom for another. Now what would this kenotic *erōs* look like when it comes to be itself, not within the blissful eternal embrace of the divine Persons themselves, but within the bitterly disjointed shambles of human history? My hunch is that it looks like, and *is* in fact, the Cross and resurrection of Jesus.[19] It is characteristic of human antagonism and sinful individualism that theology is tempted to read these events in terms of a dialectical clash of divine egos.

Now that we have re-framed the issues by setting them within the matrix of Christian spirituality, I propose developing the argument by looking at some perspectives drawn from mystical thought, looking for a way beyond the antinomy between divine suffering and divine reliability.

Persons in Love

The Holy Spirit is the ecstatic divine love by which the Father pours out the divine life, begetting Another, the Son. The Holy Spirit is the ecstatic divine love by which this Word reflects the divine Source in ever-more-particular embodiment in creation and Christ. The Holy Spirit is the ecstatic divine love who arouses that reciprocal desire by which creation goes out of itself in hunger for the divine Source who speaks this Word. Now let us consider what insights we might gain from the thoughts of those who have explored deeply into this mystery.

Augustine

I have already suggested that, for Augustine, the Holy Spirit plays a more personal role in the trinitarian life than is sometimes thought – not just *marking* the relationship of Father and Son but eternally bringing this relationship about. And the significance of this for Augustine's idea of the Trinity becomes clearer when we realize how the same energizing love draws human life into this person-constituting relationship of mutual giving.

Too late have I loved you, O beauty so ancient and so new, too late have I loved you! . . . You have called to me, and have cried out, and have shattered my deafness. You have blazed forth with light, and have shone upon me, and you have put my blindness to flight! You have sent forth fragrance, and I have drawn in my breath, and I pant after you. I have tasted you, and I hunger and thirst after you. You have touched me, and I have burned for your peace.[20]

In this famous passage from the *Confessions*, Augustine speaks of God arousing his soul to the mystical life. God's ecstatic outpouring of the divine life initiates a reciprocal yearning in Augustine for God. But notice how God does this. Neither on the one hand by simply restoring Augustine to a self-gratified wholeness in which he knows God by knowing what a fulfilled individual he, Augustine, is in himself; nor on the other hand by simply abetting Augustine in a total flight from the exigencies of himself; but rather by drawing Augustine into converted and authentic personhood. Augustine describes himself as one whose senses have all been restored to their correct functions, one who is more alive than ever *because* he is alive in response to and desire for the divine Other.

We have seen the same pattern in *The Trinity*, where Augustine has repeatedly enjoined his readers not to look for a true image of God in humanity except insofar as human life is enacted in search for God. It is insofar as the human faculties are engaged in relationship with God that humanity fulfils its potential as God's image, as truly personal and therefore relational life:

Let his memory recall, his understanding observe, and his love embrace, the greatness in that mind whereby even the Being that is everlasting and changeless can be remembered, viewed and desired; and there assuredly he will find an image of the supreme Trinity. Upon remembering, beholding and loving of that supreme Trinity, that he may recall it, contemplate it, and delight in it, he ought to make all the life in him depend.[21]

It is in giving over human nature to 'depend' on this relationship with God that the human being is consummated as image of the divine relationality. And, as I have been suggesting, the desirous love which continually draws the Father and Son into their relationship is the same love which, Augustine believes, arouses the human to true life within this trinitarian embrace: 'Thus the Holy Spirit, of whom he has given us, makes us dwell in God, and God in us. But that is the effect of love. The Holy Spirit himself therefore is the God who is love.'[22] The Holy Spirit is always God-in-the-other, God giving the other God's life so that the other may *be other* (whether divine or human) by taking part in the great 'othering' of the trinitarian life.

What I especially wish to highlight here is the fact that for Augustine this

Love, who always draws one ecstatically towards another, enables each to be most fully who they are. The Holy Spirit is God *being God* precisely by giving the divine life away (in the Father to the Son, and Son to Father), just as the Holy Spirit is the same event happening in human terms – arousing humans to be who they really are, to be consummate, relational persons by coming out of themselves in love for another. It is for this reason that Augustine is keen to stress that, as he puts it, 'the Trinity is not *in* one God but is itself one God.'[23] In us the activities of knowing, understanding and loving all belong to one person, and so the temptation naturally arises to think of God in whose image we are created as a celestial ego who has three eternal functions we have rather quaintly called Persons. This is exactly what Augustine does *not* believe. God the Holy Spirit, as the desirous love who ever draws one towards another, prevents us from ever conceiving of God apart from the relationality of the Three Persons. Augustine insists, in what is surely a crucial statement, that 'the three do not "belong" to one God but *are* one God.'[24] It is, in other words, 'by means of' the mutual self-giving of the Persons that God is God.

Rowan Williams has elucidated this mysterious giving away, this kenosis, by which God enacts and fulfils Godself.

> God gives God, having nothing else to give. . . . The Father, in eternally giving (divine) life to the Son, gives that life as itself a 'giving' agency [God the Spirit], for there is no abstract, pre-personal or sub-personal divinity; he gives the Son the capacity to give that same giving life – which, in our history, is the giver to us of the relation of gift that exists between Father and Son. . . . *Sapientia* exists *by* generating an other, it has its being as lover by being actively for another: the Father is Father, and so is concretely and actively God, by being *for* the Son. *Sapientia* exists by being eternally loved, eternally contemplated, it has its being as what receives and responds to such everlasting love: the Son is Son, and so is concretely and actively God, by being *from* the Father. And *Sapientia* exists by being, quite simply, love in search of an object, it has its being as the act of everlasting love which is given form but not exhausted by the mutual gift of Father and Son: the Spirit is concretely and actually God by being *from* or *through* the Father and the Son, in the sense of being the agency that constitutes their relation itself active or productive.[25]

God is God by giving God, and the love that arouses and is given in this giving is God the Holy Spirit. My preliminary suggestion is, then, that it is no diminution of God's power or transcendence to give Godself away to what is very much *other* than God, to sinful human history, but that this divine kenosis – consummated on the Cross – is already *included within the infinite divine giving that constitutes God as God.*

Pseudo-Dionysius the Areopagite

Clearly Augustine and other mystical writers afford a range of perspectives about this startling yet central feature of Christianity, namely the mysterious relationship between divine self-giving in salvation history and the self-giving that is itself constitutive of the trinitarian life of God. We can turn to Dionysius with some profit here, especially if we permit Augustine's thought on the divine Trinity to act as a hermeneutical 'corrective' to the Areopagite's approach.

We have been talking about God the Holy Spirit as the arousing and energizing love who draws persons, both divine and human, into the concretizing consummation of their identity by drawing them into relationship with another. In good Neoplatonic fashion, Dionysius perceives this yearning, or *erōs* to be the driving force of the whole cosmos, for the simple reason that everything that *is* yearns for the Beautiful and the Good. Dionysius goes on to claim also that

> the Cause of all things loves all things in the superabundance of his goodness, that because of this goodness he makes all things, brings all things to perfection, holds all together, returns all things. The divine yearning is Good seeking good for the sake of the Good. That yearning which creates all the goodness of the world preexisted superabundantly within the Good and did not allow it to remain without issue. It stirred him to use the abundance of his powers in the production of the world.[26]

Interpreted in more overtly trinitarian language, we might say that the divine Source is moved by the divine Spirit (yearning) to pour out that plenitude of goodness as Another, thus the Good seeks the Good: the Source gives rise eternally to the Word, the Father begets the Son. But more than this, the Areopagite is suggesting that by this same yearning activity of the Spirit which brings forth the Word, God also is 'stirred' to the 'production of the world'. In other words, there is a direct analogy between the event of God's yearning which eternally constitutes God as Trinity and the event of this same yearning in the history of creation and redemption. And, hints Dionysius, there is more at work here than a simple analogy. Dionysius says that 'the divine longing is Good seeking good for the sake of the Good'. I think we might take this to mean that this very activity of love, by which God is God, includes and seeks out within itself not only the existence of the divine Other but also the created other, that the activity of creation is in a very real sense embraced within the Father's loving self-giving towards the Son and the Son's responsivity towards the Father. It is a manifestation of the freedom and fecundity of their self-sharing.

Dionysius wants to go even further with this suggestion, for he writes that 'this divine yearning brings ecstasy so that the lover belongs not to self but to the beloved.'[27] The loving and life-giving regard of the Divine Persons for each other and for creation does not leave them as self-sufficient Cartesian egos of the stereotypical modern variety but on the contrary it is their glory to exist not for 'self' but in love and freedom for 'other'. This radical abandonment of each for the other is the radiant abyss of divine life, it is the most characteristic feature of divine love to give so freely to another, and therefore the involvement and participation of one in another is hardly a mitigation of the divine majesty but its true secret.

There are some, notes Dionysius, who think his use of this language of *erōs* with respect to God is improper or demeaning to God, but this is because their minds are clouded – not by an overheated imagining of this erotic love but precisely because they have not even *begun* to sense its singleness and intensity: 'so it is left to the divine Wisdom to lift them and to raise them up to a knowledge of what yearning really is, after which they no longer take offense.'[28] The alienation of human culture has so infected our understanding of this desirous love that we can only think of it as either a dangerous throwing away of self upon another or as a manipulative attempt to possess another for our own gratification. No wonder the absolute 'risk' involved in the self-abandonment of trinitarian life (and of the unfolding of creation within the trinitarian embrace) should seem to us as somehow grossly inappropriate to God, even a denial of God's freedom and power.

It is because we don't really know what love *is* anymore, says Dionysius, that we rather prudishly warn God off from intimacy with creation, and yet it is this very divine intimacy that identifies the trinitarian Persons and is the very condition for the possibility of creation, reconciliation and sanctification. So Dionysius pushes to the limit of human thinking about God:

> It must be said too that the very cause of the universe in the beautiful, good superabundance of his benign yearning for all is also carried outside of himself in the loving care he has for everything. He is, as it were, beguiled by goodness, by love, and by yearning and is enticed away from his transcendent dwelling place and comes to abide within all things, and he does so by virtue of his supernatural and ecstatic capacity to remain, nevertheless, within himself.[29]

In this crucial passage, Dionysius points to the vastness and goodness of the trinitarian embrace. For God is not 'beguiled' by some alien force but is drawn *in* love *by* God's *own* love (the Holy Spirit) towards the other. And even then, when God is drawn into infinite intimacy with all creation, God leaves heaven 'behind' but without ceasing to uphold, indeed even to glorify, God's own being. For this divine ecstasy of self-giving towards the created other is embraced within the infinite self-abandonment of the Father to the Son and the speaking forth of this abandonment by the Son – by means of his reciprocal self-abandonment into the hands of the Father on Golgotha. Thus God's outpouring and presence in the struggle of history is no stark opposition within the divine being, for God undertakes this involvement in all things exactly 'by virtue of his supernatural and ecstatic capacity to remain, nevertheless, within himself'. It is not that the divine nature is somehow forced ecstatically and endlessly to embody itself in another, in history, and finally in the crucified, but rather that the trinitarian Persons are God precisely in their free decision to give themselves away in perfect love.

William of St Thierry

Of all the medieval heirs of Augustine (and even the most unAugustinian medieval preferred to be thought of as deeply Augustinian – and often was!), few drew out the pneumatological possibilities inherent in Augustine's trinitarian thought more thoroughly than the one-time Benedictine abbot (and later Cistercian monk) William of St Thierry (*c*.1085–1148). What William does is to show us more clearly than ever how necessary is a proper understanding of the work of God the Holy Spirit – if we are ever to think cogently about the relationship of the creature to God. At the risk of an over-tidy systematization of things, William, we could say, draws together the *Augustinian* awareness of the Spirit's role in the trinitarian life with the *Dionysian* sensitivity to the power of this love in God's own life and in the creature's relationship to God. He draws these themes together in his concept of *affectus*, a notion that begins to clarify the activity of the Spirit as freely mediating between the trinitarian relationality and creaturely inclusion in that trinitarian life. First we need to consider the context in which William uses this concept of *affectus*, or loving-tendency-towards-good.[30]

Like all mystical writers who speak of the Trinity, William does so in terms of God's will to draw humanity into God's trinitarian existence. One cannot adequately speak of who God is without at the same time speaking of God's will for fellowship with humanity. Indeed, for the Abbot of St Thierry, this is the very basis for doing theology at all, because by exploring holy teaching (sacred doctrine) about God we realize that it is actually God who is doing the teaching; to reflect theologically is to risk being caught up in that relationship with God of which the words of theology were but the invitation. Hence the most natural prerequisite for theology is a willingness and desire to grow spiritually, to be drawn into deeper understanding by *affectus*.[31]

Our era is more than ever conscious of the *context*, the social and intellectual *location*, of any given theology. William's concerns about the migration of theology into the environment of scholasticism made him quite sensitive to this issue as well. But his response is not simply to insist chauvinistically on the preeminence of the cloister over the university as a theological venue. He takes theology to be a more radical operation than that; for him the only adequate 'social location' for the theologian is in the midst of the trinitarian event of God's own self-understanding. It is 'thence' to which the transcending momentum of theological language ought, by grace, to take one: 'the understanding of the one thinking becomes the contemplation of the one loving'.[32] What happens is that the theologian is drawn into the mutual knowing of the Father and the Son.

William is very clear that this mystical knowledge of God is not the result of the soul simply being absorbed into a union of indistinction with a putative divine oneness. True mystical knowing in William's view is possible because of two crucial features of God's own existence: 1) God in Godself is an eternal activity of knowing and loving, therefore God is infinitely knowable; 2) the human person can be, as it were, installed in this divine activity because the trinitarian self-knowledge is itself an event between Persons, and is therefore always an event of unity-in-distinction – that is, there is 'room' for the human person who comes to know and love God because this knowing takes place not by collapsing the otherness of the Mutual Knowers/Lovers but by celebrating and rejoicing in the fact that the Father and the Son *are other* to each other (thus preserving the analogous otherness of the human person in God):

> The recognition which is mutual to the Father and Son is the very unity of both, which is the Holy Spirit. The recognition by which they recognize one another is nothing other than the substance by which they are what they are. Yet in this recognition no one learns to know the Father except the Son and no one learns to know the Son except the Father and him to whom He chooses to reveal him. These are the Lord's words. The Father and the Son reveal this to certain persons, then, to those to whom They will, to those to whom They make it known, that is, to whom They impart the Holy Spirit, who is the common knowing or the common will of both. Those therefore to whom the Father and the Son reveal [Themselves] recognize them as the Father and the Son recognize Themselves, because they have within themselves Their mutual knowing, because they have within themselves the unity of both, and Their will or love: all that the Holy Spirit is.[33]

Let us consider this rich passage. William is saying that the very unity and 'substance' of God lies precisely in the mutual recognition and joy of the Father and the Son; God's existence is constituted by this trinitarian event in which the divine Persons are each drawn to know and love the other. Further, this event of recognition is no anonymous higher synthesis towards which the divine Persons are inexorably drawn, rather this mutual joy which is the very unity of the divine life is God, so to speak, 'happening again': God the Holy Spirit.

It is the activity of the Spirit to be the mutual rejoicing of the divine Persons, and therefore there is a characteristic note of mutuality and recognition-of-the-other in the Spirit's mode of enacting divine life. This is crucial since, in William's view, it is precisely this other-orientedness of the Spirit that draws the *human* other into the mutual recognition of the divine Persons; contemplatives are those in whom is poured out this mutual-rejoicing-of-the-Father-and-the-Son, who *is* God the Holy Spirit. Contemplatives 'have within themselves Their mutual knowing, because they have within themselves the unity of both, and their will or love: all that the Holy Spirit is.' Knowledge, for William, always depends on some commonality and unity between the knower and known. In the trinitarian life of God, the Holy Spirit is the personal act of this unity or likeness in which the Father and the Son are enabled to know and love each other. The Spirit works analogously in the human person, renewing the soul in that loving likeness to God which allows it to participate in God's own mutual recognition. As the Cistercian puts it: 'The Holy Spirit, the unity of the Father and the Son, is himself the love and likeness of God and man'.[34] It is now this activity of the Holy Spirit in the human person which we need to ponder.

How does the Spirit pour out this likeness in the soul? By drawing the contemplative into an awareness of God's self-expression in Christ that is so profound as to arouse in the contemplative an *affectus* which is analogous to the Spirit's own life, own love. In other words, the Spirit enacts in the creature the same activity of 'likening', or loving mutual recognition, which is the Spirit's mode of life in the Trinity. By arousing this *affectus* in the soul, the Holy Spirit enables the soul to sense, by love, the hidden presence of Christ. The soul's *affectus* (the Holy Spirit at work in the soul) leads it through the darkness into relationship with the desired Lord: 'She [the soul] loves and her love is her sense whereby she senses him whom she senses; and she is somehow transformed into what she senses, for she does not sense him unless she is transformed into him, that is, unless he is in her and she in him.'[35] Once the soul has thus been drawn into Christ, it realizes not only its new likeness to the Son but the Son's own *affectus* (Holy Spirit) for the Father and the Father's *affectus* (Holy Spirit) for the Son; such a contemplative 'somehow finds himself in their [the divine Persons'] midst, in the embrace and kiss of the Father and the Son, that is, in the Holy Spirit. And he is united to God by that charity whereby the Father and the Son are one.'[36]

We could say that the Holy Spirit enacts the same pattern of activity both within the triune life and within the creature's journey towards God. God the Holy Spirit is *affectus* because the Spirit's activity is to be *affected* by the other, being moved by delight in the divine other. This is the mutual joy of the Father and the Son – and it is this which the Spirit comes to enact within the creature, drawing the community into the 'embrace and kiss of the Father and the Son'. William explains that as creatures turn towards God, the Holy Spirit becomes for them 'what he [the Spirit] is for the Son in regard to the Father or for the Father in regard to the Son'.[37] God is God the Holy Spirit precisely in carrying out within the creature the same activity of loving recognition which constitutes the trinitarian relationality. This is the fulfilment of a human's own personhood because it is the consummation of the human's likeness to God in loving relationality.

William carefully points out that this activity, while the same in both heaven and on earth, is expressed differently within the life of God as compared with the life of the creature turning towards God. In God, says the Cistercian, the Holy Spirit simply *is* 'mutual charity, unity, likeness, recognition, and whatever else is common to both [the Father and the Son]'; but in the creature, this activity now takes place by a free decision of grace – the Spirit '*accomplishes*' likeness-to-God in the human person whereas the Spirit *is* this unity in God.[38] So while the Holy Spirit is *unity* in the life of God and *likeness-to-God* in the life of the creature, it is the same activity of loving movement towards the other (*affectus*) which is being carried out in heaven and on earth. William writes, 'there [in heaven] the mutual recognition of the Father and the Son is unity. Here it is a likeness of man to God.'[39]

What is especially noteworthy is William's notion that the event going on in both heaven and earth is the one and only eternal mutual recognition of the Father and the Son. Two points are important for us to clarify here. First, it is a characteristic of God's existence that the very act which constitutes God as God, namely the mutual joy of Father and Son in their Spirit, may happen not only in heaven but on earth; in other words, it is characteristic of the Divine Persons' mutual recognition also to include human persons in that relational life. Second, this involves no diminution of God's freedom nor does it compel God to suffer some change because of God's presence in the history of the human community. This is so because the loving relationality of the Trinity is not some necessary outcome of the divine nature per se but is rather the free act of the Trinitarian Persons, it is the event of their Personal rejoicing in each other; in the creaturely realm, God the Holy Spirit manifests the personal freedom of this mutual recognition precisely by enacting this *affectus* as a free gift of grace: 'Over the impoverished and needy love of those poor in spirit and over what they love anxiously hovers the Holy Spirit, the Love of God. That is: he performs his works in them, not through the compulsion of any need but through the abundance of his grace and generosity.'[40] This means that, on the one hand, there may be a kind of passivity about the Holy Spirit when considered purely within the trinitarian life, for there the Spirit is the *affectus*, the loving yearning for the other which is both a moving towards the other and a being-moved by the goodness of the other. But on the other hand, considered in relation to the creature, the Holy Spirit is this same *affectus* very *actively* accomplishing the creature's likeness-to-God. I would say that the availability, and mutually vulnerable yearning, of the Father and Son (which is the personal identity of the Spirit) is, for all its infinite patience and divine waiting-upon-the-other, quite naturally a powerfully *active* reality in relation to the creature who is arrested and captivated by this pattern of existence – much as the mysterious and *apparently passive* presence of the beloved exerts a powerful authority over the lover.

William was very much aware of this subtle balance in articulating the divine presence in the creature. In an early treatise he addresses God:

> We on our part hold you dear by the affection [*affectus*] of love which you have implanted in us. But how is it with you? Do you, the Creator of all things, both of the good dispositions and of the souls that are to be *affected* by them, do you love those whom you do love by some extraneous, incidental activity? And are you, the Maker of all men and all things, in some way, in some respect, *affected* in so doing? It would be ridiculous and contrary to the faith to impute such a thing to the Creator of all! Well, then, how do you love us, if you do not love us with love?[41]

William grants that love for the other puts us in a passive relationship towards the other, we are moved by our love. But, as we might expect, he goes on to say that far from God being moved by some 'extraneous' force in loving us creatures, God is therein God again, God the Holy Spirit – who *is* the mutual being-moved-by-love-towards-the-other of the Father and the Son. When we understand this about God the Holy Spirit, we understand that 'being moved' is no degradation of God but a particular pattern in God's existence – on earth as it is in heaven.

As we saw for Dionysius, God is moved by love in choosing to love the creature, but as William points out (following Augustine), this *affectus* in God is the mutual availability of the Divine Persons one for another. God's love for the creature does in a sense mean that God waits in yearning for the creature, but this yearning is derived from the trinitarian yearning of God's own life. It is an aspect of who God is to yearn for the other, and God can do that in respect of the creature with no undermining of the divine freedom for it is something that God does eternally – simply in choosing to be God by being one-for-another-in-love-and-freedom. For God to love finite creatures is a glorious manifestation of the infinite love of God for God. What we must consider now is how William's concept of *affectus*, as mediating the divine loving in history, comes to be radicalized in the next century by Hadewijch's notion of Love, or *Minne*.

Hadewijch

With this great theologian of the mid-1200s we see the trinitarian thought of the Western mystical tradition develop in powerful new directions. As I detailed in chapter two, the suffering physical humanity of Jesus and the aching dereliction of love become, by the high Middle Ages, crucial lenses for interpreting the divine–human encounter. If earlier mystical writers had stressed the need for ascesis, for the negation and transcendence of all signs in the mystical journey, this apophatic turn is now re-contextualized in the passion of Christ. The celestial *erōs* of Dionysius now begins to take on a darker hue, tinged with all the grief and sorrow of the Cross. And yet for Hadewijch and the other women who worked alongside her caring for the sick or the dying, it is the very immensity and glory of this love which is made all the clearer by its expression in the suffering of Jesus. This is what I wish to explore now: how Hadewijch's understanding of the abyss of divine love gives us a deeper ground for understanding the relations of the divine Persons and their interaction with human history.

The theme of the 'abyss of love' structures Hadewijch's thought in crucial ways. It is the powerful mystery of God's own life and also, like Dionysius's *erōs* or William's *affectus*, the motive force of our own existence. This whirlpool of love is forever pulling at the comfortable self-images we have managed to create for ourselves; the carefully groomed and rigidly separate selves we like to think we are – these are, mercifully, undone by this immense yearning which pries loose the grip we keep on our souls and frees us to abandon ourselves to another. Writing to her younger Beguines, Hadewijch urges them to discover the power of Love to release them into the truth of who they really are: 'O beloved, why has not Love [*Minne*] sufficiently over- whelmed you and engulfed you in her abyss? Alas! When Love is so sweet, why do you not fall deep into her? And why do you not touch God deeply enough in the abyss of his Nature, which is so unfathomable? Sweet love, give yourself for Love's sake fully to God in love.'[42] Love (*Minne*), the figure from courtly love literature, here functions in her gender distinction and otherness as a sign of the active and personal mystery of divine love, drawing all lovers beyond what they *think* of as themselves beyond this self towards the beloved.[43] This is an intrinsic quality of *Minne*, the original medieval Netherlandish term used by Hadewijch for Love, which in its most literal original usage meant the thought of the loved one, present in the mind of the one who loves.[44] *Minne* is the intimate presence of the one we love within us, arousing us towards the very source of our desire. And for Hadewijch, the source of our desire is also where we will find the truth of who we are created to become: '. . . you and I, who have not yet become what we are, and have not grasped what we have, and still remain so far from what is ours. We must, without sparing, lose all for all; and learn uniquely and intrepidly the perfect life of Love, who has urged on both of us to her work. . . . If you abandon yourself to Love, you will soon attain full growth' (Letter 6, p. 57). It is this abandonment in love to Love that cuts loose the bonds of human self-preoccupation and makes possible 'full growth'. Hadewijch is fairly scathing about the bondage of false selves, pointing out how quickly we are enraged by some slight done to us, and how 'we know so well what we want or do not want, there are so many things and all kinds of things for which we have an attraction or an aversion' (Letter 6, p. 61).

Minne allures us beyond these self-imposed images of ourselves and even beyond the socially-compelled roles we must play, and thus in fact liberates us into the true, relational-selves we were intended to become (in likeness to the Trinity). Hadewijch evokes the depth of this exemplary self in countless ways, pointing always to the sense that one is oneself only most fully in the rapt embrace of another. This is undergirded by an almost cosmic sense of the tide of divine life, drawing all towards each other: Father to Son, lover to beloved, soul to God and God to soul. Hadewijch develops a mystical paradox here, for she emphasizes that the drive to *union* with the other is precisely what *differentiates* each from the other: all persons, divine or human, are most distinctly *who* they are in being drawn 'out' of themselves through yearning, towards communion with the other. So there is an eternal flowing and surging: Trinity into Unity into Trinity. The divine unity exists because of the mutual abandonment of the Three, and the Three are identified eternally as the Persons they are because of the yearning which draws them into unity.

This means that for the Divine Persons, and so for human persons (who bear the divine image), it is the vulnerable bestowal of life upon the other that leads to fruition, satisfaction, and the highest happiness. Bouyer argues that for Hadewijch 'the unity beyond the Trinity is the unity of the infinite Love that is God himself. For it is this essential love according to which the Father exists only in throwing himself into the Son and the Son only in giving himself back to the Father, returning to him in the Spirit in whom is accomplished the eternal communion of *agape*.'[45] Thus Hadewijch advises her fellow Beguines that 'the most sublime life and the most rapid growth lie in dying away and wasting away in the pain of Love' (Letter 30, p. 116). This is not to be confused with simpering emotionality or a self-indulgent pining away; Hadewijch insists that the demand of true Love takes one quite beyond any such gratifying preoccupations with one's own quasi-operatic states of consciousness: 'in the experience of sweetness one is on a lower level, for people easily allow themselves to be conquered by it, and so the strength of desire diminishes' (ibid.). This kind of seeking after spiritual experiences is so dangerous, Hadewijch believes, because it satiates the very faculty that needs to be aroused to insatiability if it is to become the bearer of the infinite loving of the Trinity. Otherwise, people easily become excited over 'emotional attractions', and then 'in this delight they forget the great debt – payment of which is being demanded every hour – that Love demands of Love' (ibid.).

In Hadewijch's visionary interpretation, the eternal yearning and surging of the Divine Persons towards unity is, by God's grace, also the fundamental rhythm and momentum of history. The mutual desire of the Persons establishes a kind of vortex, an abyss, a debt of love which is the very life of God and the motive force drawing the whole creation towards its consummation. The creation is consummated, that is, as it is aroused towards participation in the eternal fruition of the trinitarian love. In one of her letters, Hadewijch pictures the manifestation in history of this vortex of love, unleashed by the mutual yearning of the Divine Persons. She pictures it in terms of the open mouth, the stretching-apart, the wounded side of crucified Jesus, drawing the very fabric of history through the wound of love into the trinitarian abyss:

> The mouth is open; the arms outstretched; and the rich Heart is ready. That fearful outstretching renders the depth of their souls so deep and so vast that they can never be filled. The fact that God opens himself so wide for them invites them at all hours to surpass their faculties. For with his right arm he embraces all his friends, both heavenly and earthly, in an overflowing wealth. And on the left side he embraces the strangers who with naked and scanty faith come to him for the sake of his friends, so that there may be fulfilled in them the full and unitive bliss that has never been lacking to him. For the sake of his good friends and his beloved ones, he gives the strangers his glory and makes them all friends of the house. (Letter 22, p. 98)

As in William of St Thierry, the passive vulnerability of the divine loving, expressed uniquely in the magnetic openness of the suffering Christ, exerts a powerful and active force on human persons, inflaming their own yearning and drawing them into the 'unitive bliss that has never been lacking to him'. Also noteworthy is the social solidarity of this vision.

It is important to see how fully Hadewijch limns the social and historical dimensions of this 'great debt . . . that Love demands of Love'. In Hadewijch's view, one abandons oneself to the this divine abyss of love at least in part by availability to the human other; when you see someone who is also seeking to fulfil the demands of love, she writes, 'pour yourself out in helping him – your heart in merciful kindness, your reasoning power in consolation, and your members in energetic service' (Letter 6, p. 57). Interestingly, the Beguine leader is quite careful about the exact form this should take. A pitying obsession with the most inveterate sinners accomplishes nothing; what will really count is 'the love we give to God, and the stronger that love is, the more it frees sinners from their sins and gives security to those who love' (ibid., p. 58). In other words, as we saw just above, God has so constituted the universe that human participation in the mutual divine self-giving is the very channel by which God has chosen to work for the good of the creatures.[46]

Hadewijch also develops that strand in Dionysius that speaks of the power of love to 'beguile' God out of heaven. In Hadewijch's terms, the triune life of self-giving yearning is the abyss which draws the whole cosmos towards fruition. Therefore when creatures freely and willingly, in likeness to the Divine Persons, give themselves to this activity of Love, there is a sense in which God is joyfully drawn into the creaturely event. It is not as if God were somehow undone or changed in these events, but rather that here and there the Divine Persons are able, through the spiritual transparency of self-giving souls, to play out the eternal dance of divine yearning which constitutes the very life of God. 'Love borrows from God the power of decision over those she loves,' writes Hadewijch, and this even means that 'Love has vanquished the Divinity by her nature. She cries with a loud voice, without stay or respite, in all the hearts of those who love: "Love ye Love!" ' (Letter 20, p.92).

The very desire by which the Divine Persons embrace thus echoes as a thundering cry in the heart of creation, and must seem to the creature to have decision even over God's own life. Reporting to her sister Beguines some of what she has sensed God to be saying in her own life, Hadewijch records the divine voice thus:

'Nothing has so much power over me as the perfect abandonment of lofty fidelity.' He added: 'Your soul's hunger disposes me to prepare everything for you, so that I, what I am, shall be yours. Through your striving to satisfy your hunger for me, you grew up to full perfection, and you became like to me: your death and mine shall be one, and therefore we shall live with one life, and one love shall satisfy the hunger of us both' (Letter 31, p. 121).

We can see here the powerful way in which Hadewijch always interprets the mutual hungering of the Trinity, into which the soul is drawn, in terms of the death, resurrection and ecstatic return into unity of the Incarnate Son. The mutual abandonment of the Divine Persons one to another is enacted in the self-giving death of Jesus, and thus the paschal mystery becomes the point of entrance for the soul into the ultimate trinitarian self-giving: 'your death and mine shall be one, and therefore we shall live with one life, and one love shall satisfy the hunger of us both.'

This is so significant because it means that, once again, the mystical tradition finds Jesus' life, death and resurrection to be very far from an ineluctable necessity to which God is subject, but rather to be the expression in time of the kenotic life of the Trinity. Because this trinitarian relationality is the implicit structure of human life, the Divine Persons are able to manifest their own life in the analogous activity of human self-giving. This is the radiant transparency to God of souls abandoned freely in love. So it becomes clear that the Love which 'has power over' God is in fact the power of trinitarian yearning. For Hadewijch, the life of the Trinity is characterized by the desire of the Divine Persons to 'content' one another, in analogy to the desire of a lover to give ever more to the beloved.

Thus she speaks of the blissful Unity of God being faced with 'the demand that the Father demands in eternal fruition from the Unity of the Son and the Holy Spirit' (Letter 30, p. 117); here the contentment desired is the eternal *coming forth* of the Son and the Spirit *from* unity – the Father, as it were, yearning for their particular personal Love and so calling them both forth eternally into the differentiated personhood of trinitarian life. This is the demand that Love makes of *Unity*, eternally to reveal its fecundity and relationality. Then again there is 'the debt that the Son and the Holy Spirit demand from the Father in the fruition of the Holy Trinity' (ibid.); this is the yearning of the Divine Persons to achieve the infinite contentment of *union* with each other. And this is the demand that Love makes of the *Trinity*, eternally to *be* the Divine Persons precisely by coming forth towards mutually self-surrendering oneness. So the demand of Love calls the Unity into Trinity and the Trinity into Unity in an eternal kenosis of self-giving.

In terms of created time and space, Hadewijch shows how the debt of Love is 'demanded' both in terms of God's cosmic plan of salvation and in terms of the believer's mystical journey. In the cosmic plan, not surprisingly, Hadewijch sees a pendulum-like rhythm of Love, flowing back and forth between trinitarian procession and the returning aspiration towards unity. 'In the Trinity, man was created. But because man did not answer the demand of the Unity, he fell. By the demand of the Trinity God's Son was born, and to satisfy the debt to the Unity he died. By the demand of the Trinity he rose again among men; and to satisfy the debt to the Unity he ascended to his Father' (Ibid.). The cosmic economy originates from the opening up of the divine rhythm of life to include the creatures within the same pattern. 'In the Trinity, man was created': humanity's coming forth is borne along within the outward 'swing' of trinitarian differentiation. But then the interruption and darkness in the created order stems from humanity's unwillingness to enter into the dance, fearful and unable to see that it is just by surrendering our selves towards unity they we are most fulfilled and consummated as persons. So 'because our will is estranged, we thwart this and fall back from this unity into our own self-complacency, we no longer grow and no longer make progress in that perfection which was thus demanded of us from the beginning by the Unity and the Trinity' (ibid.). Hadewijch opens the reader's eyes to the subtle attractions of a false imitation of true personhood, a self-enclosed 'self-complacency', in which the human person becomes trapped and stunted. The remedy for this, in her view, lies in the willingness of the eternal Son to enact his self-surrendering love within the estrangement of the human community. In this he fulfils himself by giving himself away, so re-opening for humanity the way of self-giving love, and thus restores the whole creation's means of access to Unity: 'By the demand of the Trinity God's Son was born, and to satisfy the debt to the Unity he died.'

God has invested history in this way with eternal significance, and it is in living into that rhythm, in Hadewijch's view, that the believing community fulfils its mission. For now the soul is called to realize its own true life by enacting the very pattern of trinitarian life that it has seen writ large in the story of salvation. Thus one must desire to content Love 'under the guidance of reason' and to be perfect in just works; 'in this manner one lives the Son of God'. One must also will the good with a renewed ardour, exercizing 'all the virtues with an overflowing desire'; 'in this manner one lives the Holy Spirit'. So, in this way, one's own provisional personhood comes to blossom as one enters into the particular patterns of self-giving enacted by the Son and the Spirit as they come forth into trinitarian life. Finally then, and most interestingly, one is ready to be drawn into the ultimate *self-differentiation* which is, paradoxically, to enter into the fullest *unity*, 'to grow up as loved one in the Beloved'. It is not just a question any more of emulating Jesus in the Spirit but of realizing the fullness of one's life by discovering that one in fact has come into being in enacting his life:

> to work with his hands; to walk with his feet; to hear with his ears where the voice of the Godhead never ceases to speak through the mouth of the Beloved . . . live for no one else but for the Beloved in love alone, live in him as the loved one in the Beloved, with the same way of acting, with one spirit, and with one heart; and in one another to taste the unheard-of sweetness he merited by his sufferings. Oh yes! To feel heart in heart, with one single heart and one single sweet love, and continually have fruition of one full-grown love. And lastly, that one must ever know certainly, without any doubt, that one is wholly in the Unity of Love. In this state one is the Father (Ibid., p. 118).

In this remarkable passage, Hadewijch shows how the ultimate, infinite self-giving of the Trinity, which reaches its furthest point in the life of the Incarnate Son, becomes the embracing movement of divine life, drawing creation within it, and so leading the creature back into the never-ending mystery of the divine Unity. The more one is drawn into the self-giving of Jesus, the more one is drawn into the very source and goal of that giving life; and so one discovers oneself *in the Father*.

For the Son is after all the very image of the Father, and the soul's completely abandoned unity with Jesus initiates it into his self-abandoned unity with the Father. It is important that Hadewijch clearly identifies the Person of the Father (not the divine nature per se) as the origin of the divine Unity, from which the Persons of the Son and Spirit proceed and to whom they return — bearing as expressions of their life and as tokens of love the redeemed creation. For in this way Hadewijch emphasizes more clearly than ever that the demand of Love for Unity and for Trinity is never anything other than the freely given mutual desire of the Divine Persons.

Hadewijch believes that God has chosen to find in the yearning and self-giving of the creature something of eternal cherishability. Does God then *need* the creation, redemption and sanctification of the creatures to be fulfilled as God? The Beguine writer says that when, at length, the soul comes into union with the Father through Christ there is a kind of consummate joy and fruition, certainly for the creature, but also perhaps finally for God too.

> Then the Unity for the first time obtains what it has demanded, and then the demand is first truly actualized, and then the soul can have, through the Trinity, the fruition that until now had been withheld. Then shall the Three Persons forever demand and eternally render – at one and the same time – their Unity

in one will, one possession, and one fruition. How this is, I do not dare to tell you now, for I am too far from having obtained full growth, and the love I possess is too small (Ibid., 119).

Perhaps we should take Hadewijch's demurral here in sober gratitude; perhaps there *is* something about this mystery of divine readiness to count creation into the balance of the divine life which is too great to be grasped by those whose love, as she says, is 'too small'. It seems to me we can at least do Hadewijch the justice of recognizing that while she was assuredly working within the great inheritance of Christian Neoplatonism (with its cosmic structure of oneness, procession and return), she has truly re-interpreted that scheme in light of the gospel narratives. And what she sees there is not simply that God somehow *must* enter into suffering and death but that God has – out of God's very own delight in the infinitely various ways of contenting God with love – freely chosen to include the loving responsivity of the creation *within* the self-surrender of God to God.

We can see something of this when the great Beguine poet speaks of how, in Christ, the Trinity has poured forth its name and glory over all the earth, precisely by drawing the creatures into the pattern of Jesus' mission. For after the Son's earthly life 'he returned with his name, which he had poured forth very greatly and which, now *very luxuriantly multiplied*, he now again poured into him [the Father]. His name was multiplied *although nothing was added to it*; for all things are poured out and multiplied by the fructifying oil of his sublime name, and were as great in him from all eternity as they shall be without end' (Letter 22, p. 100; my emphasis.). In a sense we could say that the whole cosmos and its responsivity to God are embraced within the infinitely fecund giving of the Divine Persons to each other. To give God to God is already an infinite gift; to include within that even the yearning self-giving of what is *not* God is to ensure that all the infinitely various possibilities of God's love are given life and voice. [47]

The Fruition of Trinitarian Life

I have tried to suggest in this chapter that by setting contemporary questions about the doctrine of the Trinity within the framework of Christian spirituality we might be able to sensitize ourselves to new possibilities and ways of thinking. Let me briefly summarize something of the argument. Again, the issue has been how to conceive of the trinitarian life of God in a way that takes the death and resurrection of Jesus as definitive of who God is but *not* so as to become reducible to a kind of gnosticism about God's inner life or a mythological slide towards tritheism.

We began by emphasizing the need to recover an awareness of our relationship with God in the Holy Spirit. For the Spirit has always been seen in the mystical traditions as the yearning love of God who draws towards unity. The Spirit represents not the bare *ontological* relationship of creature with Creator, nor the stark *historical* confrontation of the creature with the divine Other in Christ, but rather the *teleological* momentum of God's love, drawing intimacy and joy out of difference without washing out otherness or subordinating it to some higher law. The mystical writers we have considered show a fairly consistent sensitivity to the vast, yearning desire which animates the Trinitarian life. They have pointed out that this is not a kind of fourth Person, or another name for the divine nature to which the Persons are themselves subject, but is rather the freely enacted relationality by which God is who God is, mutually giving life. Yet the mystical writers have also seen that this is not a self-enclosed, self-congratulatory divine circle, but rather that the infinity and totality of the gift of the Divine Persons one to another is expressed also by the vulnerability and yearning of the divine life acting within creation. The creaturely risk of love and suffering, the hopeful but all-too-easily-avoided longing of the Son and the Spirit at work within creation – these are all aspects of God's desire to surrender all to God, to be God for God even through the very wondrousness and brokenheartedness of creation.

I have suggested *what* God is, is constituted by the free personal enactment of *who* God is.[48] So when we talk about whether God's presence in history entails some kind of change or suffering in God, we need to reflect upon this in terms of the particular personal patterns by which God is God, not by interpreting God's presence in history against the background of presupposed concepts of divine nature. This means that what is at work in God's relationship to history is never an extraneous law (to which God is subject in order to fulfil the divine nature). Rather God's presence in history is the free expression of the freely given mutual love of Divine Persons.

Elizabeth Johnson has rightly warned us of so stressing the image of self-giving love as a way of thinking about God that we end up reinforcing models of subordination which have often led to oppression for women and other marginalized groups, both in social and psychological terms. Johnson also points out, however, that trinitarian theology can and should conceive of this self-giving love in a way that points to fruition and mutuality as the *test* of its authenticity. In that case, a robust sense of constitutive trinitarian relationality can encompass suffering without being subordinated to it: 'The essence of God can be seen to consist in the motion of personal relations and the act that is love. With this in view it is possible to conceive of suffering as not necessarily a passive state nor a movement from potentiality to act. Rather suffering can be conceived of ontologically as an expression of divine being insofar as it is an *act* freely engaged in as a consequence of care for others.'[49] The Christian spiritual traditions have, I think, many fertile resources for thinking about God in this way, for re-conceiving the relationship between God's participation in our lives and God's own life of relational participation.

Notes

1　John D. Zizioulas, 'The Early Christian Community' in *Christian Spirituality: Origins to the Twelfth Century*, ed. Bernard McGinn, John Meyendorff and Jean Leclercq. *World Spirituality: An Encyclopedic History of the Religious Quest*, vol. 16 (New York: Crossroad, 1987), 28.

2　On this theme I have been greatly enlightened by the important insights of Sarah Coakley, 'Why Three? Some Further Reflections on the Origins of the Doctrine of the Trinity', chapter in *The Making and Remaking of Christian Doctrine: Essays in Honour of Maurice Wiles*, ed. Sarah Coakley and David A. Pailin (Oxford: Clarendon Press, 1993), 29–56.

3　John Thompson, *Modern Trinitarian Perspectives* (Oxford: Oxford University Press, 1994), 20–64 especially.

4　*Karl Rahner in Dialogue: Conversations and Interviews, 1965–1982*, ed. Paul Imhof and Hubert Biallowons (New York: Crossroad, 1986), 126–7.

5　See for example, Colin E. Gunton, *The Promise of Trinitarian Theology* (Edinburgh: T. & T. Clark, 1991) and Catherine Mowry LaCugna, *God For Us: The Trinity and the Christian Life* (New York: HarperCollins, 1991). Further on the range of contemporary trinitarian thought, see David S. Cunningham, *These Three Are One: The Practice of Trinitarian Theology* (Oxford: Blackwell Publishers).

6　Rowan Williams, '*Sapientia* and the Trinity: Reflections on the *De Trinitate*', in *Collectanea augustiniana: melanges T. J. van Bavel*, ed. B. Bruning (Leuven: University Press, 1990), 331–2.

7　Jürgen Moltmann, *The Crucified God: The Cross of Christ as the Foundation and Criticism of Christian Theology*, trans. R. A. Wilson and John Bowden (New York: Harper & Row, 1974), 243.

8　Cf., Thompson, *Modern Trinitarian Perspectives*, 51: 'The emphasis [in Moltmann] is so much on the three persons as subjects that the unity is underemphasized, or, to put it differently, there is a serious lack of an ontological dimension in his trinitarian formulations. This also borders on tritheism.'

9　William Temple, *Christus Veritas: An Essay* (London: Macmillan & Co, 1954), 278–9.

10　Further on the Spirit as the 'interpretive' activity of God, see Rowan Williams, 'Trinity and Revelation', *Modern Theology* 2:3 (1986): 197–21 and John Milbank,

'The Second Difference: For a Trinitarianism without Reserve', *Modern Theology* 2:3 (1986): 213–34.

11   Christos Yannaras, *Elements of Faith: An Introduction to Orthodox Theology*, trans. Keith Schram (Edinburgh: T. & T. Clark, 1991), 35.

12   See also here the highly influential work of John D. Zizioulas, *Being as Communion: Studies in Personhood and the Church. Contemporary Greek Theologians* Series, no. 4 (Crestwood, New York: St Vladimir's Seminary Press, 1985), 44: 'The ground of God's ontological freedom lies not in His nature but in His personal existence. . .   The manner in which God exercises His ontological freedom, that precisely which makes Him ontologically free, is the way in which He transcends and abolishes the ontological necessity of the substance by being God as *Father*, that is, as He who "begets" the Son and "brings forth" the Spirit. This ecstatic character of God, the fact that His being is identical with an act of communion, ensures the transcendence of the ontological necessity which His substance would have demanded – if the substance were the primary ontological predicate of God – and replaces this necessity with the free self-affirmation of divine existence. For this communion is a product of freedom as a result not of the substance of God but of a person, the Father – observe why this doctrinal detail is so important – who is Trinity not because the divine *nature* is ecstatic but because the Father as a *person* freely wills this communion.'

13   Dumitru Staniloae, *Theology and the Church*, trans. Robert Barringer (Crestwood, New York: St Vladimir's Seminary Press, 1980), 99.

14   Augustine, *The Trinity,* IX.xii in *Augustine: Later Works*, trans. John Burnaby. The Library of Christian Classics (Philadelphia: Westminster Press, 1955), 70. My emphasis.

15   Ibid, 71.

16   For what follows see especially Lossky, *The Mystical Theology of the Eastern Church* (Crestwood; New York: St Vladimir's Seminary Press, 1976); Zizioulas, *Being as Communion*; Yannaras, *Elements of Faith*.

17   Yannaras, *Elements of Faith*, 64.

18   Staniloae, *Theology and the Church*, 31.

19   No one has made this clearer to me than Herbert McCabe, OP: 'The story of Jesus is nothing other than the triune life of God projected onto our history, or enacted sacramentally in our history, so that it becomes story. . .   Imagine a film projected not on a screen but on a rubbish dump. The story of Jesus – which in its full extent is the entire Bible – is the projection of the trinitarian life of God on the rubbish dump that we have made of the world. . .   That the Trinity looks like a story of (*is* a story of) rejection, torture and murder but also of reconciliation is because it is being projected on, lived out on, our rubbish tip; it is because of the sin of the world.' (*God Matters* [London:GeoffreyChapman, 1987], 48–9).

20   Augustine, *The Confessions*, X.27, trans. John K. Ryan. (Garden City: Image Books, 1960), 254–5.

21   Idem., *The Trinity*, XV.xx, 168.

22 Ibid., XV.xvii, 160.

23 Ibid., XV.xxiii, 170.

24 Ibid., 171.

25 Williams, 'Sapientia and the Trinity', 327–8.

26 Pseudo-Dionysius the Areopagite, 'The Divine Names', IV.10, 708B in Pseudo-Dionysius: The Complete Works, trans. Colm Luibheid and Paul Rorem (New York: Paulist Press, 1987), 81–2.

27 Ibid., IV.13, 712A, p. 82.

28 Ibid., IV.12, 709C, p. 81.

29 Ibid., IV.13, 712B, p. 82.

30 For a useful brief note on the concept of affectus in William see the Appendix by Davis in William of St Thierry, The Mirror of Faith, trans. Thomas X. Davis. The Works of William of St Thierry, vol. 5. Cistercian Fathers Series, no. 15 (Kalamazoo, Michigan: Cistercian Publications, 1979), 93–5.

31 Cf. William of St Thierry, The Enigma of Faith, trans. John D. Anderson. The Works of William of St Thierry, vol. 3. Cistercian Fathers Series, no. 9 (Washington, DC: Cistercian Publications, 1974), 37–8: 'In this question of seeing God, it seems to me that there is more value in one's manner of living than in his manner of speaking. For, whoever has learned from the Lord Jesus Christ to be meek and humble of heart will make more progress in thinking about this and in praying than in reading or listening, although sometimes it is profitable both to read and to listen. However, no one should say he wants to see God if he is unwilling to expend the care worthy of so great an undertaking to purify his heart.' For an interesting recent comparison, see the remarks of a pioneer in what is often today called the 'Yale school' of theology, Paul Holmer: 'Theology does not at every juncture demand an historical-critical understanding before it can be reasserted in our day. . . . One suspects that it is far more important than most historical material to learn to hunger and thirst for righteousness, to learn to love a neighbor, and to achieve a high degree of self-concern, in order to understand the religious themes of the New Testament. There are, in short, personality qualifications that are also required. Perhaps it is even essential to have learned guilt because one has not done as he ought to have done. In any case, these forms of human consciousness are closer to the prerequisites for a Christian's understanding than is most knowledge supplied by other scholars' (The Grammar of Faith [San Francisco: Harper & Row, 1978], 9).

32 Idem., The Golden Epistle: A Letter to the Brethren at Mont Dieu, trans. Theodore Berkeley, OCSO. The Works of William of St Thierry, vol. 4. Cistercian Fathers Series, no. 12 (Kalamazoo, Michigan: Cistercian Publication, 1980), 92.

33 Idem., The Mirror of Faith, 75–6. See also a parallel passage in Enigma, p. 39: 'There, as in the Trinity, which is God, the Father and the Son mutually see one another and their mutual vision consists in their being one and in the fact that the one is what the other is, so those who have been predestined for this and have been taken up into it will see God as he is, and in seeing him as he is they will become like him. And there, as in the Father and the Son, that which is vision

is also unity; so in God and man that which is vison will be the likeness that is to come.'

34   Idem., *Enigma*, 39.

35   Idem., *Mirror*, 70.

36   Ibid., 80.

37   Idem., *Golden Epistle*, 96.

38   Idem., *Mirror*, 77.

39   Ibid.

40   Ibid., 78.

41   Idem., *On Contemplating God* in *On Contemplating God, Prayer, and Meditations*, trans. Sister Penelope, CSMV. *The Works of William of St Thierry*, vol. 1. *Cistercian Fathers* Series, no. 3 (Kalamazoo, Michigan: Cistercian Publications, 1977), 53–4. (My emphasis.)

42   Hadewijch, Letter 5.28, *Hadewijch: The Complete Works*, trans. Mother Columba Hart OSB. *Classics of Western Spirituality* (New York: Paulist Press, 1980), 56. Hereafter all references to this edition will be given parenthetically by page number.

43   Cf. Barbara Newman, *From Virile Woman to WomanChrist: Studies in Medieval Religion and Literature*, University of Pennsylvania Press Middle Ages Series (Philadelphia: University of Pennsylvania Press, 1995), esp. chapter 5, 'La *mystique courtoise*: Thirteenth Century Beguines and the Art of Love'.

44   See Hadewijch, *Lettres Spirituelles*, trans. J. B. Porion (Geneva: C. Martingay, 1972), n. 14, p. 19.

45   Louis Bouyer, *The Christian Mystery: From Pagan Myth to Christian Mysticism*, trans. Illtyd Trethowan (Edinburgh: T. & T. Clark, 1990), 243.

46   Further on the social dimensions of Hadewijch's thought, see the useful comments of Grace Jantzen, *Power, Gender and Christian Mysticism*, 142 and 295.

47   Cf. Hans Urs von Balthasar, *Mysterium Paschale*, trans. Aidan Nichols, OP (Edinburgh: T. & T. Clark, 1990), viii–ix: 'We shall never know how to express the abyss-like depths of the Father's self-giving, that Father who, in an eternal "super-Kenosis", makes himself "destitute" of all that he is and can be so as to bring forth a consubstantial divinity, the Son. Everything that can be thought and imagined where God is concerned is, in advance, included and transcended in this self-destitution which constitutes the person of the Father, and, at the same time, those of the Son and the Spirit. God as the "gulf" (Eckhart: *Un-Grund*) of absolute Love contains in advance, eternally, all the modalities of love, of compassion, and even of a 'separation' motivated by love and founded on the infinite distinction between the hypostases – modalities which may manifest themselves in the course of a history of salvation involving sinful humankind.'

48   Cf., Elizabeth Johnson, *She Who Is: The Mystery of God in Feminist Theological Discourse* (New York: Crossroad, 1993), 227: '*What* the divine nature is is constituted by *who* God is in triune relationality without remainder.'

49   Ibid., 265.

Chapter 6

THE HIDDENNESS OF GOD AND THE SELF-UNDERSTANDING OF JESUS

It is not always easy to know what people mean when they talk about Jesus. Perhaps that is appropriate for speech about one whom Christians believe is in some sense God's own speech addressed to us. Sometimes this difficulty is a matter of different contexts for the same terminology. For example when Mark's gospel has Jesus referred to as 'son of God' by two 'outsiders', a demoniac (5.7) and a Roman centurion (15.39) – what might this term mean to Mark? And what about the very same title as used by St Paul, or Irenaeus, or Anselm, or Schleiermacher, or Barth? Behind every use of such a title, or way of talking about Jesus, there lies a complex of images, narrative patterns and metaphysical entailments. It might seem, then, that to enlarge our focus – from the changing significance of a *single christological title*, like 'Son of God', to an entire *network of ideas*, like the doctrine of the Incarnation – would be to risk a fairly rapid descent into total chaos.

And yet there is a constitutive question that every kind of incarnational christology must answer: In what sense is God present in the historical human being Jesus of Nazareth? No matter how an incarnational christology may go about its business, if it bears even the remotest continuity with other eras of Christian faith, then it has to find some kind of answer to this question.

The possible answers to this question of God's presence in Christ may range from the maximally incarnational at the centre, or they may verge off to the left and right extremes of incarnational minimalisms (see the figure below).

X	X	X
Left Incarnational Minimalism (Jesus is a human being who tells us something important from God)	Incarnational Maximalism (Jesus as fully human is the speaking of the eternal Word of God)	Right Incarnational Minimalism (Jesus is the Word of God pretending to be human)

As is often remarked, the extremes of incarnational minimalism are really much easier positions to hold, for they allow one to lay aside the humanly astonishing idea that God and humanity are not mutually exclusive realities. The minimalisms are able to rest comfortably in a more immediately coherent either/or: either Jesus is a human being whom God has specially chosen or he is a divine being whose human existence holds no intrinsic significance for salvation. For nearly eighteen hundred years, talk about Jesus has gone on somewhere *between* those extremes. The Council of Chalcedon in 451 attempted to stake out the middle position of incarnational maximalism as the most adequate Christian usage; but struggles to understand this incarnational possibility (both before and after Chalcedon) have often tended to pull in one direction or the other.

Since the Enlightenment, however, there has been a growing discomfort with these terms of the discussion. The question arises: is the pre-modern incarnational idea (of a human being who is also divine) not simply a mythological conception that has taken root at the heart of Christian faith and must now be let go? The argument is not simply that Christian thinking needs to be brought into line with modern thought, but that an incarnational conception is actually a misrepresentation of the Gospel. This is of course a very deep question: have two millennia of Christians built their understanding of God and God's relation to humanity on a culturally-limited conception – one which actually distorts the Gospel by centring it on the presence of God in Christ rather than on the coming dominion of God which Jesus lived and died to proclaim?

It seems to me that before one could begin to tackle such a question, it would be wise to achieve great clarity regarding what Christians have actually meant when they have spoken of Jesus as God Incarnate. My goal in this chapter is not of course to construct a kind of proof of the Incarnation or the divinity of Jesus, and I'm quite sure that such a satisfactory proof never could be 'constructed'. My goal is rather to show by means of analogies drawn from Christian mystical traditions that the doctrine of the Incarnation is not a kind of centuries-long theological blunder. I want to propose Christian spirituality as resource for exploring in an intelligible way the notion that in this human being Jesus of Nazareth, one encounters not a truth or word about God but the actual personal presence of the eternal Word of God – who does not choose to be God apart from being human.

This does of course leave the question begging whether Christianity has, since about the time of St Paul, tended to get the real thrust of the Gospel wrong (i.e., mistakenly substituted 'incarnationalism' for kingdom of God). However, since at least part of the ground for asking this question rests on the belief that incarnational christology is unintelligible today, showing that it *is* intelligible seems a reasonable step in the discussion.

Earlier in this book I sought to give a sense of the dynamic range and momentum inherent in the *language* of mystical texts. It is good to remember this, for what we are seeking in this chapter is not so much direct mystical teaching *about* the Incarnation itself, as a feel for the kind of language that mystical discourse uses to when it speaks of human intimacy with God. In other words, we are looking at teaching about the journey into ever-deeper human encounter with God. We are doing so in order to find imagery and habits of thought by which to understand the deepest form of human intimacy with God, the Incarnation. My intention is to use these mystical analogies to explore what the christological tradition has sometimes referred to as the 'hypostatic union'.

It is important to recall that this maximally incarnational christology understands the presence of God in Christ in terms of personal identity and *not* in terms of nature or essence. This means that in thinking about how the divine and human are related in Jesus, we are *not* trying to show (though we might well be able to do so) that divine essence and human essence can somehow be held closely together, or mingled, or anything of the kind. It is this tendency which has always tended to leave the divine and human in Christ so separated as to make talk of union seem purely metaphorical, or else so to mingle the divine and human natures as virtually to undermine the integrity of either the divine or the human or both. And it was exactly this possibility that Chalcedon hoped to forestall by insisting that all talk of Jesus acknowledge him 'to be unconfusedly, unalterably, undividedly, inseparably in two natures, since the difference of the natures is not destroyed because of the union, but on the contrary, the character of each nature is preserved and comes together in one person and one hypostasis'.[1]

As this quotation emphasizes, the constitutive ground of Jesus' existence is taken in this view to be the person or hypostasis of the Word. So the model I want to explore by means of mystical analogies is one in which the personal identifying patterns of the eternal Word are the very constitutive patterns by which Jesus fulfils his life as a human being. In such a model the concern is not how, ontologically speaking, divine and human substances 'fit together' but rather how a particular divine pattern of activity (namely, the eternal procession and mission of the Son or Word) comes to be enacted in the details and struggles of an utterly human life. It is this maximally incarnational perspective that I propose for investigation. What we want to see is whether there are elements in the Christian mystical traditions that might help us to think about what goes on as human life comes to be lived more and more according to a divine pattern of life.

Michel de Certeau has described the development in the modern era of a scholarly discipline of studying and organizing the mystical life; he dubs this discipline 'mystics', in analogy with the contemporaneous development of the study of optical lenses and effects known as 'optics'. His characterization of this field of study points to a central issue in this chapter, namely that mystical texts often evoke the presence of God precisely by the virtuoso excess of their rhetoric of God's *absence*: such texts are (like the continually self-giving life of Jesus) always straining, undoing themselves, in the attempt to express their 'object'. But since that 'object' is really infinite, such a mystical text is 'never anything but the unstable metaphor for what is inaccessible. Every 'object' of mystical discourse becomes inverted into the trace of an ever-passing Subject. Therefore, *mystics* [the discipline] only assembles and orders its practices in the name of something that it cannot make into an object . . . something that never ceases judging *mystics* at the same time that it eludes it.'[2] In chapter four on hermeneutics, I suggested that Jesus' struggle to be who he is (and the journey on which this leads him through death and resurrection) might well be seen as the interpretive framework for the struggle by which mystical speech comes to be spoken and heard, written and interpreted. Now it is time to put this idea to work, to suggest that mystical speech – which comes undone and is judged in the very act of uttering the One whom it encounters – not only stems from but leads us back *into* an apprehension of the ongoing event of the Incarnation, death and resurrection of Christ.

I am suggesting, in other words, that for many writers in the Christian mystical traditions, the mystical life is fundamentally a sharing in Christ's life at the deepest spiritual level. Presumably one who is sharing the life of Christ at the most profound level will speak in language and imagery which at the very least affords us a heuristic tool for exploring the analogy between the hypostatic union and mystical union. Again, de Certeau offers us fertile thought on the self-abandonment inherent in mystical texts. He suggests something of this analogy existing between the characteristics of mystical texts and the characteristics of Jesus' life. He remarks that such texts can only speak truly of the Infinite as they 'lose themselves in what they show, like those landscapes by Turner that disappear into air and light. Modulated by pain, enjoyment, or "letting be" (the Eckhartian *Gelâzenheit*), an ab-solute (unfettered) inhabits the torture, the ecstasy, or the sacri-fice of the language that can only *say* it by effacing itself'.[3]

I am suggesting, then, that the very source of this mystical speech lies in the struggle of Jesus to be, to 'speak', the divine Word in a human community that has – by its broken-hearted fear of loving absolutely – become incapable of the only language in which the divine Word can be spoken. And for this reason, speaking the divine Word in this world entails, in de Certeau's words, 'the sacrifice of that language that can only *say* it by effacing itself'.

In general, then, it will be chiefly apophatic traditions of Christian spirituality which help us in reflection on this analogy. In these forms of negative theology, the supernal beauty and ineffable reality of God is understood to be so infinite, so dazzling to the human self, that the mystic is brought at last to the most crucial insight: loving *unknowing* is the only truthful knowing that one can have of God. Aquinas himself, rarely at a loss for words about God, knew this very well. As the Dominican Herbert McCabe puts it: 'The revelation of God in Jesus in no way, for Aquinas, changes this situation. By the revelation of grace, he says, we are joined to God as to an unknown, *ei quasi ignoto coniungamur* (*ST* Ia, 12, 13, ad 1). God remains the mystery which could only be known by God himself, or by our being taken up to share in his own knowledge of himself, a sharing which for us in this world is not knowledge but the darkness of faith.'[4] In writers of the Christian apophatic tradition such as Gregory of Nyssa, Pseudo-Dionysius, John of the Cross and Edith Stein, we can see many common elements in their presentations of the human encounter with God. Vital for our purposes is the perception that, for those still *in via*, the most intimate divine presence is experienced by the human subject as a profound darkness, as a painful longing, even dereliction – not only interiorly but in and through the actual historical contingencies of life.

In noetic terms, this is expressed as an absolute knowledge of God and self which comes by way of surrendering human pre-judgements about either divine or human existence. In existential or affective terms, this is seen as a realization of the true self by way of abandoning the self to the divine Lover who seems hidden and absent. These dimensions of abandonment (whether noetic or existential) are seen by the mystical writers as reaching a climax in which the self ceases actively to surrender itself and instead suffers the blindingly superabundant presence of God. Jean Daniélou summarizes this perspective admirably: 'The knowledge of God in the darkness is not merely negative. It is truly an experience of the presence of God as He is in Himself, in such wise that this awareness is completely blinding for the mind, and all the more so the closer it is to Him. In fact, one might also say that the darkness expresses the divine presence, and that the closer He comes to the soul, the more intense is the darkness.'[5] So it would seem that one drawing closer to God in prayer and the personal self-giving of a life-mission might well experience this deepening closeness as a dark time of mounting isolation, even abandonment.

Could this be a way of understanding the narrative dynamism of the gospels that leads Jesus towards the dark mystery of Gethsemane and Golgotha? Such at least is the generating hypothesis of this chapter: that the human self of Jesus is drawn ever more fully into reality as he enacts in our world the mission of the divine Son; Jesus' ever-greater self-outpouring in this mission leads him into an ever deeper knowledge of the Father who sends him on this mission and of himself as the Son who desires to do the will of the Father. But this is a knowledge he experiences primarily in terms of an intensifying love set amidst a gathering darkness.

All of this points to the kinds of question to which, I suggest, mystical texts may enhance our response. The range of arguments against incarnational conceptions in christology is fairly wide today. Yet there does seem to be a fundamental consensus among the critics that, simply put, we would not now understand our experience of Jesus in terms of a literal incarnation because a literal incarnation is simply unintelligible today, i.e., we don't understand the world or the human self in ways that could make sense of it. Among many others we might name the analyses of Schubert Ogden, Maurice Wiles, Karl-Josef Kuschel and John Hick as raising a number of objections along these lines.[6] Kuschel's argument seems to me the most nuanced and interesting and comes in the end, I would judge, closer to a sympathetic restatement of incarnational christology than a rejection of it as a hopeless blunder. He writes, 'the person, cause, and fate of Jesus Christ belong definitively to the determination of the eternal being of God. . . . God himself has determined himself as the Father of this Son, so that the event of Jesus Christ itself comes to have decisive, essentially real consequences for the determination of God's very being'.[7] Mystical theology is hardly an apt source of response to all the objections, but in what follows I will take up three central points of oppositon to incarnational thought and see how mystical theology might help in each case.

Objection 1: Divine and Human Existence Are Mutually Exclusive

The first and most straightforward objection is simply that divine existence and human existence are mutually exclusive; by definition the Creator is not a creature and vice versa.[8] This objection was stated perhaps most famously in recent thought by John Hick: 'to say, without explanation, that the historical Jesus of Nazareth was also God is as devoid of meaning as to say that this circle drawn with a pencil on paper is also a square'.[9] More recently Hick has put this question again and has insisted that his point is not simply about logical incoherence: 'The question . . . is not whether it is possible to give any coherent literal meaning to the idea of divine incarnation, but whether it is possible to do so in a way that satisfies the religious concerns which gave point to the doctrine'.[10]

McCabe has already suggested that this objection is not particularly helpful, even on the purely logical grounds upon which it was initially raised. For surely being God and being human do not share the same logical 'space' in the sense that a square and a circle both share the logical space we call 'shapes': 'God is not one of the items in some universe which have to be excluded if it is just man that you are talking about'.[11] So while it is true that there is no sense in which a human being could be any other creature, God is not, obviously, in the category of 'creature'. This means that it cannot be part of the definition of 'human being' to be exclusive of God.

Furthermore, how well do we really know 'what' God is, after all? If the mystical writers accomplish nothing else, surely they awake in us their own nose-wrinkling distaste for that subtlest of theological odours, the refined scent of the most perfect theory about God, the idolatrous perfume of that glittering and glistening godling: necessary being. Not for nothing did Pseudo-Dionysius drench his pages in all those astringent prefixes: God, he writes over and over, is *super*-existent being, *super*-intelligible intelligence, *super*-meaningful meaning.

So perhaps we need to respond to the objection that divine being and human being are mutually exclusive by asking whether this objection doesn't tend to lock God up into a coffer which has been studiously labelled 'divine being'. As God discloses Godself in the events concerning Jesus, we discover one who exists by a free activity of love, by an eternal trinitarian mutual self-giving: God's existence is not a kind of bleak and bare necessity, but rather God exists by the free decision to give Godself away – Father to Son, Son to Father in the Holy Spirit. God, in other words, is not the captive of some predetermined divine nature but exists in the free personal acts of triune self-giving.

What makes God so unknowable, so hidden, is not simply the suspiciously Olympian purity of the divine 'nature' but precisely the unfathomability of this trinitarian self-sharing. In contrast to our way of existing as individuals ever opposed to each other, fretfully fencing ourselves round against the other – in contrast to creaturely being, the mystery of divine being lies precisely in the immensity of the love by which the three divine Persons *are*, exactly not by choosing to grasp or protect their divine equality but by abandoning their all, one for another, in love and freedom. The real hiddenness of God, I want to suggest, does *not* result from the putatively unutterable oneness of the divine essence (a oneness about which, after all, philosophy has been able to say rather a lot quite apart from anything discovered in Christ). Rather God's hiddenness has to do with the heart-stopping, breath-taking freedom of the three divine Persons to give themselves away in love to each other, and so to us and all creation – it is this which is truly incomprehensible.

But what of Hick's argument that every time theologians try to understand what the doctrine of the Incarnation means, they end up depriving it of the very religious concerns out of which it originated and 'which gave point to the doctrine'?

Here we need to recollect that we're thinking about the Incarnation not in terms of the divine and human natures per se, but in terms of the *personal identifying activity* (hypostasis) in which Jesus' life is grounded (hypostatic union). And we need more than ever to hang on to the idea that God is a mystery to us not because God zealously shoos away any impertinent inquirers into the divine being, but because in our world the trinitarian life of freely giving yourself away in love to the other is an act of blinding – even incomprehensible – foolishness. And yet it is precisely the particularity of this trinitarian pattern of existence to which we must attend. That is, we don't want to keep on puzzling over logical conundrums regarding how divine nature and human nature are somehow meant to be jiggled together. It is just this queasy mesmerism of trying to fit divine part A into human part B that has given us all those furrowed brows from Nestorius to Eutyches and Schleiermacher to John Hick and Co.

Jesus is the Word incarnate, Christians say. What this means of course is that this is *who* Jesus is. The fact that Jesus is a divine Person doesn't mean that he is not human, for the person he is tells us precisely *who* he is not *what* he is. The problem for us, of course, is that we have managed to make a world in which being human in this particular way gets you crucified, in which the joyful receiving of all you are from God and the loving giving away of all you are to others and so to God means identifying yourself, signing yourself with the Cross.

As we all know very well, being marked with the Cross doesn't change us from being human to being angels or any other kind of being; but it does begin to hold before our eyes another way of being *who* we are, another way of being human – a way that corresponds to the way of God's Beloved into the far country: for being human means losing yourself, being caught up in the mission of Jesus.

The correlate of this in mystical thought is the idea that the mystical journey does not involve the *overcoming* of human nature but rather the *participation* of human life in that identifying pattern of activity or mission which is Christ's. So, for example, when John of the Cross surveys the mystical journey, he wants his readers to be firmly aware of the *context* of this journey. And that context, for John, is the mission of Christ. The mystical journey is in fact an interior sharing in the spiritual states of Christ as he makes his own journey through life and death and into glory.

Over and over John of the Cross explains that one must not flinch from spiritual dryness or desolation, even from a sense of self-loss, because these are simply the mystic's share in the stages of Christ's self-giving and self-abandonment. Among many examples: 'It happens that . . . when the pure spiritual cross and nakedness of Christ's poverty of spirit is offered them in dryness, distaste, and trial, they run from it'.[12] Or again: 'Because I have said that Christ is the Way and that this Way is a death to our natural selves in the sensory parts of the soul, I would like to demonstrate how this death is patterned on Christ's. For he is our model and light' (*Ascent*, II.7.9, p. 97).

We see a similar pattern in Edith Stein's thought as she reflects on John: 'As, in the desolation of his death, Jesus surrendered himself into the hands of the invisible and incomprehensible God, so the soul must enter the midnight darkness of faith, which is the only way to this God'.[13] For John of the Cross as for Stein, it is not simply that the human spiritual journey echoes Christ's, but rather that it takes place *by means of* Christ's. We saw (in chapter 2) the same point made by Bonaventure at the climactic moment of his *Journey of the Soul to God*, where the soul is encouraged to enter into the Passion/Passover of Christ: 'Let us, then, die and enter into this darkness. Let us silence all our cares, our desires, and our imaginings. With Christ crucified, let us pass out of this world to the Father'.[14]

Already we can see here that, for these writers, the mystical journey is not a bare impersonal encounter with God but an entrance into the trinitarian life; that is, the mystic comes to experience God not as a blank Other, but from within the reality of the Son and gazing towards the infinite (and so hidden) glory of the Father in their Spirit. The God whom the mystic encounters, writes Edith Stein 'is overflowing love, in which the Father generates the Son and gives him his Being, while the Son embraces this Being and returns it to the Father; it is the love in which the Father and the Son are one, both breathing the Holy Spirit'.[15] The consummation of the mystical journey, then, is not simply to share in divine existence per se. Rather it is to share in the eternal Son's particular mode of enacting this existence. The soul comes to experience itself as the total gift of the Father; the soul discovers its personal freedom and identity by loving this Giver in a reciprocal act of total self-giving. The soul, says Stein, 'loves the Father with the love of the Son'.[16]

As we have seen, these mystical writers (and many others) are convinced that the best understanding of the mystical life is as a participation in Christ and, therefore, they are also convinced that a fundamental analogy exists between the soul's mystical journey into God and the historical incarnational journey of Jesus as he carries out the mission of eternal Sonship. The point of all this is to remind us that it is not abstract divinity which Christians claim to be incarnate in a human life, but that particular pattern of personal existence whom we call the divine Son. So there are logical problems (as McCabe showed) entailed by arguing, as our first objection does, that God per se cannot be human. But even beyond these, the religious concern involved is *not* in any case to say that bare deity can also be human, but rather that the eternal pattern of filial love (divine sonship) can be enacted divinely and *also humanly as well*.

This point was made some time ago in the context of a sermon by John Henry Newman on the mystery of divine self-humbling. Newman's approach to this subject is thought-provoking, for he is working to draw his listeners not merely to an intellectual apprehension of divine kenosis, but to a personal trust, indeed personal sharing, in that mystery. He sets his hearers rather artfully in a contest of understanding between the cold and clever individual reasoner of today (whom he elsewhere calls 'the self-wise inquirer') and, on the other hand, the ardently involved early Christians. These latter, he says, 'felt that in saying Christ was the Son of God, they were witnessing to a thousand marvellous and salutary truths, which they could not indeed understand, but by which they might gain life, and for which they could dare to die'.[17] Newman's hearers are invited to feel the disparity in understanding between a life thus lived within the dynamic of Christ's own self-sacrifice and the pallid curiosity of the present age.

He goes on to suggest that while early Christians sought to know Christ contemplatively, entering into the mystery of his divine source, the present age too easily stops short at mere formulas and, 'under the pretence of guarding against presumption, denies us what is revealed' (586). As ever with Newman, *what* is known follows closely *how* it is known. This is the key, for in Newman's estimation it is precisely the present age's lack of participation in the mystery of Christ which leads it into an unsettling disquietude of thought. By refusing to enter contemplatively into 'what is revealed', modern people are unable to sense the inner logic of the Incarnation and instead are left with a bare incongruity, an unintelligible conjunction of divine and human.

> We speak of [Christ] in a vague way as God, which is true, but not the whole truth; and, in consequence when we proceed to consider His humiliation, we are unable to carry on the notion of His personality from heaven to earth. He who was but now spoken of as God, without mention of the Father from whom He is, is next described as if a creature; but how do these distinct notions of Him hold together in our minds? We are able indeed to continue the idea of a Son into that of a servant, though the descent was infinite, and to our reason, incomprehensible; but when we merely speak first of God, then of man, we seem to change the Nature without preserving the Person. In truth, His Divine Sonship is that portion of the sacred doctrine on which the mind is providentially intended to rest throughout, and so to preserve for itself His identity unbroken (586–7).

At last the point of Newman's sermonic placement of his listeners *within* the mystery of Christ's relationship to the Father becomes apparent. One can begin to understand what it means for a son to enact his sonship one way in eternity and another way within constraints of a broken world – yet it is the same personal identity, that same particular pattern of filial activity, which is at work in both cases. By contrast the merely curious reasoner has not developed the contemplative sensibility that would enable one to see beyond the seemingly abstract transition from divine to human nature.

Newman, like John of the Cross and Edith Stein, is not simply proposing a kind of fideism – just believe in the Incarnation a little more religiously and then you shall understand it! – but is suggesting that contemplative participation in Christ's life and destiny does afford an important and probative vantage point. For it introduces the contemplative believer into that particular pattern of receptive and self-giving love which identifies the Son, that pattern of trinitarian relationality which distinguishes the Son from the Father and the Spirit. It is this same pattern that identifies Jesus as who he is and distinguishes him as a person. The fact that he lives out these characteristic features of his personhood as a fully human historical individual is what constitutes him as the Incarnation of the Son, for that is whose personal activity he lives out – nowhere more completely than on the Cross.

As Austin Farrer put it, preaching in the same city as Newman over a century later:

> We cannot understand Jesus as simply the God-who-was-man. We have left out an essential factor, the sonship. Jesus is not simply God manifest as man; he is the divine Son coming into manhood. What was expressed in human terms here below was not bare deity; it was the divine sonship. God cannot live an identically godlike life in eternity and in a human story. But the divine Son can make an identical response to his Father, whether in the love of the blessed Trinity or in the fulfilment of an earthly ministry.[18]

The mystical apprehension of christology from within, from the vantage of participation in the Son's earthly mission, is the basis of this awareness. The reality of the Incarnation is no longer conceived as a logical conundrum about mutually exclusive natures being fitted together (as though God's 'nature' were a kind of super-celestial stuff alongside our merely mortal stuff). Instead, incarnational christology is drawn back into what are most likely its origins, the church's participation in Jesus' trinitarian existence, in his relationship with the One he called 'Abba' through the Spirit.

Perhaps it will be objected that to say that Jesus lives out *humanly* the same pattern of life that distinguishes the divine Son from the Father and the Spirit is still not quite the same thing as to say, straightforwardly, that the eternal Son became human as Jesus. If, however, we recollect something of Maximus's christology (discussed in chapter 2), it should be apparent that to speak of this filial pattern of activity is precisely to speak of the *tropos* or mode of being of the Son; in other words, it is exactly this *tropos* which constitutes the distinct hypostasis or person of the Son. So what we have been proposing, drawing on this mystical approach to christology, is simply another way of talking about the hypostatic union. The fully human individual, Jesus, is identified by the personal pattern of life he lives, and that pattern is the Son's – that is *who* Jesus is, the eternal Son.

He is the eternal Word speaking the Father's love in the lamed and disjointed language that we have made of human existence. It is by God's mercy that the speaking of this eternal Word should take the form of a fully human being, who is willing to go on loving, and so being human, no matter the cost; it is by our sin that this Word could only be spoken in our world in suffering, betrayal and death. This approach to pondering the doctrine of the Incarnation *does* seem to me, Hick's views to the contrary notwithstanding, to speak of the Incarnation in a 'way that satisfies the religious concerns which gave point to the doctrine'.[19]

Objection 2: Insufficient Knowledge of Jesus' Self-Understanding

A second objection holds that one cannot make theological sense out of the idea that this human being Jesus is actually the Second Person of the Trinity because historical critical approaches to the Bible simply do not any longer support such a reading. Numerous questions are raised here. In the first place, the historical critics do not believe that Jesus' historical self-consciousness can in fact be known with much certainty. Second, what they do think might legitimately be surmised about Jesus' self-understanding is hardly sufficient to identify him as a divine Person existing humanly. The fundamental question then arises: if Jesus is the eternal Word acting within humanity to rescue humanity, ought not we be able to say with more certainty that this is in fact Jesus' self-understanding?[20]

So this argument usually attempts to frame a dilemma. If Jesus is the Word incarnate it would seem likely that he would have some consciousness of his identity, but would such knowledge really be consonant with a truly human existence? On the other hand if Jesus is not humanly conscious of his identity, in what sense can we coherently speak of a literal incarnation of the divine Word in this human life? Of course this critique acknowledges the attempts of other eras to answer these questions but, on the basis of new biblical research and modern understandings of God and the human self, these earlier answers are seen as being unworkable.

First we might simply remind ourselves of something that emerged in the previous section, namely the *kind* of consciousness of God that develops as one enters into the patterns of Jesus' life, death and resurrection. At the level of greatest intimacy with God, human self-understanding may develop not so much in terms of propositions about one's own identity but in terms of relationship with the Father who gives all and to whom one longs to return all in reciprocal love. In other words, it can hardly count against Jesus' divinity that the historical critics believe he never went around detailing with metaphysical exactitude his status as the Incarnate Son; we do however have historical reason to believe that he did understand himself profoundly in relationship to the One he called 'Abba' and of whose Kingdom he may well have believed himself to be the bearer.[21] As Farrer put it once, 'To *be* the Son was to *know* the Father, not for the Son to know himself'.[22]

But if we turn now to the specifically noetic aspects of Christian apophatic traditions we may find further tools for thinking about these questions. Here we encounter the conviction that the ultimate knowing of God, the kind that shares in God's own knowing of Godself (i.e., the Son's knowing of the Father in their Spirit), is most likely to be experienced by the human self as an overwhelming darkness that yet remains grounded in love. I turn first to Gregory of Nyssa, whose re-construal of the Origenian mystical itinerary in the light of a new emphasis on the divine infinity is so important for Christian spirituality.[23]

The hypothesis I want to explore is this: Gregory (and many another of apophatic perspective) describes the highest levels of divine presence to the soul as a luminous darkness, an unknowing, and an unsatiated desire; this insight provides a mystical analogy helping to explain the manner of Jesus' consciousness of his own identity. In other words, we might be able to find in this analogy a way to do justice both to incarnational christology and to a realistically human interpretation of Jesus' historical self-consciousness. Let me now offer at least the preliminary outline of such an argument.

Vladimir Lossky, among others, has pointed out that for Origen and Evagrius, darkness remained a sign of all that *separates* the soul from the light of God; but for Gregory of Nyssa the dark cloud of Sinai and the shimmering night of the Song of Songs represent a far more perfect 'mode of *communion* with God'.

> If God appears first as light and then as darkness, this means for Gregory that of the divine essence there is no vision, and that union with God is a way surpassing vision or *theoria*, going beyond intelligence to where knowledge vanishes and only love remains . . . . Desiring God more and more, the soul grows without ceasing, going beyond herself; and in the measure in which she unites herself more and more to God, her love becomes more ardent and insatiable.[24]

Lossky summarizes all our themes here, but for the moment just note the sense that this powerful yearning for God, which draws the soul beyond the self, is not a diminution of the self but the means of its growth: the human self is drawn into fuller and fuller existence by the lure of God.[25]

In his treatment of the Song of Songs, Gregory describes the divine Lover as wooing the bride into true beauty, from a kind of *provisional* existence into the concreteness of *actual* reality. 'The bride says, "My beloved is mine and I am his who feeds among the lilies," the same one who has transformed human life from shadowy phantasms to the supreme truth.'[26] The bride recognizes herself as one who is given identity precisely by her delight in the bridegroom, and Gregory (like Hadewijch centuries later) clearly sees this as a mystical paradox: an ecstatic passing-beyond-the-self to the other – which is in fact the *constitution* of the self, the drawing of the self from phantasm into truth.

Suppose we allow these perceptions to serve as a matrix within which we interpret the historical existence of Jesus: his human existence is literally drawn into being by union with the Word, and this need not be seen as a static ontological fixity but as something perpetually achieved anew – the human being Jesus coming to fuller and fuller self-expression precisely as Jesus hungers and thirsts with an ever more fateful urgency 'to do the will of the Father' (i.e., to enact the filial pattern of existence).

If we turn more directly to the much vexed question of Jesus' knowledge of God, it will be salutary to remind ourselves what kind of genuinely human 'knowledge' one can have of God in any case. Since God is not among the items of the universe, one would surely not expect God to be an 'object' of knowledge per se. Whatever it could mean to 'know' God would seem to be connected to a sense of spiritual darkness and perhaps of being grasped by a necessity beyond one's understanding (Gethsemane). 'We can say that it is an intellectual experience of the mind's failure when confronted with something beyond the conceivable.'[27]

Daniélou has catalogued the various ways in which Gregory of Nyssa depicts this experience of God's infinity: darkening of the intelligence, images of inebriation, vertigo, dizziness – all point to 'the soul's complete confusion in the presence of a reality for which there is no common measure'.[28] The bride's restless search for the absent beloved causes her to realize 'that her sought after love is known only in her impossibility to comprehend his essence' (CSS, 131). So in Gregory's view, a sense of unknowing and unclarity are the virtual hallmarks of authentic knowledge of God.

And beyond this there is perhaps an authentic unknowing knowledge of God that is distilled as *a new sense of self*. This knowledge of God is, in other words, embodied not as information in the mind but as a sharpening sense of mission and identity – the soul comes to define its own existence more and more in terms of its yearning for the absent One and its desire to fulfil the wishes of this One. In a similar vein, Dionysius speaks of the highest knowledge of God being given only to one who 'belongs completely to [God] who is beyond everything. Here, being neither oneself nor someone else, one is supremely united by a completely unknowing inactivity of all knowledge'.[29] In other words, one experiences an ultimate intimacy with God as a sense of belonging to the divine Other, a sense of *self as constituted by relationship to God*.

But because God is infinite, the soul's intimacy with God can continue to deepen infinitely so that, in the words of John of the Cross, 'the soul becomes aware of being attracted by the love of God and enkindled in it, without knowing how or where this attraction and love originates'; as this progresses, 'the longings for God become so intense that it will seem to individuals that their bones are drying up in this thirst' (*Dark Night*, I.11.1, p. 187). A curious phenomenon happens at this point: the more the soul gives itself to God and draws close to God, the more the soul's longing for God intensifies, and the more the soul is painfully aware of the infinity of God which it lacks. John says that at this stage 'it seems God is against them . . . . that God has rejected them' (*Dark Night*, II.5.5, p. 202).

The christological analogies here are stark enough to note quite readily. If Jesus is truly a human being existing by means of his identity as the eternal divine Son, we would not expect him to know this in any purely discursive rational manner. Rather, if the mystical union is any guide, we might expect Jesus to have a pervasive sense of the enrapturing and infinite goodness of God ('Why do you call me good? No one is good but God alone.' [Mk 10.18]), to have an intensifying sense of personal calling, and a desire to abandon himself to the will of the One who becomes ever more absent and unavailable – think of the strange thirst and cry of dereliction on the Cross.

For Jesus to be experienced by the earliest Christians as, literally speaking, constituted by the gift of the Father's love and by his desire to respond to this love – this is, in the apophatic tradition, an authentic sign of the infinite intimacy of God's presence to Jesus.[30] Whatever we might mean by Jesus' self-understanding, the apophatic analogy suggests that we ought to look not for propositional details of cognition, but for a pattern of self-giving action and love even in the face of seeming rejection.

Does this mystical approach in terms of the negative knowledge of God threaten to undermine the human consciousness of Jesus altogether? Gregory describes the bride as saying: 'I have sought him [the bridegroom] by my soul's capacities of reflection and understanding; he completely transcended them, and escaped my mind when it drew near to him' (*CSS*, 220). The soul's experience is not anti-noetic in the sense of implying that the quest for God demands an infamous sacrifice of the intellect, rather it is an awareness (with a very definite intellectual component) that the source of one's desire is beyond the grasp of the intellect. This is not, therefore, a humanly diminishing mindlessness but a kind of amazement that is exhilarating and liberating for the whole person; drawn closer to God in this way, Gregory implies, the human self is invited into a realm of possibilities it would never have imagined. We might note the simple analogy of a truly overwhelming work of art: the beholder stands mutely riveted in delighted wonder before an expression of unutterable depth; while one clearly will never begin to fathom the work, one is marvellously engaged by a world of meaning whose existence one had never even dreamt of. This experience is by all accounts among the most life-giving and ennobling one can have.

Jesus feels himself constituted by his desire to respond to God, (in ways that far outstrip the power of his own understanding). In the apophatic mystical tradition this signals a momentum towards greater fulfilment as a human being as well as betokening God's presence. Commenting on the dark night of the soul in John of the Cross, Denys Turner makes an important point: the apophatic traditions we have been considering are all based on the conviction that the real roots of our identity our hidden in God. This means that the more fully we have 'understood' who we really are, the less we are likely to feel securely in 'possession' of some graspable self.

> Our deepest centre, the most intimate source from which our actions flow, our freedom to love, is in us but not of us, is not 'ours' to possess, but ours only to be possessed by. And so faith at once 'decentres' us, for it disintegrates the experiential structures of selfhood on which, in experience, we centre our-selves, and at the same time draws us into the divine love where we are 'recentred' upon a ground beyond any possibility of experience.[31]

To risk the plunge into the unfathomable waters of one's vocation is precisely to be decentred in this way, for it is to discover the true meaning of one's life in the darkness and void that lie beyond one's control.

The soul experiences this deepening darkness not only in intellectual but also broadly existential ways. Jesus' experience of abandonment and isolation in the final stages of his life could thus be read in terms of the unfathomable presence of God – drawing Jesus into an intimacy so infinite that our world can only experience it as absence, forsakenness, the ultimate decentring. He may never have known or fulfilled himself more consummately than in the final self-surrender of the Cross. In short, earlier incarnational christologies may have relied on super-human evaluations of Jesus' knowledge and high readings of his self-understanding; but the mystical analogies we have been considering suggest that such construals are neither necessary for, nor even consistent with, a maximally incarnational view of Jesus.

Objection 3: Incarnational Christologies are Inevitably Docetic

Our third objection holds that the doctrine of the Incarnation inherently leads to severely vitiated or inconsequential renderings of Christ's humanity. However much the Chalcedonian definition may declare that Jesus is fully human, it seems hard to find an accepted orthodox christology that accords much significance – so the criticism runs – to the real human struggle of Jesus' historical existence. Can a human being be a divine Person and really still be human? As Frances Young put it: 'Jesus cannot be a *real* man and also unique in a sense different from that in which each one of us is a unique individual. A literal incarnation doctrine, expressed in however sophisticated a form, cannot avoid some elements of docetism, and involves the believer in claims for uniqueness [of Christ] which seem straightforwardly incredible to the majority of our contemporaries.'[32]

Now there is a problem with this line of argument, at least as it is articulated here. Young implies that whatever it is that would make Jesus unique (beyond the usual kind of uniqueness we all have as individuals) must necessarily also make him other than human. We are trapped here in the old essentialist thinking of the worst kind, I fear. What seems to lie behind this view is the persuasion that Jesus' divine-and-human status must somehow vitiate his full humanity; as though the divine 'nature' were a heavenly substance which had to be filtered into Jesus so that, at the end of the day, he could hardly still be called human at all. Yet I have been arguing all along that what distinguishes Jesus from other human beings is *not* anything at the level of *nature*, but precisely that which distinguishes us all from one another as individuals, our *personal identity*.

The fact that Peter and Paul carry out the mission of the gospel in very different ways is part of what distinguishes them from each other, for it is bound up with their personhood, namely, the way they enact the particular pattern of life which is *who* they are. The fact that their *personal identities* are different does not, however, make either of them less than fully human (whatever they may sometimes have thought of each other). It is true, then, that Jesus' personal identity is different from anyone else's, just as is every individual's personal identity, yet this is not the category which tells us *what* Jesus is but rather *who* he is. And *who* he is, is the eternal Word of God, but that does not mean that *what* he is is other than fully human.

Again, the achievement of Chalcedon is to clarify that if we persist in talking about the mystery of the Incarnation in terms of the category of nature, we are likely to run into exactly the kind of puzzlement that Young's concern exemplifies. The union of divine and human in Christ does not take place at the level of nature, essence, or *ousia* but at the level of person or *hypostasis*. It is precisely this *distinction* between nature and person, developed by the Cappadocians in the context of trinitarian reflection, which allows us to see that our personal identity is not constrained or determined by our nature. Rather our personhood is the developing result of our free and individualizing enactment of our existence through *relationship with others*.[33] Whether Jesus' full humanity is necessarily rendered nugatory simply because the personhood he comes to enact is *characterized by a very particular relationship* (i.e., sonship) to the One he called 'Abba' and their Spirit is what we must now consider.

Putting aside Young's particular formulation of the docetism charge, we may still grant that, historically, many incarnational christologies have indeed seemed to find little significance in Jesus' humanity, even while they might not have intended in any way to deny it. Here is where the more affective themes of desire and ecstasy in the apophatic tradition become especially helpful. Just as the soul enters into *knowledge* of God by the way of darkness or unknowing, so the soul *embraces* God by an endless *erōs* that is never satiated but rather draws the soul beyond itself. In fact Gregory of Nyssa speaks of the soul being continually led from her 'place' by desire for God (*CSS* 218–20). Or as Daniélou puts it, 'As God's adorable presence becomes more and more intense, the soul is, as it were, forced to go out of itself by a kind of infatuation'.[34] The crucial mystical paradox, as we have seen before, is that this *ekstasis* towards God is also the soul's consummate *enactment* of its human existence.

The point of construing Christ's ever greater momentum of self-giving in terms of a continual *ekstasis* like Gregory of Nyssa's is not to suggest that Jesus was some kind of ecstatic in the technical sense, but rather to offer this theme of being-drawn-beyond-oneself as a way of illuminating the fullness of Jesus' humanity. The deepening sense of necessity, even of fateful self-surrender, implicit in the gospels might be read in this way as pointing to the intensity of desire being aroused in Jesus, and thus to the intimate presence of the One who stimulates such desire. What is crucial to note here is that in this apophatic tradition there is absolutely no sense in which a full divine presence diminishes or subverts the fully authentic humanity of the individual. Quite the reverse. The ever-fuller intimacy of the divine presence to the soul draws the soul beyond the usual limits, stretches it to the fullest and highest extent of human existence.

Such an ecstatic existence, that is, an existence in which Jesus' humanity comes to ever greater fulfilment precisely as it is drawn into the eternal mission of the divine Son – such an existence is, the mystical tradition declares, the fullest realization and actualization of human selfhood. This ecstatic existence literally means, says John of the Cross, that the human being comes to live the very life of God on earth:

> Just as the soul, according to St Paul, will know then as she is known by God [1 Cor 13:12], so she will also love God as she is loved by Him. As her intellect will be the intellect of God, her will then will be God's will, and thus her love will be God's love. The soul's will is not destroyed there [in the state of union],

but it is so firmly united with the strength of God's will, with which He loves her, that her love for Him is as strong and perfect as His love for her, for the two wills are so united that there is only one will and love, which is God's (*Spiritual Canticle*, stanza 38.3, p. 279).

If again we offer this description of mystical union as at least an analogy for what takes place in the hypostatic union of the Incarnation, then the inference is clear: far from undermining the significance of Jesus' humanity, such a union permits the truly human intellect and will of Jesus to act with the strength and significance of God.

Does this mean that Jesus' humanity is in some sense absorbed, lost in the divine, so that his acts are not his own, not free acts? It is true that apophatic mysticism emphasizes a radical abandonment of the self; John of the Cross even uses the disconcerting term 'annihilation'. But what such writers mean by this is a free movement of the human being beyond all the constraints of the ego's desire to manipulate, possess and control persons and things for the ego's own ends. Such an ecstatic freedom, says Edith Stein, means to discover the foundations of one's true self; the higher the soul ascends into God, 'the deeper it descends into itself: the union [of the soul and God] takes place in the innermost sphere of the soul, in its deepest ground.'[35] So the journey into God is seen not ultimately as a loss of self but as a homecoming to the divinely-beloved self, beyond the false selves projected onto the soul by prevalent ideologies, mass marketing, dysfunctional childhood, even (perhaps especially) by religious asceticism of the self-possessive sort.

The highest union with God, Stein suggests, could never mean a loss of the human self or its freedom: 'For the indwelling [of God in the soul] demands from both sides an interior being, i.e., a being that embraces itself interiorly [*das sich selbst innerlich umfasst*] and is capable of receiving another being within itself, so that a uniting of being is effected without destroying the independence of either the receiving or the received being.'[36] Thus to speak of Jesus as existing enhypostatically, in the Person of the Son, need not at all be seen as a denial or loss of his human selfhood. Indeed the gospel narratives might well be read as pointing to a genuine search on Jesus' part for the truth of his selfhood and his mission, a truth he intuits not with a stultifying fixity but through the historical human struggle of his whole life – baptism, misunderstood teaching, agony of Gethsemane, and all the rest. And in fact this is what we would expect in one who is grappling to discern his true identity within the mystery of his union with God.

None of this is to suggest that the harsh realities of Christ's life and death are only a dispensable visual aid for some supposedly more real interior drama of his soul. The point is to see that even the viciously mundane details of Christ's suffering speak of his share in the human separation from God. That is, Jesus' sorrowfulness and his thirst are not merely a kind of 'spiritual' desolation somehow quite other than the actual brute facts of his existence in the world; no, the desperate thirst of his soul is fully and really lived out in his *ekstasis* from Jerusalem to Golgotha, in his self-abandonment into the hands of the other, both human and divine.

By reading this desolation in terms of the apophatic tradition we begin to see how entirely his dereliction might be the fullest sign of his union with God. In a crucial passage, John of the Cross remarks that Jesus accomplishes his mission most fully in the utterly broken-down human failure of the Cross:

> this was the most extreme abandonment, sensitively, that He had suffered in His life. And by it He accomplished the most marvelous work of His whole life surpassing all the works and deeds and miracles that He had ever performed on earth or in heaven. That is, He brought about the reconciliation and union of the human race with God through grace. The Lord achieved this, as I say, at the moment in which He was most annihilated in all things (*Ascent of Mount Carmel* II, vii, 11; p. 97).

In the language of mystical paradox, then, one might even say that Jesus is most divine (most fully enacting the eternal mission of the Son) and the Incarnation is most fully consummated exactly at Golgotha, when the aching physicality of his humanity is unlimited and the unknowing of himself and God is entire. Jesus does not need to be 'super-human' to be the Incarnation of the Word, suggests the mystical tradition; the very struggles and frailties of human life are radicalized in him – wounded tokens of his union with God in a world where God is rejected.

At the very least the usual criticism that incarnational christology is unintelligible for moderns seems unconvincing. The fullest, most intense expressions of Jesus' *human existence*, when construed in correlation to apophatic traditions, are seen as the most coherent signs of his infinite intimacy with God. So perhaps christology today might turn with legitimate hope to the insights of mystical theology, to the witness of those who have sought to know Christ by the shattering and re-creative sharing of his own life from within.

Yet if contemporary christology is going to understand something of the fullness of the Word's humanity, it will need not only to *draw* on the mystical journey of others as a source, but also to venture some way along the path itself. Austin Farrer reflected on the daily struggle of Jesus to discover and to enact his true identity as a human being; but Farrer pondered these things in a way that pointed to our own participation in Christ as the best means to real understanding – of both Christ's human life, and his identity as God's Word.

> [Jesus] made himself, he built his human greatness stone by stone, choosing love daily and rejecting evil. Every such choice renewed and affirmed his union with his Father's life. By every act he committed himself wholly, so far as any man can commit himself by any act. But our human condition does not allow us to prefabricate our moral future. Today's acts make us what tomorrow will find us, and yet, being what we are tomorrow, we shall have to remake ourselves then by fresh decisions. The situations will be new, the temptations new. Though every act of Christ's was perfect, none of them was final except the last, nothing irrevocable but voluntary death. . . . Such, then, was the life of Christ. . . . It was not a pattern of moral choice forestalling all surprises, it was divine Sonship, filial love.[37]

For Farrer, the vitality and fullness of Jesus' humanity is forged in his passionate desire to do the Father's will. And Farrer, like Newman before him, locates us in this same relationship. 'Whatever our future hopes', he writes, 'our present concern is to live ourselves into the living Christ, the man whom God the Son has become by his life and death.' We become most fully human persons, ultimately, as we come to live into the eucharistic act by which Jesus – through the whole course of his giving life – gives himself away to those who need him and so finally into the hands of his Father: 'Christ is his accepted sacrifice, that is his present being. Taken into his sacrifice we are ourselves both sacrificed and accepted, for we are brought into Christ.'[38] We become who we are as Christ came to be who he is, by giving self away freely in love.

Notes

1 The Council of Chalcedon's 'Definition of the Faith' in *The Christological Controversy*, trans. and ed. Richard A. Norris, Jr (Fortress: Philadelphia, 1980), 159. The literature on the history of christology is of course enormous. See especially, Alois Grillmmeier, *Christ in Christian Tradition*, trans. John Bowden. 2nd edn (London: Mowbray, 1975).

2 Michel de Certeau, *The Mystic Fable*, vol. 1, *The Sixteenth and Seventeenth Centuries*, trans. Michael B. Smith (Chicago: The University of Chicago Press, 1992), 77.

3 Ibid., 15.

4 Herbert McCabe, *God Matters* (London: Geoffrey Chapman, 1987), 41–2.

5 Jean Daniélou, Introduction to *From Glory to Glory: Texts from Gregory of Nyssa's*

    Mystical Writings, trans. and ed. Herbert Musurillo (Crestwood, New York: St Vladimir's Seminary Press, 1979), 31–2.

6   See, e.g., Schubert Ogden, *The Point of Christology* (New York: Harper & Row, 1982); Karl-Josef Kuschel, *Born Before All Time? The Dispute over Christ's Origin* (New York: Crossroad, 1992); John Hick, *The Metaphor of God Incarnate: Christology in a Pluralistic Age* (Louisville, Kentucky: Westminster/John Knox Press, 1993); for Maurice Wiles see John Hick, ed., *The Myth of God Incarnate* (London: SCM Press, 1977).

7   Kuschel, *Born Before All Time?*, 495.

8   See the useful summaries of these kinds of objection in Richard Sturch, *The Word and the Christ: An Essay in Analytic Christology* (Oxford: Oxford University Press, 1991), 17–25.

9   John Hick, ed. *The Myth of God Incarnate*, 178.

10   Idem., *The Metaphor of God Incarnate*, 4.

11   McCabe, *God Matters*, 57–8.

12   John of the Cross, *The Ascent of Mount Carmel*, II.7.5 in *John of the Cross: Selected Writings*, ed. Kieran Kavanagh, OCD (New York: Paulist Press, 1987), 95. All citations from John will be from this edition.

13   Edith Stein, *The Science of the Cross: A Study of St John of the Cross*, trans. Hilda Graef (London: Burns & Oates, 1960), 89.

14   Bonaventure, *Journey of the Mind to God*, VII.6, trans. Philotheus Boehner, ed. Stephen F. Brown (Cambridge: Hackett Publishing Company, 1993), 39.

15   Stein, *Science of the Cross*, 126–7.

16   Ibid.

17   John Henry Newman, 'The Humiliation of the Eternal Son' in *Parochial and Plain Sermons*, vol. 3 [1836] (San Francisco: Ignatius Press, 1987), 581. Subsequent quotations are from this edition and are given parenthetically.

18   Austin Farrer, *The Brink of Mystery*, ed. Charles C. Conti (London: SPCK, 1976), 20.

19   Hick, *Metaphor of God Incarnate*, 4.

20   This is a frequently raised objection; see for example in Hick, ed., *Myth of God Incarnate* points made by Wiles and by Cuppitt at pp. 5 and 136 respectively.

21   See on this especially E. P. Sanders, whose nuanced reading of Jesus' eschatological expectations includes a definite role for Jesus himself in the coming Kingdom; *Jesus and Judaism* (Philadelphia: Fortress, 1985).

22   Austin Farrer, 'Very God and Very Man' in *Interpretation and Belief*, ed. Charles C. Conti (London: SPCK, 1976), 136.

23   See the helpful placement of Gregory in Bernard McGinn, *Foundations of Mysticism*, 139–42. See also the very useful survey by Anthony Meredith, 'The Idea of God in Gregory of Nyssa', in *Studien zu Gregor von Nyssa und der Christlichen Spätantike*, ed. Hubertus R. Drobner and Christoph Klock (Leiden: E. J. Brill, 1990), 127–47 (pp. 138–44 analyse the concept of God in the *In Canticum Canticorum* and in the *De Vita Moysis*).

24   Vladimir Lossky, *In the Image and Likeness of God*, ed. John H. Erickson and

Thomas E. Bird (Crestwood, New York: St Vladimir's Seminary Press, 1985), 37.

25 'The essential element of any ecstasy as I. Hausherr has rightly said, is "a going out of oneself, not by an unconsciousness involving the suspension of sense activity, but by a kind of projection of the soul beyond the laws of reason under the impulse of love" ' (Jean Daniélou, Introduction to From Glory to Glory, 33).

26 Gregory of Nyssa, Commentary on the Song of Songs, trans. Casimir McCambley (Brookline, Massachusetts: Hellenic College Press, 1987), 130. Hereafter references to this source will by given in the text as CSS and page no..

27 Lossky, Image and Likeness, 13.

28 Daniélou, From Glory to Glory, 41.

29 Pseudo-Dionysius the Areopagite, Mystical Theology I.3, in Pseudo-Dionysius: The Complete Works, trans. Colm Luibheid and Paul Rorem, Classics of Western Spirituality (New York: Paulist Press, 1987) 137.

30 I am grateful to my Loyola colleague, John Haughey SJ, who suggested to me the apt phrase 'infinite intimacy' for describing this definitive characteristic of Jesus' life.

31 Denys Turner, The Darkness of God: Negativity in Christian Mysticism (Cambridge: Cambridge University Press, 1995), 251.

32 Frances Young, 'A Cloud of Witnesses', chapter in Hick, ed., The Myth of God Incarnate, 32.

33 Further on the development of the distinction between nature and person, and its theological implications, see John D. Zizioulas, Being as Communion and the same author's more recent summary essay, 'The Doctrine of the Holy Trinity: The Significance of the Cappadocian Contribution' in Christoph Schöbel, ed. Trinitarian Theology Today: Essays on Divine Being and Act (Edinburgh: T. & T. Clark, 1995); also Christos Yannaras, Elements of Faith: An Introduction to Orthodox Theology, trans. Keith Schram.(Edinburgh: T. & T. Clark, 1991).

34 Daniélou, From Glory to Glory, 43.

35 Edith Stein, Science of the Cross, 116.

36 Ibid., 132.

37 Austin Farrer, Lord I Believe: Suggestions for Turning the Creed into Prayer (Cambridge: Cowley Publications, 1989), 45–7.

38 Ibid., 48–9.

Chapter 7

LOVE FOR THE OTHER AND DISCOVERY OF THE SELF

The origins of Christian theological anthropology are dialogical and relational in structure. In the earliest Christian eucharistic communities (as we saw in chapter 2), the human person is seen as created in the image of God – and as being drawn into the fullness of that likeness through incorporation into the Body of Christ. This process of becoming who one most truly is takes place, in other words, by means of relationships, by means of love for the other – both divine and human.

Modernity's conception of the autonomous self did manage, however, to reframe the Christian understanding of the human person to an enormous extent. Just as the Christian doctrine of God was newly minted on the grounds of natural reason, so Christian anthropology was reconfigured as a direct correlate of that same Enlightenment argument about the deity. God is a particularly powerful and invisible subject who acts over against human subjects, and must then withdraw in order to permit their freedom to act autonomously (as though God were one of the acting subjects of the world who only happens to be more powerful than the others and so gets to be God instead of some other possible candidate). Likewise the human person comes to be understood as a human subject over against whom exists the range of objects for potential mastery or subordination.

Indeed it would be hard to say what exactly was the difference between the Enlightenment deity and the Enlightenment self. Perhaps, as Feuerbach later saw, they were only really distinguished from each other by their mutual exclusivity. And this feature was nicely codified by giving the divine subject a securely cordoned-off supernatural realm, thus bestowing on the human subject the 'real' world of nature in which to carry on being self-sufficient and autonomous.

As Louis Dupré has astutely observed, the withdrawal of God's intimate involvement with creation (beginning with late medieval nominalism), led also to questions about the source of meaning in the world:

> Whereas previously meaning had been established in the very act of creation by a wise God, it now fell upon the human mind to interpret a cosmos, the structure of which had ceased to be intelligible. Instead of being an integral part of the cosmos, the person became its source of meaning. Mental life separated from cosmic being: as meaning-giving 'subject', the mind became the spiritual substratum of all reality. Only what it objectively constituted would count as real.[1]

As a the new modern self thus accrued more and more tasks, its preeminence over cultural location, moral imperatives and linguistic structures was necessarily assumed. These features of reality, it was fancied, are constituted by the exigencies of human subjectivity and are best explained in terms of the *self's own inner life*.

Even in the thought of Schleiermacher and Rahner, who were concerned to re-establish anthropology in terms closely connected with Christian experience, the consciousness of the inner self is fundamentally unthematized – primordially cocooned from any concretely relational and linguistic transaction. The relation of the human subject to the transcendent divine reality may once again have become an important consideration; but it is disconcertingly hard to be sure whether, for Schleiermacher and Rahner, this is really a 'relationship' between the Creator and the creature (enacted in irreducibly historical terms), or if it is more nearly an inherent aspect of human subjectivity that is everywhere always the same. In other words, the gospel sense of the slow and costly strain of discipleship as the *matrix for the constitution of the human person* seems washed out in favour of a more interior and, in a sense, timeless self-consciousness. One does not become who one is by taking up one's cross and losing one's 'self' for Christ so much as one discovers that this discipleship is a particular cultural (even mythological) objectification of the universal structures of human consciousness.

It scarcely needs saying that the modern perspective on the self has, to put it mildly, come into question from that line of thought which is often referred to as postmodernism. From Nietzsche, through Heidegger, and French post-structuralist philosophy, postmodern writers have raised serious questions about the distinction of subject and object, and who gets to define them – about whether there is such a thing as a 'subject' in the modern and Romantic sense at all. In what follows I shall draw on the work of Emmanuel Levinas, Edith Wyschogrod and Michel de Certeau to suggest some of the questions and issues at stake in a postmodern reading of the self. Against this background, I think we will be able to see all the more clearly some of the most significant features of Christian anthropology framed in terms of mystical traditions as this is exemplified in the writing of Marguerite Porete and Meister Eckhart. We shall then be able to see the contemporary form of this approach in the thought of Edith Stein and Simone Weil.

But we also need to raise some of the troubling ambiguities that contemporary writers, especially feminist thinkers, have pointed to in postmodern notions. Specifically, for example, one wonders why the subject seems to be disappearing now in the endless deferral of discourse – just when women are achieving some social status as independent subjects themselves, no longer defined simply as objects for the real (male) subject. Does talk of the radically ecstatic self, abandoned for the other, function to legitimate oppression? How exactly does the postmodern or mystical subject get delineated – and by whom? When we return later in the chapter to mystical texts, we will be able to address these questions in the context of trinitarian spirituality, the very setting in which both Stein and Weil find the ultimate basis for all talk of person and self.

Postmodern Anthropology

This is hardly the place to develop a complete survey of postmodern anthropological thought, but I do want to sketch some ideas that will allow us to see how certain themes in Christian spirituality might easily find themselves in conversation with postmodern concerns.

Levinas

Few postmodern writers have more directly pondered the question of the human self than Emmanuel Levinas. Like Edith Stein and Simone Weil, Levinas – a Jew – suffered during the Nazi era in Europe; and his thought, like theirs, is doubtlessly sharpened and made all the more urgent by these experiences (which for him included a lengthy period of forced labour in a prisoner of war camp). His thought about human subjectivity is marked by such words as trauma, obsession, insomnia and restlessness. In fact we might say that Levinas begins with the awareness that behind its façade of self-sufficiency and control, the modern ego is a troubled creature, gnawed at by an inescapable call which is 'there' before it can even begin to hide in the thickets of its own essence.

The source of this call is the infinite, which Levinas does not hesitate to refer to as God. In his thought-provoking work, *Otherwise than Being or Beyond Essence*, Levinas points to the divine activity of creation as the beginning of this call: 'In creation, what is called to being answers to a call that could not have reached it since, brought out of nothingness, it obeyed before hearing the order'.[2] The paradox of this situation is highly suggestive: even before there is any self, any ego, or determined essence of the human, there is a responsivity. And this responsiveness is ineluctably also a responsibility towards the call; it is not, in other words, simply the static constitution of some personal substance but rather a momentum towards whatever calls. It is not a self, but, as Levinas puts it, the response of 'here I am'. So this responsibility towards the other who calls is not an existing ego's free choice; the prior call of the other evokes a responsivity, and so, ultimately, a self, into being. Whatever there comes to be of personal being is, so to speak, dependent upon this prior relation between the call and the response.

Levinas offers a less transcendental example in his imagery of awakening and insomnia. Just as we all like to slip back into the most delicious languors of a contented sleep, so, Levinas suggests, the ego would like to rest languorously in the comforting solidity of its essence as a self. Maddeningly, however, the ego is ever and again set on edge, aroused, sobered up, and a kind of insomnia overtakes it. My fatal (and all-too-complete) *dream* of being a self-sufficient self is troubled, so that what *could* be real about me may indeed be drawn into reality: 'Awakening is like a demand that no obedience is equal to, no obedience puts to sleep . . . it is the spirituality of the soul, ceaselessly aroused from its state of soul'.[3] Whoever 'I' am is only something that can be worked out in practice, a practice of obedience that is never completed in terms of some putative self-fulfilment on *my* part, but leaves a perpetual state of watching for the *other*.

What constitutes this awakening? Again, Levinas suggests that the very idea of God, 'but God already breaking up the consciousness which aims at ideas' is a kind of infinite awakening, calling me into being prior even to there being any 'me' which could comprehend or be the subject of this idea.[4] For Levinas, I do not come to be as a subject by some judicious manipulation of my own ideas or circumstances. Rather, whatever reality I have is coincident with the 'trauma of awakening', the inescapable calling of the Infinite within my finitude in an 'undergoing that no capacity comprehends' and which 'devastates its site like a devouring fire':

> It is a dazzling, where the eye takes more than it can hold, an igniting of the skin which touches and does not touch what is beyond the graspable and burns. It

is a passivity or a passion in which desire can be recognized, in which the '*more in the less*' awakens by its most ardent, noblest and most ancient flame a thought given over to thinking more than it thinks . . . . The negativity of the *in* of the Infinite – otherwise than being, divine comedy – hollows out a desire which cannot be filled, nourishes itself with its very augmentation, and is exalted as a desire, withdraws from its satisfaction in the measure that it approaches the desirable. It is a desire that is beyond satisfaction, and, unlike a need, does not identify a term or an end. This endless desire for what is beyond being is dis-interestedness, transcendence – desire for the Good.[5]

But, as Levinas quickly goes on to point out, it is precisely the characteristic of God as the Good to *reorient* my desire towards the other. God, in other words, does not call me into personal being by filling me up with goods, but by compelling me to goodness, God's 'absolute remoteness, his transcend-ence, turns into my responsibility – non-erotic par excellence – for the other': for there is no game of self-discovery, or self-fulfilment 'when the neighbour approaches – that is, when his face, or his forsakenness, draws near'.[6]

It is this neighbour, whose face draws me out of my self, who is the trace of the infinite God. In fact there is a more than coincidental analogy between the way in which I exist at all by virtue of God's call to me before I was, and the way in which I grow into some kind of human person precisely by my responsivity to the neighbour. What emerges in this relationship with the other is not so much an ego as an identifiable responsibility, a responsiveness which is unsubstitutable, namely me: 'it is a being torn up from oneself for another in the giving to the other of the bread out of one's own mouth . . . . The identity of the subject is here brought out, not by a rest on itself, but by a restlessness that drives me outside of the nucleus of my substantiality.'[7] So it is not the case for Levinas that there is simply no such thing as personal identity; the richness and uniqueness of that identity (coming to be as 'me') are not discoverable in an analysis of my *inner consciousness*. Rather, the discovery of what makes me *me* is something that takes place when my neighbour appears before me; it is the moment when 'a subject becomes a heart, a sensibility, and hands which give'.[8]

'I' am not simply a subject who, perhaps through a benign effort at consciousness-raising, has managed to be more aware of the needy; Levinas's proposal is far more radical than that. 'I' am rather the name given to this locus or event of self-giving. My love for my neighbour is what constitutes me as a human person. And for Levinas this is not to be understood on some highly elevated theoretical level but in the very quotidian concreteness of life. It is through the call to me of God's infinite otherness in the neighbour, and the responsibility this claims from me, that I become myself – 'designated without any possibility of escape, chosen, unique, not interchangeable, and – in this sense – free'; and so my freedom as a human person is discovered in just this 'hearing of a vocation which I am the only person able to answer – or even the power to answer right there, where I am called'.[9]

Thus the very feature most central to the modern notion of the self, my individual freedom to act and interpret reality, is re-read by Levinas in terms of *vocation*; I am free insofar as I am the one who at any given moment can answer the call of my neighbour. My freedom is always a freedom-for-the-other, but it is nonetheless the identifier of my self; for *I am never more myself than when I give myself away for my neighbour in love.* As Levinas puts it, 'It is as though the unity and uniqueness of the ego were already the hold on itself of the gravity of the other'.[10]

De Certeau and Wyschogrod

Many of the themes we have cursorily surveyed in Levinas are set to work in helpful historical or practical contexts in the writing of Michel de Certeau and Edith Wyschogrod. Whereas the latter addresses these issues in conscious dialogue with other postmodern thinkers, especially Levinas himself, de Certeau does so a bit less directly even while he puts his finger on some of postmodernism's most vexing anthropological questions.

In her important work, *Saints and Postmodernism*, Wyschogrod seeks to show that, fears to the contrary notwithstanding, the whole project of ethical relationship need not run aground on the shifting sands of postmodernity. There are ample resources for a new praxiological reading of moral life in the characteristic postmodern turn to the other. In her writing, the Levinasian troubled and awakened self takes more particular form as the saint who comes to *be* precisely through self-abandonment to the needs of the other. 'Such saintliness is not a nostalgic return to premodern hagiography but a postmodern expression of excessive desire, a desire on behalf of the Other that seeks the cessation of another's suffering and the birth of another's joy.'[11]

While Levinas is aware of the problem that the call of the other might somehow be grasped or used as a project for self-fulfilment, Wyschogrod moves very quickly to deal with this loss of the other's alterity. On the one hand, she points out, there is the danger that the other may simply fill up the place of the self-abandoned self, 'substituting for the self as a content' so that the other functions purely as an adjunct to the self (33). On the other hand, if 'saintliness is a total emptying without replenishment, there is no subject to engage the Other' (34). Wyschogrod provides a helpful clarification of these questions by suggesting that while saintly life is characterized by renunciation and *loss* of self, the consequent action of the saint in respect of the other is an *empowerment*: 'the power to bring about new moral configurations is authorized by the prior renunciation of power' (58). So the practical dialectics of saintly existence preclude any self-abandonment that would *either* subvert the other's capacity for moral empowerment *or* undo the saint's personal identity so as to disable any work for the other's good. This discriminating point will be useful to bear in mind.

Again as in Levinas, Wyschogrod sees the other as stimulating the saint to the divestment of self. The exposure of the saint to the world opens the saint to the other 'as a pressure, even a wound or trauma, replete with moral meaning' (174). Wyschogrod seems to see this as more of a remedial work, the scraping bare of false self-construction, the uprooting of the self's interests in favour of the needs of the other; whereas Levinas is more concerned to indicate that there would not be any subject at all in the first place, apart from the call of the other. Nevertheless it is this 'hagiographic imperative', as Wyschogrod calls it (183), that leads for both thinkers to the awakening and developing of a true persona.

Wyschogrod raises another important clarification when she points out that the complete vulnerability of the saintly self, which appears to leave it open 'to the violence and aggression of others' is not to be confused with masochism; saints are not those 'seeking pain in order to derive satisfaction in suffering' (98–9). Rather the saintly self is vulnerable precisely to the 'Other of lack and destitution' (98). While this does not at all rule out the possibility that the saint's openness will be met with violence, it does clarify that what awakens personal identity is not self-destitution per se, but availability to the other as characterized by the poor and suffering.

Finally, I want to note the ecstatic character of saintly existence in Wyschogrod's reading. She is of course concerned to show that this going out of the self is not in itself a delirious cultivation of the self's most exalted ambitions. The real ecstasy of the self lies in the unboundedness of the saint's desire for the other's beatitude. 'The saintly desire for the Other is excessive and wild' (255). What singularizes the saint is the singularity and alterity (sheer otherness) of the other; that is, the other is never reducible to some algorithm of the saint's own self but is always a 'more' that can never be encompassed by saintly intention. There is never a time when the self-abandonment of the saint is satiated, for there is always more to the other who calls the saint forth.

'From this perspective, saintly singularity is desire released from the bonds of a unifying consciousness, a desire that is unconstrained and excessive yet guided by the suffering of the Other' (256). This means that what constitutes personal identity is, as with Levinas, not some interior aspect of the saint's essence as subject or any putative deep level of pre-linguistic experience, but rather the particular character of the relationship engendered by the call of the other. It is in going out of self into this unbounded encounter that saints become who they are.

Turning briefly to de Certeau, we are given a glimpse of a historical setting in which many of these themes find their particularization in the mystical life. With the seeming vanishing of God in the early modern era, the mystical problematic becomes the quest to express in some way this newly felt divine *absence*. The mystical self becomes, in de Certeau's view, a locus for this divine absence, a kind of speech that sounds only by dwindling into silence. I would judge that in these circumstances the Neoplatonic sense of desire and yearning, whose intensity is a measure of the desired other's absence, emerges with a new poignancy. As de Certeau remarks: 'It remains to be known *who* or *what* says "I". Is the "I" a fiction of the other, which offers itself in its place? St Teresa, when discussing the crystal-castle that is the soul, speaks of a disappearance (ecstasy) or death that constitutes the subject as *pleasure* [*jouissance*] in the other. "I is an other" – that is the secret told by the mystic long before the poetic experience of Rimbaud, Rilke, or Nietzsche.'[12] Here we have more than a hint of Wyschogrod's enucleated self given over to the calling of the other – indeed, *constituted* by the desire and pleasure in the other. In de Certeau's reading of this period in the history of Christian mysticism, the self is, if anything, even more radically at the disposal of the other. It is not easy to judge whether this is because, in his view, the painful absence of God drives the self all the more out of itself in a hopeless desire for the divine other, or if this radical abandonment is simply the characteristic of mystical anthropology with its intense focus on the intimacy of the divine–human encounter.

We have some sense of this push to extremes in de Certeau's comments on John of the Cross and his poetry: 'Like the musician in [Hieronymus] Bosch's *Garden of Earthly Delights*, who is caught in his harp, his arms outstretched as though dead or passed out, played by the song that sends him into ecstasy, insane from being imprisoned in his instrument, that is, in the body of the voice of the other – the poet, too, is *robbed* by that excess which names but remains unnameable.'[13] Clearly in de Certeau's reading, the imperative and trauma of the other is just as paramount as for Levinas and Wyschogrod. And again there is also the characteristic note of *infinite* calling; the development of human identity, in other words, is not a manageable human process that reaches some reasonably satisfying conclusion: it is a journey into the unboundedness of the other's reality. 'An ecstasy constitutes the "I" by the loss of the ego – it is an "I" carried to incandescence, in-finite, because the other is not a particular, but only the signifier of a forever unlocalizable, in-finite exteriority.'[14]

This infinite deferral of the self does not mean, in de Certeau's view, that there is no characteristic patterning to the subject. The divine unboundedness which can only be expressed in terms of absence, this very realm of deferral, calls forth the particular identity of those (mystics) who seek to 'be' only by speaking for what is not. De Certeau points to the entire panoply of new spiritual practices whose orchestration in early modernity marks the feverish attempt to provide some concrete locus for communion with the absent Other. Mounting obsession with methods of prayer, rules for spiritual guidance, codification and ever more refined distinction between varying types and stages of prayer, the devising of the whole microcosm of the 'retreat' – all these social and linguistic practices emerge as a kind of new machinery by which the self begins to construct its identity as the locus of divine communion.

And the key move, suggests de Certeau, is the making of absolute resolutions to deny nothing to God: 'With this founding act, the subject enters a retreat, it goes where the world's objects are absent. The subject is born of an exile and a disappearance. The "I" is "formed" – by its act of willing *nothing* or by (forever) *being incapable of doing* what it wills – as a "desire" bound only to the supposed desire of a Deity. It is created by the state of being nothing but the affirmation of a will.'[15] Here perhaps we see something of the strange play of passivity and activity in the mystical self. On one hand the 'I', as de Certeau suggests, is formed by its act of handing itself over to the divine other; but on the other hand, the personal traits and vehemence by which the 'I' makes this resolution mark it as a subject. Indeed as de Certeau developed at length in his puzzling and remarkable work, *The Mystic Fable*, this passionate desire to be the location of the divine (non)speech leads to a blossoming elaboration of the soul and its tantalizing maze of public and private spaces. So that, in the best known example, Teresa's *Interior Castle*, the soul by its fervent desire to be for the Other pays more attention to itself than ever, imagining the increasingly baroque fictional space – now crystal, now castle – 'in which it can mark its movements' and identity itself as 'but the inarticulable echo of an unknown Subject'.[16]

Mystical Anthropology

With these postmodern readings of human subjectivity, we can see (especially in de Certeau) a range of points for discussion with Christian spiritual understandings of the self. So I want to turn now to some historical examples of mystical thinking about the self, in the hope of isolating a regularly-used set of 'tools' for thinking about the human person.

Augustinian selfhood

It might be objected that mystical anthropology is fertile ground for growing the most individualistic, even solipsistic, notions of the self. After all, if as de Certeau suggests, the passionate desire for the divine other leads to an ever more refined inner world, a theatre of the divine (non)speech, then it would be easy for the alterity of the other – who is supposedly being indicated in this scheme – to be submerged under the fascinating faculties of the soul. It is a pretty standard line of argument today that the original culprit in this regard is Augustine of Hippo, whose mesmerizing analysis of his own soul in the *Confessions,* and so-called psychological model of God in *The Trinity,* are regarded as opening the flood-gates of Western introspective subjectivity – leading, supposedly, straight to the hegemony of the modern autonomous self.

As usual with Augustine, however, one is advised to have second, or even third, thoughts. Rowan Williams has argued with great cogency that what we have in Augustine is something altogether more *relational* than is usually supposed.[17] The key distinction, as Williams points out, is between the *image* of God in us and the mere traces of triadic structure in the functioning of the human mind. Common readings of Augustine's trinitarian thought would point to these various triadic patterns (variations on memory, understanding and will) as constituting the human subject's imaging of the divine subject. This would mean that in *both* cases (God and human subject) we have a self-sufficient, inner-directed activity as the very essence of the self.

But Williams's point is that the true image of God in us is only 'realised when the three moments of our mental agency all have God for their object. The image, in other words, is *not* the mind's self-relatedness'.[18] The human subject is not really even able to know itself accurately if it does not know itself as that which *is* by the continual loving of God. So it is not as if the human being, just in its own structures of consciousness, represents a little version of the divine being. The fundamental characteristic of divine being is the life of giving to the other and establishing the inherent patterns of relationship:

> For [the mind] to see itself as acted upon by God is to know that it is known and loved by God; and in this knowledge it acquires *sapientia*, the knowledge of what is eternal. And what is eternal is the self-imparting activity of God as creator, as giver of the *justitia* and *sapientia* by which we come to share in divine

life, to actualise the divine act in our own temporal and finite context. The image of God, in short, is realised when we come to be in conscious relation to the divine act that establishes the possibility of relation; when we see ourselves as acting out the self-imparting love of God by consciously yielding ourselves to be known and loved by God. Since that being known and loved by God is the foundation of our reality in the first place, since we exist because God desires to impart his love, knowing ourselves as loved creatures is the only way of knowing ourselves truthfully.[19]

So the human self comes to be at all by virtue of the infinite relationality of God as Trinity, knowing and loving not only Godself but also what is other than God, and embracing even what is opposed to God into that trinitarian relational life.

As we saw with the postmodern writers above, human personal identity is constituted by limitless reciprocal ecstasies: the human person has its *origin* in the primordial ecstasy of the divine call to it, awakening a 'Here I am' out of nothing; it also has its *telos* in the desire to surrender itself back into the divine infinity, an ecstasy that constitutes the self-in-relation to that Other who 'is' without end. For Augustine, it is important that this 'return' is not so much an *act* of the human subject, as an *availability* to be drawn into the divine activity of knowing and loving.

Denys Turner's recent analysis of these issues in Augustine provides some further evidence to support Williams's reading. For Turner as well, the self is not the image of God by means of some purely internal structures of subjectivity, but only because the self is created to participate in the relationality of the divine knowing and loving.[20] It so often seems in Augustine as if the self has this inward drive of its own, an extensive pre-linguistic world of meaning and longing that is there quite independently of anything or anyone else.

But as de Certeau hinted with regard to Teresa of Avila, this inwardness is only a place, the opening of a space for the speaking, hearing and searching that *God* is doing. Turner comments: 'The primary agent of Augustine's seeking is not Augustine but God. It is because – indeed, emphatically, it is *only* because – God has been and is seeking out Augustine that Augustine seeks God.'[21] What seems like this very private inner realm is really the focused intensity of the call of the divine other. What seems like the inner play of enchantingly incommunicable pre-linguistic experiences is really the event of ultimate speech (even in silence) – namely the activity of God's self-communication calling Augustine into responsivity and thence to personal identity.

It is worth noting at this point that the divine calling and the human responding are virtually the same activity viewed from different perspectives. For God to seek out Augustine through all eternity takes the form, in time, of Augustine seeking out God. And most significantly, this does *not* mean that the divine and the human agents are really only the same single being, manifesting itself in different forms – nor does it mean that the human agency is merely a cipher, a frame for that nothingness which is the ultimate absent-presence of God in the world. For Augustine as for Aquinas, the divine agency is the fount of very real and distinct human agency, indeed the more God is consciously present to Augustine the more really present Augustine comes to be to himself. Together, the divine and human agencies work a single activity – knowing and loving – but this does not mean the inevitable absorption of either agent in the other; for divine agency is rather the very foundation of the creaturely participant.

Porete and Eckhart

By the later Middle Ages we have the development of a more radically apophatic anthropology in the brilliant and puzzling insights of Marguerite Porete (d. 1310) and Meister Eckhart. I have been suggesting thus far that there are two distinct but reciprocal elements to mystical anthropology. There is, first, what we might call the originary dynamic: the variably described scheme by which God evokes or calls a human personal identity into being. There is, second, what we might call the ascetical dynamic: the practices or spiritual stance by which a human person responds to this call and, in some sense, fulfils itself by struggling towards the boundlessness of the other. Both of these elements seem to me to be present in all the postmodern and mystical approaches to anthropology we have considered so far – though, as I say, the terms in which they are envisioned vary considerably. These features are crucial to the thought of Porete and Eckhart, who treat them in ways that might almost be considered postmodern before their time.

Both Porete and Eckhart hold to a 'principial' (or exemplary) eternal presence of the soul in God – as the eternal object of divine love. Porete speaks of the soul's aim as a return to her 'prior being', to this One, which 'is when the Soul is melted in the simple Deity, who is one simple Being of overflowing fruition, in fullness of knowledge, without feeling, above all thought'.[22] This seems to suggest that the fruitfulness of the divine life includes within it the eternal reality of whatever it is that, in creaturely existence, we would come to know as human persons. This principal existence of human persons can only (because of the divine simplicity) be an element in God's own eternal self-knowing and self-willing; so, considered from this primordial standpoint, the human person-to-be is in no way distinct from the divine being.

Eckhart points to this notion in the famous *German Sermon* 52: 'In the same being of God where God is above being and above distinction, there I myself was, there I willed myself and committed myself to create this man. Therefore I am the cause of myself in the order of my being, which is eternal, and not in the order of my becoming, which is temporal.'[23] Eckhart already announces here the same impetus that Porete will identify as the originary 'push' of the soul into created existence, namely the act of will. For Eckhart, the prior unity is more dramatically depicted by this language of the soul (in its principial indistinction from God) choosing and willing *itself* to become a distinct creature.

Porete uses what may seem at first less radical language here, saying that God 'created me without myself by His divine goodness'.[24] Then, however, Porete specifies how Uncreated Goodness leads the soul into its distinct created existence by remarking that 'Uncreated Goodness possesses properly of herself free will, and she gives us free will also by her goodness, free will beyond her power, without any why except for our sakes that we might be of her goodness. Therefore we have will, departing from her goodness and outside her power, in order for us to be even more free.'[25] The divine Goodness places us 'outside her power' precisely by means of a gift of free will, by the distinguishing of a creaturely will from the eternal will of Goodness. And again later Porete specifies this gift of free will as the originary gift to the human creature, for by this gift of free will God 'wills that the one who has no being might have being according to such a gift from Himself'.[26]

So one might begin to argue that the distinction of the creaturely self is not an ontological distinction at all, that at its ground (as Eckhart says) the soul's being and God's being are one being, or, alternatively, that the being of the creature is literally no-thing, nothingness, in the sense that the divine existence is not an *item* of reality. What does in fact call the human person into creaturely existence is its gift of will, along with its intentionality and responsivity to the other who arouses this will.

It is not surprising then that Porete presents the *handing back of this will* as the proper consummation of the human soul's creaturely existence. The creature who has fallen into the temptation of wilfully manipulating life has come to be identified with this problematic will: 'Now I cannot be, says Unrighteous Will, what I ought to be until I return to where I was before I departed from Him, where I was as naked as He is who is, to be as naked as I was when I was who was not.'[27] And how is this return to be effected? It happens when the Divine Light overflows the soul and 'gives itself to such a will in order to dissolve this will into God, not being able to place itself there without such Light'; this moment is so crucial because it strips the soul of her illusions about creaturely existence, showing her 'the nothingness of her nature and of her own will' and so enabling her to see 'that the will must will the Divine Will alone without any other will, and that for this purpose this will was given. And thus the Soul removes herself from this will, and the will is separated from the Soul and dissolves itself, and [the will] gives and renders itself to God, whence it was first taken, without retaining anything of its own in order to fulfil the perfect Divine Will.'[28]

Such passages as this suggest that the ultimate state of the soul's identity is only achieved through union or re-union of the divine and creaturely wills as one will. Presumably for Porete, the *fulfilment* of the particular person who had existed as a creature comes with a return to its eternal principial state as an 'idea' in God.

Amy Hollywood has also emphasized other (even more dramatic) language in Porete, arguing that beyond this volitional unity there is 'a transformation of the soul into the divine through its annihilation'.[29] I would argue that this state of the annihilated soul should not be taken to mean a total loss of all personal being but rather the abandonment of those patterns of selfhood and creaturely will that cause the soul to remain separated from God. Once these have been abandoned, Porete still speaks of the soul, but of the soul who no longer knows herself except through God's self-knowledge: 'She is so dissolved in Him that she sees neither herself nor Him, and thus He sees completely Himself alone.'[30] At this point the soul's personal reality is fulfilled in the trinitarian personal knowing and loving of God. As Ellen Babinsky comments:

> the annihilated soul is thus united by the power of the Holy Spirit to the Trinity, in whom she is dissolved and melted so that the one divine will of the Trinity wills in her. When the Holy Spirit fills the soul, she receives the fullness of divinity and at that moment is lifted into divine existence in union with the Trinity. By this melting and joining of the soul to the Trinity, the *soul is made completely transparent*, so that God sees only Godself, which is, for Marguerite, the goal and limit of spiritual perfection that can be attained in this life.[31]

In fact it is precisely the trinitarian generativity that, in Porete's view, draws the human person towards consummation – by aligning the soul's patterns of existence with the divine trinitarian patterns. The Father as 'eternal substance', the Son as 'pleasing fruition' and the Holy Spirit as 'loving conjunction' generate exactly these structures of existence in the increasingly 'transparent soul' so that the soul begins itself to share in this trinitarian generativity: 'From the eternal substance the memory possesses the power of the Father. From the pleasing fruition the intellect possesses the wisdom of the Son. From the loving conjunction the will possesses the goodness of the Holy Spirit.'[32]

As a result of this restructuring of the self according to the generativity of the Trinity, the Holy Spirit is able (as the personal conjunctive activity of God) to unite the soul with the whole trinitarian life. Porete gives us a strong sense of the abiding personal reality of the soul, now free from any possessive individualism. The sovereign Lover, she says:

> shows that there is nothing except Him from Whom all things have being. And so nothing is except Him in love of light, of union, of praise: *one* will, *one* love, and *one* work in *two* natures. One sole goodness, through conjunction of the transforming power of love from my Lover, says this Soul who is at rest *without obstructing* the outpouring of divine Love. By such divine Love, the divine Will works *in me*, for me and without my *possession*.[33]

This is a rather extraordinary passage. It hints, at least, of an enduring essential distinction between the divine and human ('*one* work in *two* natures'). But it also clearly points to the role of the consummated human being: *to be personal* by sharing in that supremely personal life of the Trinity – wherein the personal reality of one neither *obstructs* nor *possesses* the other, but pours out love continually and mutually.

Eckhart follows a number of the themes articulated by Porete. Since it often happens that the startlingly monistic-sounding texts in Eckhart receive particular attention, it may be useful here to note how Eckhart amplifies the explicitly *trinitarian* language which we have seen in Porete. What I have called the ascetic dynamic of the self, that is, the process by which it responds to the divine gift of being and seeks to discover the truth of its being – this dynamic begins for Eckhart with the birth of the Word in the soul. This is a reciprocally ecstatic moment in which God has 'come completely out of himself for love of you' and the soul is urged to 'go completely out of yourself for God's love':

> when these two have gone out, what remains is a simplified One. In this One the Father brings his Son to birth in the innermost source. Then the Holy Spirit blossoms forth, and then there springs up in God a will that belongs to the soul. So long as the will remains untouched by all created things and by all creation, it is free . . . . If this will turns away from itself and from all creation for one instant, and back to its source, then the will stands in its true and free state, and it is free.[34]

The birth of the Word is both the originary moment, the production of 'a will that belongs to the soul' and it is also the source to which the distinct human self (distinct by virtue of its own will) can return to discover 'its true and free state'. In Eckhart, the ascetical dynamic of the self is marked by a relentless stripping of the self of all illusions about itself, a freeing of it for that moment of ecstatic breakthrough into the place of the simplified One where it is free to exercise its will exactly as the exercise of God's will.

In Porete we saw how this ultimate state of human being consists in coming to share the personal relationality of the Trinity. It is sometimes suggested that the ultimate state of the soul for Eckhart is a oneness with God which is so simple and unitary as to 'surpass' even the trinitarian relational unity. I remain unconvinced. Richard Woods has argued persuasively that when Eckhart says that God begets 'me' as his Son, he does not mean that I am coming to be a creaturely son in *the* Son, a beloved mirror of *the* Beloved. Rather, Woods points out, for Eckhart there is only one (eternal) Son; we do not come to be multiple, miniature, proportional reflections of the Son, but actually are drawn into the single filial pattern of divine life.[35] Thus the consummation of my personal identity is to become free of all that prevents me from sharing by adoption and grace in the eternal Sonship – a sharing, therefore, in that oneness which is infinitely relational.

This would mean that the ultimate breakthrough into the divine ground is not a leap into a monistic oneness but an ecstasy into that eternal receiving and responding which is the Word's personal pattern of trinitarian life. Consider this passage, for example, where Eckhart writes that 'in the breaking-through, when I come to be free of will of myself and of God's will and of all his works and of God himself, then I am above all created things, and I am neither God nor creature, but I am what I was and what I shall remain, now and eternally'.[36] What I am suggesting is that just as the self comes to be free of its distinct creaturely willing, so it comes to be free of God insofar as God is seen as a divine object 'out there' over against the creature; for as the soul journeys into its ground – namely, the coming forth of the Second Person of the Trinity – there is no more 'God' as an object to a creaturely subject but only the eternal trinitarian mutuality of the Son's relationship to the Father in their Spirit.

But what about that famous Eckhartian 'spark' in the soul that 'wants to go into the simple ground, into the quiet desert, into which distinction never gazed, not the Father, nor the Son, nor the Holy Spirit. . . . this ground is a simple silence, in itself immovable, and by this immovability all things are moved, all life is received by those who in themselves have rational being'?[37] Of course one way of reading texts like these is to assume, as has lately been assumed (wrongly, I think) of Augustine, that they point to the ontological priority of a divine essence, a divine unity that is somehow the originary source of the trinitarian persons.

The metaphysics of this debate need not paralyse us here, for surely the *consistent ascetical logic* of Meister Eckhart should guide us. What could be more self-possessive, more 'undetached' than a divine oneness? It seems at least plausible to me that Eckhart, with his trinitarian metaphysics and noetics, would view the 'simple ground' not as a possessive oneness *behind* the Trinity but as the *silent fecundity and mutuality of the trinitarian life*, ceaselessly enacting the divine unity by self-dispossession in favour of the other. The 'quiet desert' into which our titles for God – Father, Son, and Holy Spirit – 'never gazed' would not be something other than the Three in God but precisely their ineffable relationality, their infinite giving of each to each.

Denys Turner comments on Eckhart's refusal to allow either God or the self to be 'appropriated within some intelligible, meaningful, desirable, possessible structure of selfhood'; this is so because, 'for Eckhart, "my" self is not in the last resort *mine* at all. And any self which I can call my own is a false self, a self of possessive imagination. To be a self I must retain within myself the void and the desert of detachment'.[38] This void of detachment (I suggest, following Levinas) is the infinite call of divine one to other, in which each of the Three is only constituted by abandoning any claim to *be* at all apart from the eternal giving away. In this sense the divine Persons are who they are precisely by refusing any 'possessible structure of selfhood' (in Turner's phrase), and by instead enacting their identities in the desert of infinite detachment, of self-*abandon*. They are Persons, in other words, precisely by being *relations*. Thus the consummation of human personal identity, for Eckhart, is found in breaking through to this paradoxical trinitarian life where one *is* only by being wholly for the other. So it would seem that 'I' am not so much constituted by some mysterious inner self which lies behind my outgoing relationship with others; rather, I am who I am exactly *in virtue of* that outgoing relationality.

Edith Stein and Simone Weil

Where do I come from and where am I going? Who am I after all? For Edith Stein and Simone Weil these were not questions of idle curiosity, but critical ambiguities – whose significance was all the more unmistakable in the gathering darkness of Hitler's plans for the peoples of Europe.

I begin with the originary dynamic of the self, the question of what it is that draws me to be here and offers a provisional sense of my identity. Stein and Weil answer this question quite differently, influenced, I think, by their respective philosophical proclivities: phenomenology and Thomism in Stein's case, and Plato and Kant in Weil's case.

In her doctoral dissertation completed in 1916, Stein developed a phenomenological analysis of empathy as an approach to understanding human personhood. 'We found,' she writes, 'the spiritual subject to be an "I" in whose acts an object world is constituted and which itself creates objects by acts of its will.'[39] The modern machinery of the autonomous subject who is defined by its ability to turn everything else into objects is hovering over these early pages pretty closely. But even here Stein is already aware that 'if we take the self as the standard, we lock ourselves into the prison of our individuality. Others become riddles for us, or still worse, we remodel them into our image'.[40] This sense that the other is more than just an object to the self (but rather, perhaps, a clue to the true meaning of the self), continued to deepen in Stein, especially during her years of lecturing on the requirements of adequate education for women – who were, in 1930s Germany, becoming ever more of an 'object' to the growing construction of the Aryan master self.

'To arrive at being all, desire to be nothing.' These famous words of John of the Cross were printed on the prayer card for Edith Stein's clothing ceremony as a novice in the Carmelite Order, held on 15 April 1934. During the period of eight years in Carmel before her death in 1942, Stein began to reflect more and more systematically on the possibility that the real human self only comes into being as it becomes nothing, or goes out of itself towards the other. Stein's final work, *The Science of the Cross*, was an analysis of John of the Cross's mystical theology. She included a section attempting to clarify the great Carmelite's theory of union with God by her own analysis of the human soul.

Her approach is interior and even somewhat psychological, as in the dissertation she had written twenty-six years before. But now she is concerned to say that the innermost core of the human person is marked by two crucial features: first, it is only identifiable as such, as the constitutive centre of human being, because it is there that *God* is present (there is an Other in the self to begin with); and second, this innermost being is inaccessible for the reason that the soul cannot know itself except insofar as God calls and draws it into relationship. The human person has a self, an identity, in other words, but it is only able to actualize that provisional reality by existing in relationship with the Giver of that personal identity.

This understanding of the original provisionality of the self may be made clearer by considering Stein's view of human freedom. For her, the human being is 'destined to live in his innermost being and to master himself in a way that is possible only from this inmost sphere . . . Yet he will never know his inmost being completely. This is a mystery of God.'[41] Nevertheless, she adds, the human person has perfect freedom over this inmost life: 'the soul has the right to decide its own fate, it is the great secret of personal freedom that God himself respects it.'[42] Yet this freedom can only be consummated by the soul's self-surrender to God (there is a very close parallel here to Porete); placing itself in God's hands allows the soul to fulfil the potential of its freedom – because it then begins to stand in a new relationship to God: no longer does the self-surrendered soul stand on *one* side with God as the ultimate object on the *other*.

No, in the bestowal of the self to the divine Other, the soul enters into the eternal triune relationality in which an infinity of freedom is exercized precisely through the mutual giving and receiving of one's all. Stein writes:

> [In this self-surrender] God will work everything in the soul, itself will have to do no more than to receive. Yet its share of freedom is expressed in just this receiving. Beyond this, however, freedom is involved even far more decisively, for in this state God works everything in the soul only because the soul surrenders itself to him perfectly. St John himself describes the mystical marriage as the voluntary mutual surrender of God and the soul and attributes to the soul at this stage of perfection so great a power that it can dispose not only of itself, but even of God.[43]

I interpret Stein to mean here that, standing within the trinitarian self-surrender, the soul participates in that infinite giving of God to God which is both the ultimate kenosis and the eternal constitution of the divine existence. As for Wyschogrod, the saintly self-abnegation is not an ultimate dissolution of personal being but the empowering of the human to effect new possibilities. And as for Levinas, the self only becomes real as it is woken up and called into the surrender of its freedom for the other.

If we consider these same questions now from the perspective of Simone Weil, we see a differently-imaged but highly compatible point of view. In the essentially Neoplatonic vision of Weil, the infinite giving of God as the Good has led to the finitizing of this goodness in the creaturely realm. We only exist as creatures (by means of God's self-abnegation and self-bestowal) in order for us to realize that, ultimately speaking, we *are not*: we are moments of God's hoping, elicitations of God's love seeking a response and a return. 'Our existence is made up only of [God's] waiting for our acceptance not to exist. He is perpetually begging from us that existence which he gives. He gives it in order to beg it from us.'[44] What we *think* is our existence as selves is only a kind of test of love in which we become fully who we are by handing ourselves over to God. 'It is like one of those traps whereby the characters are tested in fairy stories and tales on initiation. If I accept this gift it is bad and fatal; its virtue becomes apparent through my refusal of it. God allows me to exist outside himself. It is for me to refuse this authorization.'[45]

Clearly Weil thought that this recognition of the self's nothingness was itself a positive moment in the stripping away of illusions, illusions imposed both by one's own self-image and constructed by social roles. Even our ability to know and act positively is liberated, in Weil's view, by the abandonment of the self. She comments wryly that 'subjectivist theories of cognition are a perfectly correct description of the condition of those who lack the faculty, which is extremely rare, of coming out of themselves'.[46] Not to recognize our status as acts of continual divine self-dispossession is, in effect, to misperceive reality and also to stultify it, to freeze into manipulable possession. We cannot really *be* who we have the potential to be unless we give up trying to be this self-construed, autonomous, object-making subject: 'We have to die in order to liberate a *tied up* energy, in order to possess an energy which is free and capable of understanding the true relationship of things.'[47] Again, as for Wyschogrod, what is sought is not the disability of the human person, but that self-dispossession which is empowering, which releases what had been constrained.

As with Stein, Weil is willing to talk of a 'real' part of the human self, but only in terms of its relationship with God. It is significant that when Weil speaks of the nothingness of the self, it is primarily in the starkly oppositional language of God and the creature; but when she hints at the radical possibility of real selfhood, she shifts to overtly trinitarian language. In Weil's view the nothingness which we think of as creation is akin to the abyss of chaos over which the divine breath or Spirit hovers in Genesis. It is a nothingness with a potential. In the final years of her life, after all her own attempts at solidarity with workers and peasants, and in the midst of repeated attempts to be allowed back into France as a member of the Resistance, Weil began to point to a deeper self energized with possibilities. The Holy Spirit, she writes, is:

> the seed which falls on every soul. To receive it, the soul must become simply a matrix, a vessel; something plastic and passive, like water. Then the seed becomes an embryo, and at last a child; Christ is born in the soul. What used to be called 'I' and 'me' is destroyed, liquefied; and in place of it there is a new being. . . . It is a different being that has been engendered by God, a different 'I', which is hardly 'I', because it is the Son of God.[48]

As we saw with Eckhart, the discovery of our true self is the discovery of our place in the trinitarian self-expression and self-giving. This passage speaks of a kind of dissolving of the self, as the mere shell, which Christ bursts. But in another place Weil draws on the long mystical tradition of the uncreated element in the soul, Eckhart's ground; when whatever obscures that has been relinquished, then the 'uncreated part of the soul, which is identical with the Son of God' is revealed.[49]

Now we must turn to the second element in mystical anthropology, namely the ascetical dynamic by which the possibility of human personal being is consummated. For both Stein and Weil this involves a mystical participation in Christ's suffering and in a kind of total availability to human others as well as the divine other. It is here that we see how fully Stein and Weil develop what I would call a self-in-solidarity, which in many respects fulfils some of the trajectories of the postmodern interest (obsession) with relationality.

Edith Stein was born on the Day of Atonement and remarked that her devoutly Jewish mother always considered this obscurely significant. Certainly the image of the high priest entering the Holy of Holies on behalf of the people seemed to bear a powerful resonance for her. In an essay written for her fellow Carmelites just two years after beginning the novitiate, Stein used this imagery of the high priest to frame a discussion of the Christian church's prayer. For Stein, the prayer of the church is really nothing else but a listening in, a participation in the mysterious inner dialogue of Jesus with the Father in their Spirit: 'The Saviour's high priestly prayer unveils the mystery of the inner life: the circumincession of the Divine Persons and the indwelling of God in the soul. In these mysterious depths the work of salvation was prepared and accomplished itself in concealment and silence'.[50] For Stein, the salvific work of Christ opens out in two directions. First, there is a vertical opening to the inner life of God, for in Stein's view, the self-giving of Christ is the enactment in time of the eternal self-giving of the trinitarian Persons. But second, Christ's saving work is the secret wellspring of the church's life as Christ's body, constantly attempting to fulfil its identity as the incarnation of God's sacrificial love; and through the visible church this sacrificial power becomes hiddenly present in the often unknown work of souls in solidarity with all who suffer.

Stein had a strong sense that 'the work of salvation takes place in obscurity and stillness. In the heart's quiet dialogue with God the living building blocks out of which the kingdom of God grows are prepared'.[51] The self fulfils itself, achieves 'the highest elevation of the heart attainable by this co-suffering presence to others through surrender to God'; for in their hiddenness in God they are empowered to make their greatest act as persons, to 'radiate to other hearts the divine love that fills them and so participate in the perfection of all into unity in God'.[52] Indeed Stein felt convinced that any occasion of suffering could, if offered intentionally, become a sharing in Christ's saving struggle. Like Wyschogrod, she carefully distinguishes this from 'the mania for suffering caused by a perverse lust for pain', and goes on to insist that an authentic desire to suffer with and for others is a sign that one has (consciously or not) entered into the person-making community of Christ's suffering body.

In what is perhaps one of her most remarkable passages, Stein addresses her sister Carmelites on the contemporary state of affairs in Europe and calls them to realize the powerful possibility inherent in the self-dispossession entailed by their religious vows. It was mid-September 1939: 'the world is in flames, the battle between Christ and the Antichrist has broken into the open'.[53] Now is the time when we have to decide how best to spend our lives, she says to her sisters. In effect she is asking them to consider their religious vocation as a political act – to consider their self-abandonment to God as an empowering blow against a new culture of violence and self-assertion. By allowing their religious vows to become an authentic act of self-emptying, they will become fully available for everyone, 'then the flood of divine love will be poured into your heart until it overflows and becomes fruitful to all the ends of the earth'.[54]

Brilliantly Stein plays on the no doubt strong feelings in the convent that they should be *doing* something, should find out once and for all who they are as women by *acting*. We know that Stein herself felt just this way during the First World War, giving up her university studies for a period to work at a field hospital. But now, she says, perhaps we discover the true secret and power of our identities – by relinquishing our sensible practical ideas and abandoning ourselves to the hidden possibilities of our vocation to prayer:

> Do you hear the groans of the wounded on the battlefields in the west and in the east? You are not a physician and not a nurse and cannot bind up the wounds. You are enclosed in a cell and cannot get to them. Do you hear the anguish of the dying? You would like to be a priest and comfort them. Does the lament of the widows and orphans distress you? You would like to be an angel of mercy and help them. Look at the Crucified. If you are nuptially bound to him by the faithful observance of your holy vows, your *being* is precious blood. Bound to him, you are omnipresent as he is. You cannot help here or there like the physician, the nurse, the priest. You can be at all fronts, wherever there is grief, in the power of the cross. Your compassionate love takes you everywhere, this love from the divine heart.[55]

We know that Stein's final days were a terrible test of these words, a test for her sense of identity. Who had the final right to say who Edith Stein was, or to say who she would be? Was she to be defined by the brutality of Auschwitz as a mere number, yet another so-called degenerate herded to the 'showers'? Stein certainly believed that she had found in her self-abandonment to God another self, a true self which lives not by fleeing from the suffering of others and herself but by weaving them into the eternal divine giving, the trinitarian abandonment of God to God. 'Come, Rosa. We are going for our people.'

Three years before that final train ride to Auschwitz, Stein wrote: 'I joyfully accept in advance the death God has appointed for me . . . . Please permit me to offer myself to the Heart of Jesus as a sacrifice of atonement for true peace'; she asked especially to offer herself for the needs of the church, the convents where she had lived, and 'for the Jewish people'.[56]

For Simone Weil as well, struggle for the consummation of the real self is seen as a sharing in the Cross. In her view, the uncovering of the hidden self entails the process not of destruction but of 'decreation'. Decreation in her words is 'to make something created pass into the uncreated', whereas destruction is 'to make something pass into nothingness'.[57] Undoubtedly there is in Weil a pervasive sense that, as the particular individual she is, she is only in the way: 'I must withdraw so that God may make contact with the beings whom chance places in my path and whom he loves. It is tactless for me to be there. It is as though I were placed between two lovers or two friends . . . . If only I knew how to disappear there would be a perfect union of love between God and the earth I tread, the sea I hear.'[58]

Nowhere is this sense that she is somehow only an unlovable obstacle more poignantly expressed than in the strange, Song of Songs-like untitled lines she wrote just a few months before her death. In this brief scene a Christ-figure calls someone to come with him. He takes the other, who speaks in the first person, to a church where she (or he?) tells him that she hasn't been baptized (one of the difficult decisions in Weil's life – possibly resolved only on her deathbed). He takes her to a small garret apartment where the two talk and eat bread and wine. Finally after some days he tells her to go. As she goes in confusion she realizes she cannot find her way back:

> I have never tried to find it again. I understood that he had come for me by mistake. My place is not in that garret . . . . Sometimes I cannot help trying, fearfully and remorsefully, to repeat to myself a part of what he said to me. How am I to know if I remember it rightly? He is not there to tell me. I know well that he does not love me. How could he love me? And yet deep down within me something, a particle of myself, cannot help thinking, with fear and trembling, that perhaps, in spite of all, he loves me.[59]

This knife-edge struggle to sense one's place in relationship to what is most ultimate is truly painful. It seems very far from Stein's sense that the abandonment of the self to God would allow God to fulfil the self as a channel of grace to others. And yet even this passage is not without hope, a 'particle' of the person cannot help thinking that 'in spite of all, he loves me'. It is that hope that makes it possible, in Weil's view, to turn suffering into affliction, and affliction into union with God and solidarity with fellow sufferers.

Unlike pity, which simply wants to help someone so as not to have to think about them any more, compassion, says Weil, 'consists in paying attention to an afflicted man and identifying oneself with him in thought. It then follows that one feeds him automatically if he is hungry, just as one feeds oneself'.[60] Levinas had said that becoming real was like giving someone the bread out of your own mouth, becoming responsible for their suffering. And in this concrete giving away of self to the other, says Weil, one discovers the true basis of real life: 'Because, just as the gift of bread is simply the effect and the sign of compassion, so compassion is itself the effect and sign of being united to God by love.'[61] Suffering embraced by hope, in the face even of the appalling silence of God, can become 'affliction' (*malheur*), affliction that brings those who persevere in love to the foot of the Cross.

And this is really the key to understanding Simone Weil on the self, namely her trinitarian understanding. As for Eckhart, Weil sees the divine outpouring in *creation* as embedded within the *eternal* divine outpouring which is the infinite speaking of the Word by the Father. The whole universe exists in this opening up of the divine being, in the risky stretching apart of the love between the First and Second Persons of the Trinity. The Spirit who sustains the bond between God and God is the love who sustains us also in our afflictions. So for the human subject 'our misery gives us the infinitely precious privilege of sharing in this distance placed between the Son and his Father'.[62]

In other words, Weil, like Stein, sees the giving away of the self, even in suffering, as the constitution of the self—precisely in terms of the emplacement of the self within the intra-trinitarian self-giving. God approaches the soul again and again, 'like a beggar' asking to 'possess us', 'if we consent, God puts a little seed in us and he goes away again . . . . We have only not to regret the consent we gave him, the nuptial yes'.[63] And of course what God plants in the self — the little seed — grows into the Cross; our willingness to go on loving the other in affliction is what allows the secret Christ-identity to grow in us and to emplace us in the Word's own trinitarian relationship:

> A day comes when the soul belongs to God, when it not only consents to love but when truly and effectively it loves. Then in its turn it must cross the universe to go to God. The soul does not love like a creature with created love. The love within it is divine, uncreated; for it is the love of God for God that is passing through it. God alone is capable of loving God. We can only consent to give up our own feelings so as to allow free passage in our soul for this love. That is the meaning of denying oneself. We are created for this consent, and for this alone.[64]

It is this trinitarian risk of being-for-the-other which, in Simone Weil's thought, can be the only goal of the created being. It is important to be clear here. Weil is not saying that the fulfilment of personal being is found simply in loving others even though it may 'stretch' you a bit – as though the human self, in being for the other, were thus consummated as a self-sufficient earthly mirror of the divine being-for-the-other.

On the contrary Weil emphasizes that such a love for the other in affliction is not possible for the creaturely self per se. To rest there with a benign concern for the other will only perpetuate the opaque, illusory self, the block between God's love and the creature. It would maintain myself as a kindly giving subject for all those needy others, who exist sadly but conveniently as objects for my self expression. It is precisely Weil's trinitarian radicalism that undercuts such a scheme, by insisting that no creature ever remains simply an object to the divine subject but is, rather, destined to share in the eternal mutuality of giving and receiving of the divine Three. The human self can only truly love when it has allowed itself to love in this way, namely in the eternal abandonment of one to the other for love of the other, to become a participant in this triune event of loving.

And it is, I would argue, finally their fundamental turn to trinitarian language that may save both Stein and Weil from a dangerous way of speaking. For as many have pointed out, the Christian tradition is full of calls to self-denial and self-abnegation, usually calls that men seem to have issued and women were expected to heed. Susan Hekman has summarized the concern: 'The argument that women have been denied subjectivity for too long for them to reject it just when women are successfully challenging their inferiority is a compelling one'.[65] For both Stein and Weil the crucial element to note is that the trinitarian mutuality of self-dispossession is an eternally affirming, life-constituting reality. In Stein's words, 'The eternal Father in unconditional love has given his entire being to his Son. And just as unconditionally does the Son give himself back to the Father'.[66] No Person of the Trinity can *be* except by giving the whole divine essence to the others, yet that absolute – indeed infinite – kenosis is not the termination of the divine life but its very basis and meaning.

And it is because this loving self-giving is Spirit, in Stein's view, that the human person can be drawn into the personal relationality of God; 'thus the soul lives its life of grace through the Holy Spirit, in him it loves the Father with the love of the Son and the Son with the love of the Father'.[67] So on the one hand, this self-abandonment is not the loss but the basis of divine Personal being; it is what constitutes God as God, as Trinity. On the other hand, neither is it the loss of personal subjectivity for the human person, but rather a new kind of subjectivity which can never be frozen into an interior self – it is always a dispossessing of the subject in the play of giving which constitutes the subject.

And for Simone Weil, as we have seen, the human self is most real when it becomes *fully transparent* to the infinite divine event of self-giving: 'The love which unites Christ abandoned on the Cross to his Father at the infinite distance dwells in every saintly soul . . . . In such a soul the dialogue of Christ's cry and the Father's silence echoes perpetually in a perfect harmony.'[68] This 'saintly soul' is hardly a 'nothing', in spite of Weil's frequent talk of the total renunciation of self. As a participant (even a vehicle) of the trinitarian dialogue, the soul is not destroyed or rendered functionless but is rather freed of the limitations of creaturely subjectivity.

Moreover, the trinitarian dialogue is not a self-enclosed entity but an infinite personal loving – who, in Weil's view, has mysteriously chosen to risk the inclusion of the creature within the dialogue.

> God produces himself and knows himself perfectly . . . . Before all things, God is love. Before all things God loves himself. This love, this friendship of God, is the Trinity. Between the terms united by this relation of divine love there is more than nearness; there is infinite nearness or identity. But, resulting from the Creation, the Incarnation, and the Passion, there is also infinite distance . . . . The love between God and God, which in itself *is* God, is this bond of double virtue: the bond that unites two beings so closely that they are no longer distinguishable and really form a single unity and the bond that stretches across distance and triumphs over infinite separation.[69]

The unity of the Trinity is an infinite unity; it does not need to convert what is *other* to the *same* in order to embrace the other. And yet the other is welcome. My proposal is that mystical anthropology grounded in this fully economic vision of the Trinity may offer a fruitful source for contemporary theological anthropology. Here is a conception of the self as that which is called forth by the infinite giving of God, a self who only discovers what it means to have fully personal identity in the bestowal of its freedom towards the other, a self for whom the other never becomes an object but a friend in a mutuality which is infinite love. As Simone Weil wrote: 'Pure friendship is an image of the original and perfect friendship that belongs to the Trinity and is the very essence of God. It is impossible for two human beings to be one while scrupulously respecting the distance that separates them, unless God is present in each of them.'[70]

While I want to avoid a premature and undoubtedly artificial 'synthesis' of the ideas we have considered in this chapter, it may be useful to draw them a little together in order to search for common points of reference. I set up some elements in postmodern thought as a background for the discussion, and we may note several helpfully critical points.

Levinas warns against the appealingly reassuring assumption of some primordial self which only needs to be activated by contact with the other. For Levinas, this would be to hold the relational dialogue with God as a kind of necessary second moment for the self; whereas Levinas is suggesting that it is precisely this address of God, this attending of God to what is not God, that calls a responsive self into being at all. Edith Stein's roots in the psychological and phenomenological traditions might have led her in the direction of such a mysterious inner self, held incommunicado until pierced by the awakening divine presence. Yet as we have also seen, for Stein there never was such an inner self apart from the divine presence at the heart of it. So in that sense at least, to be human is not so much to discover the secret of one's own inner life as it is to discover the secret relationship with God which has all along been the source of one's personhood.

Wyschogrod raised two especially important critical points. The most obvious being that a truly authentic self-giving is not a form of masochism, which might covertly feed a wounded ego by subjecting it to the painful risk of the other's demands. Perhaps this concern must be raised in connection with aspects of Simone Weil's thought. How do we discern the point at which self-renunciation seems to verge into self-hatred? Certainly Weil emphasizes the nothingness of her self, but as we know this can be correlated with mystical traditions in which the self is most fully alive and active when it is transparent to its eternal exemplary status in the divine self-uttering (as in Eckhart's notion of the birth of the Word in the soul). Weil insists that the point of our created existence as human persons is to *hand over* our created being to the divine Giver of that being. But to what end? Is the long struggle of personal life only an illusion for Weil?

Again, I would argue that placing her understanding of the self in the trinitarian context avoids such a reduction. For Weil, God is constituted by the unity that holds the trinitarian persons together *and* equally by the outgoing love of that very unity – which allows the trinitarian Persons to be truly *other* to each other, to be other in a kind of infinite act of 'othering'. This openness of the Trinity to the other sustains not only the infinite othering of the divine persons but also the *finite* other of human persons. For that reason I would argue that human self-renunciation, in Weil's view, does not unmask the human person as a nullity or an illusion but rather frees it to pass over into its only real basis for being a distinct 'I' at all, namely its rooting and placement in the relational othering of the trinitarian Persons. And this othering sustains the unity and mutuality of life-in-God *without* collapsing every other into a monarchical divine 'I' – no matter whether that other is divine or human.

Wyschogrod's second critical point is directly related to this: another gauge of authentic self-donation is that it neither converts the other into a convenient adjunct to the self (a handy repository for its need for self-emptying), nor renders the subject so absent that no further relationality or mutuality can be sustained. Mommaers helpfully points out common features of the mystics' self-forgetfulness in terms parallel to Wyschogrod's criteria: 'Theirs is not a self-emptying undertaken in anticipation of being filled up again by something outside of themselves. Nor is it simple self-sacrifice undertaken in a blind trust. They are first overwhelmed by an Other and as a result lose track of themselves. They disappear from their own consciousness because they are caught up in a living reality too different to be related to the ordinary self.'[71] What often reads like a complete *displacement* of the self in favour of the other is, in this view, as likely to be a complete freedom from self-preoccupation – an extreme attentiveness to the other which is actually the vitalizing of the self and its empowering beyond its 'ordinary' self-conception.

A crucial observation of de Certeau's is that the journey of the self is an open-ended journey. The ultimate basis of our subjectivity is located in the infinite play of the divine life. This helps to ward off the mistaken idea that once the self has 'handed itself back' to God in Porete (and Weil) or entered the divine ground in Eckhart, it has somehow reached a point of stasis or closure. It also reminds us of the importance of Rowan Williams's point regarding Augustine and the *imago dei*: the fundamental basis of the human person as image of God does not lie in the comfortable closure granted by a self-sufficient mirroring of trinitarian relationality *within* the human subject. Rather the self only comes to know and love itself truly (to *be* in a more than provisional sense), by being known and loved by God, by being drawn into the deepest basis of our being within the trinitarian life of God.

It is not that there is a substance called 'selfhood' here, infinite in God and doled out in finite quantities to human persons. The idea is rather that the divine activity of being God, namely the infinite self-bestowal of the trinitarian persons one to another, is the eternal mutual activity of 'selving' which alone sustains particular identity. It is this activity that evokes human identity in the first place, and it is by ever-less-obstructed participation in this activity that human identity flourishes.

So the reality we call human selfhood is constituted by its basis in the infinite self-giving of the trinitarian life. Yet this is not a foreclosure but an invitation to something that transgresses the boundaries of what we tend to think of as human being; it is an invitation to a form of absolute self-gift to the other which is simultaneously the very energizing of the one who gives. It is clear that this infinite dimension, this making of the human person by participation in the infinitely self-bestowing creativity of the divine life, must also encompass the costly sacrifice of self on behalf of the other, as we see in Edith Stein. In the eternal play of the trinitarian life this absolute renunciation of the self on behalf of the other may be an infinite event of bliss and joy, but in the broken shards of human moral history the very same event may necessarily be enacted in painfully sacrificial terms.

Nevertheless it is the underlying endless (trinitarian) resource, empowering this act of self-sacrifice, that preserves it from masochistic self-negation or any other constraints of human sin. Granted that Edith Stein's self-giving led to her death. And yet, she believed, our ultimate self-bestowal is not *only* into the hands of the oppressed who need our solidarity most desperately, nor even finally into the hands of the Auschwitz planners and executioners (who also and perhaps more desperately than any need the gift of sacrificial love). But rather, in and through and beyond those finite gifts of ourselves we are being invited into that infinite act of self-bestowal which is the very constitution of God's life. And if it is into the hands of God that we ultimately place ourselves by giving ourselves away in love for the other, then perhaps we catch a glimpse at last of what is meant in 1 John 3.2: 'Beloved, we are God's children now; it does not yet appear what we shall be.'

Mystical theology thus suggests that Christian anthropology finds its roots in a consideration of trinitarian life. In such a perspective, being human means being drawn into that endless resource and generativity which may lead one in love for the other beyond what seem like the very bounds of human existence into the death of self. But that same giving life leads thereby, Christians believe, to the death of death, to that ultimate creation of the human being which we call resurrection and which has irreversibly begun in the resurrection and ascension of Jesus Christ.

Notes

1 Louis Dupré, *Passage to Modernity: An Essay in the Hermeneutics of Nature and Culture* (New Haven: Yale University Press, 1993), 3.
2 Emmanuel Levinas, *Otherwise than Being or Beyond Essence*, trans. Alphonso Lingis (Dordrecht: Kluwer Academic Publishers, 1991), 113.
3 Idem., 'God and Philosophy' in *The Levinas Reader*, ed. Seán Hand (Oxford: Blackwell Publishers, 1989), 170.
4 Ibid., 173–5.
5 Ibid., 176–7.

6   Ibid., 178–9.

7   Idem., *Otherwise than Being*, 142.

8   Idem., 'God and Philosophy', 182.

9   Idem., 'Revelation in the Jewish Tradition' in *The Levinas Reader*, 207, 210 n.10.

10 Idem., *Otherwise than Being*, 118.

11 Edith Wyschogrod, *Saints and Postmodernism: Revisioning Moral Philosophy* (Chicago: University of Chicago Press, 1990), xxiv. Hereafter all page references to this text will be given parenthetically.

12 Michel de Certeau, 'Mystic Speech' in *Heterologies: Discourse on the Other*, trans. Brian Massumi (Minneapolis: University of Minnesota Press, 1986), 96.

13 Ibid., 97.

14 Idem., 'Surin's Melancholy' in *Heterologies*, 109.

15 Idem., 'Mystic Speech', 92.

16 Idem., *The Mystic Fable*, vol. 1, *The Sixteenth and Seventeenth Centuries*, trans. Michael B. Smith (Chicago: University of Chicago Press, 1992), 189.

17 Two essays in particular by Rowan Williams are very helpful in this regard: '*Sapientia* and the Trinity: Reflections on the *De Trinitate*' in *Collectanea augustiniana: melanges T. J. van Bavel*, ed. B. Bruning (Leuven: University Press, 1990), 317–32; and '"Know Thyself:" What Kind of an Injunction?' in *Philosophy, Religion and the Spiritual Life*, ed. Michael McGhee. Royal Institute of Philosophy Supplement 32 (Cambridge: Cambridge University Press, 1992), 211–27.

18 Williams, '*Sapientia* and the Trinity', 319.

19 Ibid., 320.

20 Denys Turner, *The Darkness of God:Negativity in Christian Mysticism* (Cambridge: Cambridge University Press, 1995) e.g., 100: 'The immortal self [in Augustine] *is* a participative image of the Trinity: it is not something else, *plus* image, for its reality consists in its being "like" God.' (And God is fundamentally relational.)

21 Ibid., 59.

22 Marguerite Porete, *The Mirror of Simple Souls*, trans. Ellen L. Babinsky. *Classics of Western Spirituality* (New York: Paulist Press, 1993), #138, 219–20.

23 Meister Eckhart, *German Sermon 52: Beati pauperes spiritu* in *Meister Eckhart: The Essential Sermons, Commentaries, Treatises, and Defense*, trans. Edmund Colledge and Bernard McGinn. *Classics of Western Spirituality* (New York: Paulist Press, 1981), 198.

24 Porete, *Mirror*, # 111, p. 183.

25 Ibid.

26 Ibid., #118, p. 191.

27 Ibid., #111, p. 183.

28 Ibid., #118, pp. 191–2. See also #138, p. 220: 'This simple Being does in the Soul through charity whatever the Soul does, for the will has become simple. Such a simple will has nothing to do in her, since it conquered the necessity of the two natures [distinct eternal and creaturely forms of existence] at the moment when the will was given up for the sake of simple being. And this simple will, which

is divine will, places the Soul in divine being.'

29   Amy Hollywood, *The Soul as Virgin Wife: Mechtild of Magdeburg, Marguerite Porete, and Meister Eckhart. Studies in Spirituality and Theology*, vol. 1 (Notre Dame: University of Notre Dame Press, 1995), 109.

30   Porete, *Mirror*, #91, p. 167.

31   Ellen L. Babinsky, 'Introduction', *Mirror*, 41. My emphasis.

32   Porete, *Mirror*, #115, p. 185.

33   Ibid., pp. 185–6. My emphasis.

34   Eckhart, *German Sermon* 5b, in *Meister Eckhart: The Essential Sermons*, 184.

35   Richard Woods, '"I am the Son of God": Eckhart and Aquinas on the Incarnation', *Eckhart Review*, June 1992: 27–46.

36   Eckhart, *German Sermon* 52, in *Meister Eckhart: Essential Sermons*, 203.

37   Idem., *German Sermon* 48, in *Meister Eckhart. Essential Sermons*, 198.

38   Turner, *The Darkness of God*, 184

39   Edith Stein, *On the Problem of Empathy. The Collected Works of Edith Stein*. Sister Teresa Benedicta of the Cross, vol. 3 , trans. Waltraut Stein (Washington: ICS Publications, 1989), 96.

40   Ibid., 116.

41   Idem., *The Science of the Cross: A Study of St John of the Cross*, trans. Hilda Graef (London: Burns & Oates, 1960), 120.

42   Ibid., 121.

43   Ibid., 122.

44   Simone Weil, *Gravity and Grace*, trans. Emma Craufurd (London: Routledge, 1963), 28.

45   Ibid., 35.

46   Idem., *First and Last Notebooks*, trans. Richard Rees (London: Oxford University Press, 1970), 362.

47   Idem., *Gravity and Grace*, 30.

48   Idem., *First and Last Notebooks*, 287–8.

49   Ibid., 283.

50   Edith Stein, 'The Prayer of the Church' in *The Hidden Life: Hagiographic Essays, Meditations, Spiritual Texts. The Collected Works of Edith Stein*, Sister Teresa Benedicta of the Cross, vol. 4, trans. Waltraut Stein (Washington: ICS Publications, 1992), 12.

51   Ibid., 15.

52   Ibid., 15–16.

53   Idem., 'Elevation of the Cross, September 14, 1939' in *The Hidden Life*, 94.

54   Ibid., 95.

55   Ibid., 96.

56   Edith Stein, letter and testament, quoted in Waltraud Herbstrith, *Edith Stein: A Biography*, trans. Bernard Bonowitz, 2nd edn, (San Francisco: Ignatius Press, 1992), 168–9.

57   Simone Weil, *Gravity and Grace*, 28.

58   Ibid., 36.

59   Idem., 'Come With Me' in *The Simone Weil Reader*, ed. George A. Panichas (Mt Kisco, NY: Moyer Bell, 1977),410–11.

60   Idem., *First and Last Notebooks*, 327.

61   Ibid.

62   Idem., 'The Love of God and Affliction' in *Waiting for God*, trans. Emma Craufurd (New York: Harper & Row, 1973), 127.

63   Ibid., 133.

64   Ibid., 133–4.

65   Susan J. Hekman, *Gender and Knowledge: Elements of a Postmodern Feminism* (Boston: Northeastern University Press, 1990), 93.

66   Edith Stein, 'Exaltation of the Cross, September 14, 1941', in *The Hidden Life*, 104.

67   Idem., *The Science of the Cross*, 126–7.

68   Simone Weil, *First and Last Notebooks*, 94.

69   Idem., 'The Love of God and Affliction', 126.

70   Idem., 'Forms of the Implicit Love of God', in *Waiting for God*, 208.

71   Paul Mommaers and Jan van Bragt, *Mysticism Buddhist and Christian: Encounters with Jan van Ruusbroec. Nanzen Studies in Religion and Culture.* (New York: Crossroad, 1995), 66.

INDEX

Printed in Great Britain
by Amazon.co.uk, Ltd.,
Marston Gate.